Who Does That Bitch Think She Is?

CRAIG SELIGMAN

Who Does That Bitch Think She Is?

DORIS FISH AND THE RISE OF DRAG

PUBLICAFFAIRS

New York

PublicAffairs
Hachette Book Group
1290 Avenue of the Americas, New York, NY 10104
www.publicaffairsbooks.com
@Public_Affairs

Printed in the United States of America

First Edition: February 2023

Published by PublicAffairs, an imprint of Perseus Books, LLC, a subsidiary of Hachette Book Group, Inc. The PublicAffairs name and logo is a trademark of the Hachette Book Group.

The Hachette Speakers Bureau provides a wide range of authors for speaking events. To find out more, go to www.hachettespeakersbureau.com or call (866) 376-6591.

The publisher is not responsible for websites (or their content) that are not owned by the publisher.

Print book interior design by Amy Quinn.

Library of Congress Cataloging-in-Publication Data

Names: Seligman, Craig, author.
Title: Who does that bitch think she is? : Doris Fish and the rise of drag
    / Craig Seligman.
Description: First edition. | New York : PublicAffairs, 2023. | Includes
    bibliographical references and index.
Identifiers: LCCN 2022036158 | ISBN 9781541702165 (hardcover) | ISBN
    9781541702189 (epub)
Subjects: LCSH: Fish, Doris, 1952-1991. | Drag queens--Biography. | Drag
    performance--History.
Classification: LCC HQ76.98.F57 S45 2023 | DDC 792.02/8092
    [B]--dc23/eng/20220809
LC record available at https://lccn.loc.gov/2022036158

ISBNs: 9781541702165 (hardcover), 9781541702189 (e-book)

LSC-C

Printing 1, 2022

To my old friend Jay Carey

CONTENTS

INTRODUCTION
DORIS AND HIS TIMES

Doris Fish was a made-up person (in both senses: invented and cosmetically enhanced) who became one of those characters who define an era. That era, from the early 1970s to the early '90s, when he was variously shocking the public and cracking it up with the aggressive glamour of his bad-girl drag, has receded so quickly in our collective consciousness that it can be hard to remember how totally beyond the pale drag queens used to be. And not just drag queens: Across a large chunk of the globe, gay men and lesbians were in a far shakier place at the beginning of those years than they were at the end. Drag queens were a flash point in the culture wars that raged during that era of change.

Left: Photo by Martin Ryter. *Right*: Photographer
unknown. The mustache was a stick-on.

Doris was brazen in the delight he took in his frocks, his wigs, his high heels, and above all his makeup. "I'd paint my eyeballs if I could," he said. He had to settle for painting his teeth. But he was nothing like the stereotyped ditzy drag queen. He had a sharp intelligence and reservoirs of kindness hidden behind his quick, cutting wit, and he was extremely grounded. He touched everyone he encountered, including me, though I was only on the periphery of his world. Why does his memory still haunt me, all these years after his death? Perhaps because Doris was the freest person I've ever known, even while, as an artist, he was also one of the most disciplined.

Everyone who knew him was aware of the way he compartmentalized his life. There were effectively three Dorises—the artist, the drag queen, and the prostitute—and he embraced them all. I've never known anyone who loved being himself so much. All three of those personas centered on his gayness, at a time when homosexuality was just beginning to make its way toward the center of the conversation in both of the countries he called home. But if Doris was, in some ways, emblematic of our gay generation, in the end he was too exceptional a person to be emblematic of anything but himself.

His name still resonates in Sydney, his hometown, and in San Francisco, his adopted one. During his abbreviated life, Sydney metamorphosed from a homophobic backwater where gay sex was against the law into the cosmopolitan backdrop of the biggest and showiest gay-pride celebration in the world, the Sydney Gay and Lesbian Mardi Gras, where Doris was a star. At the same time, San Francisco progressed from a city without a single gay elected official to the one with arguably the best organized, most politically effective gay community on the planet. They evolved as Doris evolved, and in the end, both cities honored him with acclaim.

Back then our understanding of gender fluidity wasn't what it is now, and a person who called himself (or herself) a drag queen might occupy a wide range of places on the sexual spectrum. Within the Sluts a-Go-Go, the San Francisco drag troupe Doris led, the fragile and ebullient Tippi was a person we would now easily recognize as trans, while the formidable Miss X was a bisexual man whose most profound attachments were to women. Doris himself had no uncertainty about his own gender or his sexuality. Though he was thoughtful about his feminine side and a student of all things womanly in cosmetics and apparel, he loved his male body, nurtured it, and got tremendous pleasure out of it. And so did a lot of other men.

He began as a visual artist, attending art school in Sydney, and he never stopped painting portraits on canvas and paper. But his real medium was the living face. Doris could completely erase a face—his own or someone else's—with base and powder, and then, once he had it down to a blank slate, paint an entirely new one on top of it. He was a constant presence in Sydney and San Francisco drag shows and pride parades. But Doris's face, if not his name, was famous beyond those local stomping grounds, owing to a yearslong series of wacky greeting cards on which he appeared in dozens upon dozens of guises. The cards were big sellers and a good source of income (he was always scrambling), but they were also something no one recognized at the time: a cultural marker. That middle Americans were scooping up these artifacts of high-camp humor to send to family and friends showed that the society had progressed to the point where a gay sensibility no longer had to disguise itself. Suddenly the wider world was in on the joke.

Doris started performing in Sydney as a member of Sylvia and the Synthetics, a psycho troupe that, like San Francisco's Cockettes, represented the first anarchic flowering of gay creative energy in the post-Stonewall era. Gender-bending was in the zeitgeist. The male members of Sylvia and the Synthetics made no attempt to hide their maleness—sequins and taffeta went on over furry chests and hairy legs. The group would hurl things at the audience, and the audience loved it. The Synthetics' hostility and, sometimes, outright violence were fueled by the repressed anger in the room and outside it. That fury was looking for an outlet, and soon it would take on an identifiable shape in the aesthetic of punk. But by then Doris had moved on.

He made his first trip to San Francisco in 1975 and fell hard for the city. In the '70s San Francisco was a paradise for horny gay guys like

Doris: Rents were cheap, sex was everywhere, and all the rules seemed to have vaporized. He made his debut on the alternative-entertainment scene in 1977 after winning a contest to join a three-week engagement with the city's resident rock screwballs, the Tubes. Thereafter, he became the driving force behind a decade-long series of sidesplitting drag shows that were loved as much as you can love throwaway trash—which is what everybody thought they were. No one, Doris included, perceived them as political theater, when in fact they were accomplishing satire's deepest dream: not just to rail against society, but to change it. From *Sluts a-Go-Go* through *Nightclub of the Living Dead* and beyond, Doris's work belonged to a creative movement that was reshaping attitudes toward, and thus altering the status of, queer people in much of the world.

A lot of onlookers, however, accused him of doing the opposite. In the 1970s, drag queens, up till then a marginalized minority within a marginalized minority, suddenly became flaming-hot potatoes in the angry debate over how homosexuals should represent themselves in the face of the backlash that started with Anita Bryant's Save Our Children campaign. Drags were not then the antic and lovable TV personalities we know them as today. They terrified straight people, and they horrified those gay people who were bent on proving to the heterosexual world that homosexuals deserved equal rights because we were just like everybody else. Drag queens didn't want to be like everybody else. "What is the point of our years of struggle," Doris wrote in a popular San Francisco gay newspaper, "if people who present a 'negative image' are to be hidden and excluded from our community media and from their full rights as citizens of this planet?"

In retrospect, we can see how the Anita Bryants of the world undermined their own agenda. Ranting about homosexuality brought it into day-to-day discourse, familiarizing gay men and women to a public that previously hadn't given them all that much thought. The same can be said of AIDS. Of course, no one would claim that this silver lining was worth the hundreds of thousands of deaths that accompanied it. Still, the epidemic filled the news with images of gay people, and those images went a long way toward making the public realize that gay people were their daughters and sons and siblings and friends and colleagues. Once the epidemic swept San Francisco, Doris became a ubiquitous performer on the benefit circuit, as well as one of the city's best-known AIDS patients himself. By the time he died, in 1991, he was celebrated far beyond drag circles for his public-spiritedness, his openness about his own suffering (though that took him a while), his unflagging wit, and his courage. His death was front-page news, which would have delighted him—though he would have shrugged off the celebrity treatment as only proper.

I FIRST MET DORIS LATE IN 1983, AT A COCKTAIL PARTY GIVEN BY my boyfriend (he's now my husband), Silvana Nova. He and Doris had just finished performing together in the first episode of *Naked Brunch*, a drag-heavy soap opera that had become an unexpected hit at Club 181, a hip San Francisco nightspot with a mixed gay and straight clientele.

To repeat myself: It's difficult in this ostensibly more enlightened era to get across the kind of alarm with which drag queens were then viewed. Homosexual acts were still against the law in much of the United States and Australia; variances on the sexual spectrum were barely acknowledged, much less discussed. I was a serious young journalist, and a drag queen was about the last thing I envisioned as boyfriend material, though it felt very bohemian to be able to say I was going out with one. Silvana, in any case, wasn't a professional like Doris: he had a day job (in the art department of a magazine, where we'd met), and by the time we got together he was doing drag mainly for special occasions, like shows and marches.

Doris and his cohort Miss X came to Silvana's cocktail party directly from a shoot for West Graphics, the greeting card company where they were star models. They weren't just in drag but in space-alien drag: blue faces, scarlet lips, and eyebrows penciled on like lightning bolts. (The cutline on the card that resulted, with the two of them glaring and weighed down with shopping bags: "NINE PLANETS IN SEVEN DAYS, NEVER AGAIN!") Miss X I found charming and easy to talk to (despite the terrifying side he was reputed to have), and we're friends to this day. Doris was cooler—cordial, as you would be to a friend's boyfriend, but not one to linger with a stranger irrelevant to his career.

No doubt they'd come up with the interplanetary theme because they were then in the middle of filming their outer-space drag extravaganza, *Vegas in Space*. Silvana had been cast as a shopgirl in the movie's extraterrestrial shopping mall, and early the next year I visited him on the set. He was costumed in whiteface, a voluminous white wig, and a Kansai Yamamoto giraffe-print jumpsuit out of his own stuffed closet. A snapshot of the two of us taken that evening, with Sil standing a foot taller than me in his heels (he's tall anyway) and me looking bemused, has sat on my desk ever since; it always amuses me when visitors to our house see his picture and ask, "Who's that?" (It's been less amusing when, more recently, they've started asking, "And who's that next to him?")

Though Doris fascinated me, he remained more acquaintance than friend. (He always loved Silvana.) I got to know him a little better a couple of years later, when I proposed a profile of him to the editors of the Sunday magazine of the *San Francisco Examiner*. Doris, I knew, would jump at the publicity. Two years earlier such a topic would never have been approved, but attitudes had already shifted to the point that an article about a drag queen whose name was by then well known around town was no longer too dangerous a proposition for a family newspaper, though I know it caused some nervousness.

Only in retrospect do I understand to what extent the editors' consent was a marker of real change. By that year, 1986, AIDS had put gay men all over the news, often in a sympathetic light, since it was hard for journalists, in San Francisco or anywhere, to be hateful about the dying. Though the reasons were horrible, we had reached our greatest visibility since Anita Bryant's antigay campaign of the late 1970s—during which Harvey Milk, the country's best-known gay politician, had noted that "more good and bad, but *more* about the word *homosexual* and *gay* was written than probably in the history of mankind." Now AIDS, perversely, was having the same normalizing effect.

I interviewed Doris and several of his friends and colleagues, and because I was an inexperienced writer of profiles I spent far more time with everyone than a four-thousand-word article required. In retrospect, that overwork was lucky, since Doris and Tippi are no longer around, and much of what follows comes out of my interviews with them.

THEY'RE NOT AROUND BECAUSE AIDS KILLED THEM. THE STORY OF Doris and his circle is also, inevitably, the story of the AIDS catastrophe. Recent narratives of those years have centered mainly on ACT UP, the group of largely East Coast activists who responded to governmental indifference in brilliantly creative—and effective—ways. (The Reagan administration found it easier to ignore the mostly gay men and needle users infected with HIV than to risk alienating the Christian right, which thought HIV was what they deserved.) But angry activism wasn't the whole story, especially in San Francisco, a famously gay-friendly city whose government responded to the emergency with both compassion and funding.

AIDS had other significant effects both for the community in general and for drag queens in particular. One was that resentments that had simmered for years between lesbians and gay men over issues of power hogging in the movement (not unlike the ones that earlier had created a rift between white women and women of color who felt sidelined in feminist circles) were put aside. AIDS was a family crisis. Those lesbians who had viewed drag as deeply insulting to women came to appreciate the ballsiness that drag queens—many of them, like Doris, sick themselves—brought to rallying a traumatized community. Of course, I'm generalizing; serious antagonisms are never healed that easily. But the worst of the bitterness never quite returned. AIDS was a big part of what transformed drag queens, in a remarkably short time, from social lepers into culture heroes.

A WORD ON THE VEXED SUBJECT OF PRONOUNS. DORIS DIDN'T SUFFER from gender dysphoria: he was a man who considered himself a man (in current terms, a cisgender male) and who enjoyed having sex with other men. A lot. Outside of some childhood fantasies, he never had a serious desire, as far as I'm aware, to be a woman. It's true that when I knew him, in the 1980s, everyone in his circle and in the wider gay community referred to him with feminine pronouns—"Her new look is sluttier than ever!"—which is how he referred to his gay male friends, too. But this usage had nothing to do with gender confusion; it was a timeworn mannerism of oh-Mary camp banter. In those days I would have felt discourteous calling Doris "him," but I was following the lead of those around me. I don't think he cared that much.

When, years later, I started interviewing people about his life, I found that those feminine pronouns were by no means universally used, especially among his Australian friends (his family never used them), which is why I've decided not to use them myself. I like the dissonance that the words "Doris" and "him" introduce when you put them together. They give a sentence a glimmer of drag. But I've retained feminine pronouns when quoting other people, and if this convention causes occasional confusion . . . well, Doris practiced the art of confusion. In the case of men who renounced their maleness, such as his close friends Jacqueline Hyde and Tippi, I would feel disrespectful referring to them by any pronouns other than the ones they chose for themselves.

DORIS EMBODIED A NEW STAGE IN THE EVOLUTION OF DRAG culture. What it had been in the generation before ours is laid out in what's probably the best-known and the most widely influential of the many books about drag, Esther Newton's 1972 *Mother Camp: Female Impersonators in America*. Newton, who was born in 1940, was a graduate student in anthropology at the University of Chicago when she went to her first drag show, in 1965—watching it, as she wrote in a coda to the book, with "mingled shock and fascination." Drag queens became her dissertation topic, a daring one at a time when social science, she recalled some years later, regarded homosexuals as "the object solely of psychological, medical, or even criminological study." In 1965 gay sex was, in fact, illegal in every state except Illinois, which had repealed its antisodomy law only three years earlier. "The insight that gays were not just a category of sick isolates, but a group, and so had a culture," she continued, "was a breathtaking leap whose daring is hard to recapture now, when the term 'gay community' is familiar even to most straight people." In the usual pattern, her groundbreaking work threatened to demolish her career—she was denied tenure at her first teaching post—until it made her celebrated.

She completed the dissertation in 1968 and published a revised version as *Mother Camp* four years later. The book is consistently astute and often prescient, not to mention well written. Newton was excited by the taboo-breaking potency of her subject. She understood that the "drag queen symbolizes an open declaration, even celebration, of homosexuality. The drag queen says for his gay audience, who cannot say it, 'I'm gay, I don't care who knows it; the straight world be damned.'" And thus "homosexuality is symbolized in American culture by transvestism," which in turn was why, though at the time this insight may have seemed startlingly counterintuitive, "drag, like violence, is as American as apple pie. Like violence, it is not an accident or mistake, nor is it caused by a few people's weak character. It is an organic part of American culture—exactly the 'flip side' of many precious ideals." Foremost among these ideals was the strict definition of sex roles that reigned in postwar America (and Australia).

The parallel with violence is intentionally unsettling. "Professional drag queens," Newton wrote, "are, therefore, professional homosexuals; they represent the stigma of the gay world."[*] Ouch. "Stigma,"

---

* On the subject of stigma, the transgender performer and activist Kate Bornstein, who was a friend and admirer of Doris's, has offered this revelatory observation: "Assuming that gay men and lesbians are more consciously excluded by the culture for violations of *gender* codes (which are visible in the daily life of the culture) than for actual sexual practices (which usually happen behind closed doors and in private spaces), then lesbians

"downfall," "degradation," "dishonor": *Mother Camp* is shot through with condemnatory words like these, although Newton, who's gay, wasn't making moral judgments herself. She was talking about how drag queens were viewed by Americans—and not just straight Americans. Many gay men, she noted, had an attitude of "condemnation combined with the expression of vast social distance between themselves and the drag queen," while others tended to "deplore female impersonators for 'giving us a bad name' or 'projecting the wrong image' to the heterosexual culture." This loathing had only deepened by Doris's time. In the course of a long interview for this book, Miss X surprised me with a sudden tirade: "We were the lowest rung on the ladder! We knew it! We were hit in the face with it over and over again! I mean, my God, we couldn't even get a good review out of the *gay press*! Through our whole career!"

Newton further observed that the widespread disdain for drag queens extended to the queens themselves. The ones she got to know were a disturbingly self-hating group: "Impersonators do not often deny society's judgment of them, and they even cooperate by blaming themselves more than the straight world for their lowly estate. They tend to describe the profession and often their own persons with such words as 'sick,' 'rotten,' 'tainted,' and 'shitty.'" I would have dismissed this derogatory aspect of Newton's book as shards from a vanished past before X's outburst exposed an old wound. Taken aback, I pointed out that Doris never had a low opinion of himself. "No, of course not," X replied. "She was a goddess. You could never say that Doris was humble! But I made up for it."

When Doris, early in his San Francisco drag career, rolled around on filthy floors and wet streets ("What a mess! I looked fabulous!" he wrote to a friend after a party in 1977), he was turning this self-loathing into parody. To him it was ridiculous—which shows how fast

---

and gay men actually share the same stigma with 'transgendered' people: the stigma of crimes against gender. And while 'transgendered' people may not in fact practice gay or lesbian sex, and so may not themselves be lesbian or gay, gays and lesbians are invariably perceived as 'transgendered.'"

times were changing. *Mother Camp* had appeared in print only five years earlier.

Newton also highlighted the chasm between glamour drag and comic drag. When she was doing her fieldwork, a drag queen was either stunning or funny—capable in the former case of fooling an audience into thinking it was watching a born bombshell, or in the latter of drawing comedy both from his acid wit and from the stupefying role reversal offered by a man in a dress. But Doris bridged those roles: He could be gorgeous and still make fun of himself, and of everyone else in the room. Which is why Doris's wit, even at its cruelest, never had the bitterness common to the queens who came before him. It was good-natured cruelty, because there was no self-hatred in it.

The reason was the momentous shift that had taken place between our generation of homosexuals and the generation before. Among the few things Doris and I had in common was our immunity to the shame that had tormented so many older gay men and lesbians. This kind of self-acceptance characterizes the vast majority of gay people I've known—though in fairness I should add that I have friends whose childhoods were sunk in shame and who bridle when I put forward this argument. Which is hardly surprising, since when Doris and I were coming of age the prohibition against homosexuality was unquestioned. (A 1968 poll found 64 percent of Australians opposed decriminalizing homosexual acts between consenting adults. The gay scholar Dennis Altman, writing in 1971, pointed to a survey suggesting "that homosexuals are considerably more disliked by the American public than ex-convicts, ex–mental patients, gamblers, or alcoholics.") And yet as soon as it was seriously questioned—as soon as a crack appeared in the wall—the wall crumbled and collapsed.

That shift is part of the answer to one of the questions that spurred me to write about Doris: How did we get from there to here—from a world in which homosexuals were despised (or, at best, invisible) to one in which same-sex couples no longer raise eyebrows? It had already started happening in the 1960s, as the counterculture flowered and gay men and lesbians began coming out of the closet in ever-larger numbers. In April 1968 the playwright Mart Crowley managed to secure five off-Broadway performances for *The Boys in the Band*, his tragicomedy about his own generation of gay men, considered uncommercial because of its subject matter. It ran for a thousand and one. By early in the morning of June 28, 1969, when a battle at the Stonewall Inn in Greenwich Village between cops and a crowd that was heavy on drag queens heralded the Lexington and Concord of the gay-rights movement,* "Out of the closet and into the streets" had become a slogan with the peal of inevitability. The activism that followed Stonewall is often referred to as gay liberation, but the movement had become possible because by then so many gay men and women had already freed themselves from the shame of previous eras.

I was seventeen when I saw *The Boys in the Band* in Atlanta in 1970, using a fake ID to gain admittance to the adults-only production. It was my first full-on exposure to the gay culture I knew I was preparing to enter, and its camp one-liners became a study tool for me and for thousands of other young queens who were just learning, in David M. Halperin's resonant phrase, how to be gay. But it also had a self-pitying side that didn't ring true to me: "You show me a happy homosexual," goes one of its most famous lines, "and I'll show you a gay corpse." Doris was a living retort to that dictum. Happiness and fulfillment didn't seem unattainable to our generation of gay men—not, at least, insofar as we were gay. Our consciousness was raised. We were liberated. The task was to liberate everybody else. And on that front Doris was a leader.

His influence on drag style is very much with us in the ironic drag queens of today—performers like Peaches Christ, Bianca Del Rio, and Sasha Velour, to name only a few. Doris was playing with notions of gender at a moment when those notions had started to shift toward what we currently call the nonbinary. He wasn't what we would now

---

* Earlier instances of militant resistance to police harassment had taken place at Cooper Do-nuts in Los Angeles in 1959 and, on a larger scale, at Compton's Cafeteria in San Francisco in 1966. The Stonewall uprising occurred at a psychologically apt moment and, unlike the earlier incidents, benefited from extensive press coverage.

identify as trans—far from it—but he did give a lot of thought to masculinity and femininity and the liberating thrill of traveling between those two continents. His strong sense of self encompassed an unusually fluid concept of identity.

Previous drag queens had presented themselves as women manqué. Nobody in his first group, Sylvia and the Synthetics, bought in to that aesthetic. As Doris matured, his drag got more complex, but it always remained, to use his term, *crook*. The aim was never to pass for a woman—which, as he pointed out, wouldn't get him the attention he craved, because no one would notice him then—but rather to savor the freedom of being who you wanted to be and not who somebody else thought you were supposed to be. He was a walking celebration of the gamut of identities available to us and the rush that comes with getting to choose for yourself.

SOME RECURRING NAMES

The Mills Family

Mildred June Harrison Mills, Doris's mother
Ace or **Tony (Anthony Clargo) Mills,** Doris's father
Liz (Elizabeth)
Marianne and her husband, **Tony Haid**

Philip Clargo Mills, a.k.a. **Doris Fish**
Michael
Andrew
Gina (Georgina)

Sylvia and the Synthetics

Jacqueline or **Jackie Hyde**
Miss (Danny) **Abood**
Jasper Havoc (Peter McMahon), Doris's childhood friend

Clayton MacDonald (Cockroach Clare), Jackie's boyhood friend
Carmel Strelein, a fashion radical

Visual Artists

Peter Tully, the first artistic director of the Sydney Gay (later Gay and Lesbian) Mardi Gras Workshop
Ron Smith, the second artistic director of the workshop

David McDiarmid (pronounced "McDermott"), the third artistic director of the workshop

San Franciscans

The Sluts a-Go-Go

Miss X
Tippi, formerly Miss Leading

Phillip R. Ford, a director and
performer
Sandelle Kincaid, the only
biologically female Slut

Drag Queens

Ambi Sextrous, a bearded queen
with a trust fund
Arturo Galster, a talented singer
Freda Lay, a spacey friend
Ginger Quest (Greg Foss), holder
of the lease at 422 Oak Street

Lulu, a blonde frenemy of Doris's
Silvana Nova, a frequent
collaborator and the author's
husband
Tommy Pace, a brilliantly funny
performer

More Friends and Colleagues

Anne Block, an actor
Bob Davis, a musician who became
Tippi's boyfriend
Carmela Carlyle, a dancer and
psychologist
Connie Champagne, a singer
David Weissman, a filmmaker
Gwyn Waters, a fan
Jane Dornacker, a tall comedian
Janice Sukaitis, a performer and
writer

Jennifer Blowdryer, a
rock-and-roll singer
Marc Huestis, a director and
producer
Pearl E. Gates, later Pearl
Harbour, a rock-and-roll
singer
Peggy Darm, Doris's nurse
Robin Clark, an artist and
cinematographer
Timmy Spence, a musician

Note: The spelling of some names changed over time (*Sandal* became *Sandahl*, then *Sand-elle*) or from week to week (*Freda/Freida*). To avoid confusion, I've stuck with one spelling.

1
MANLY VALE

T HE OUTRÉ PERFORMER AND OUTSIZE PERSONALITY WHO
would one day be known as Doris Fish was born Philip Clargo
Mills on August 11, 1952, in the Sydney suburb (as the city's districts
are called) of Manly Vale. We used to laugh about that *Manly*. The joke
turns out to be etymologically valid, by which I mean that the name
commemorates a real attribution of masculinity and not just some public servant whose name is funny in retrospect. It dates from 1788, the
earliest days of Australia's colonization, when Captain Arthur Phillip, the commander of the First Fleet of convict exiles and the new
settlement's governor-to-be, described to the British home secretary,
Lord Sydney, a shipboard encounter with some twenty Indigenous

The Mills siblings, 1959: Marianne, Philip, Liz (holding baby
Gina), Michael, and Andrew. Courtesy of Andrew Mills.

Australians whose "confidence and manly behaviour" so impressed him that it "made me give the name of Manly Cove to this place."

Philip entered the world auspiciously. "He was a stunner," according to Elizabeth Mills Byrne, the oldest of his five siblings. "Out of all the babies I've ever seen, he was the most beautiful. He didn't make a fuss—calm, peaceful, just that kind of child. And then he went on to *be* that kind of child."

"I was perfect," Doris, speaking to me in 1986, concurred. "Even then."

He spent an unremarkable childhood in an unremarkable decade. The Australia of the 1950s—conformist, politically paranoid about the Communist threat, emotionally rather gray—was much like the United States of the same period. His siblings remember a tranquil boy sitting on the living room floor of their home on Horning Parade, or later at a table, drawing industriously. He didn't bother anybody. His two younger brothers, Michael and Andrew, were mostly out of the house, running around with the multitude of other kids on the street. So was Georgina, or Gina, the youngest sibling and something of a tomboy. The older girls, Liz and Marianne, lounged around doing their makeup and watching TV and taking advantage of Philip's agreeable nature: "Phiiiiil . . . can you get us a drink of water?" He would genially comply and return to his drawing.

His first primer contains his earliest extant sketches: a rabbit and a goose and, inside the front cover, a princess on the balcony of her turreted castle, standing next to what appears to be a potted plant and surveying her realm. After his father bought him a big box of Derwent pencils, he applied himself to drawing his new passion: automobiles. When he was a little older, he assembled and painted plastic models. American Duesenbergs of the '20s and '30s were his favorite—he admired their "lovely lines." There were toy trains, too; his father helped him screw together two old doors to make the base for a papier-mâché fantasy of mountains and valleys and rivers and trees and tunnels for the little trains to travel through and stations for them to stop at.

Then eyes. He left eyes everywhere, on envelopes and magazines and scraps of paper, up until the end of his life. From paper to skin was a natural progression. In time his expertise at eye makeup was such that he could not only decorate a face but remake it entirely. Once, for a fancy-dress party in the freak years, he painted eyes on Liz's eyelids, so that when she closed them there was still a pair of open eyes staring at you.

The Mills children grew up in a happy, chaotic household, although the chaos teetered just this side of dysfunction. Their parents, Ace and Mildred, married in 1947. Liz arrived in 1948, and after that the babies just kept coming—Marianne in 1950, Philip in 1952, Michael in 1955, Andrew in 1958, and finally Gina in 1959. Liz would think, "Another bloody baby! She's having another baby! Oh, just go away, all you babies!" Mildred, who hated solitude and loved activity and never stopped talking for a minute, would have welcomed half a dozen more. Or that's what she claimed.

"Poor Millie was exhausted," Marianne says. "All the time. You'd come home from school and you'd say, 'Mum! Mum!' and she would always—I quite understand now—be having a nap, trying to catch a few minutes' sleep before we all descended again." Meals were a free-for-all, with everyone grabbing for food and talking over everybody else. Mountains of laundry piled up in the basket. "Our household chores," Liz told me, "were a disaster. We'd have a roster system for a week, and then that would be the end of that. We used to have a chute which fed down into a laundry at the bottom. If any visitors were coming"—which was often—"Mildred would just grab everything in the room and throw it down the chute. That was her idea of housekeeping."

Which isn't to say they remember her as anything other than a wonderful parent. Somehow, she attended the six-thirty Mass every morning and still had eggs or porridge on the table when the children got up, chattering as she served. She sent them off to school with lunches that became legendary among the local schoolkids, who themselves came provisioned with meager little jam sandwiches. Mildred's sandwiches—thick slices of bread exactly buttered all the way to the edges and stuffed with meat and copious vegetables, by lunchtime half vermilion from leaching beet juice—became such a hot item that Michael could sell his, buy himself a meat pie, and have pocket money left over.

IT WASN'T THE LIFE HER PARENTS HAD PLANNED FOR HER. MILDRED June Harrison was born in 1922. Her father had come home a hero from World War I and opened hardware stores in Manly (next to Manly Vale) and nearby Balgowlah. He was something of a good-time Charlie, but there was enough money for the parents to spoil their two daughters. They were upright Methodists whose deep suspicion of Catholics can be epitomized in the nasty stories Mildred heard as she was growing up about the tunnels that ran between the priests' quarters and the nuns'. And so they were appalled when she fell in love with one.

Anthony Clargo—first Tony, later A.C., which mutated into Ace—Mills was born three years after his future wife, in 1925. He was a dark-haired, burly man with a large head, a wide jaw, and a big nose, frank but not gregarious—he was no Mildred. She, by contrast, was an effervescent beauty, with voluptuous breasts and lush, cascading auburn hair that she set off with crimson lipstick. They met when Ace was just back from the war and had gotten in on the bottom rung of the public service, and Mildred was working in downtown Sydney as a stenographer-secretary. To the horror of her parents, Ace insisted, when he proposed, that she convert.

She didn't just convert. "She became the Catholic of all Catholics" is how Michael puts it. "Every single day she went to church. She never missed. She had miracles, everything." Philip and his siblings were the victims, as they saw it later, of a seriously Catholic childhood. They all attended Catholic schools. "Sitting around saying the rosary"—Michael again—"that was big. Turn off the telly and all get down on your knees!" Ace was strict in those days, and anyone who giggled in the middle of devotions got the strap. On Sunday mornings they would make the long trek down from Horning Parade to St. Kieran's for the eight-thirty service; then a big breakfast of eggs, with toast and straw-berry jam prepared by Ace for dessert.

"I was a perfect Catholic child, even going to Mass as an altar-boy during the week," Doris wrote later. "The nuns thought I was some kind of saint when I sent the Pope a hand-colored Christmas card at the age of seven." He grew out of it, of course ("When Catholics go 'bad,' they go whole hog")—they all did, including Ace. By the time of Doris's death, Mildred was the only member of the family still in the church.

They hardly wanted, but food and shelter and parochial-school tu-ition for six children on a government clerk's salary meant they didn't dine out, they didn't take vacations, and they left the floors uncarpeted. A law degree was a prerequisite for getting anywhere in public service, and so Ace began studying nights, making him much less present for the younger kids. While Liz and Marianne remember the fun they had with him at the nearby Mermaid Pool, Michael and Andrew recall the closed door of the den just off their parents' bedroom. Not that entry was forbidden; you were welcome to come in and spend a few comfort-ing minutes on his lap. But he was driven. If you got up in the middle of the night, he would still be in there working.

As the boys entered adolescence, their parents' distractedness had its advantages. "By the time I came around," Andrew says, "they'd given up on trying to keep us in line." He and Michael headed out to the beaches to surf; Philip discovered the nighttime world of clubs. This freedom, of course, didn't simply stem from the overwhelming mob of children and the demands of Ace's work. The '60s arrived, and the world changed.

But that was later. "For my parents, my early years were trouble-free," Doris wrote in 1990. "I was well behaved and quiet. They never suspected." The placid young introvert drawing at a table suggests the kind of child who might easily have grown into a loner. But Philip al-ways had friends, and just as the imaginary worlds he constructed at home presaged the ones he would later build on stage and screen, out-side the house he was the embryonic performer. From an early age he was close to his three-years-younger neighbor Moira Batley. Her mother and Mildred saw each other daily at St. Kieran's, and Philip and Moira, who were usually in tow, became playmates. *Play* for them might mean simply sitting together and drawing and talking, sometimes about their fears: Moira, who was tiny, of the big, mean girls on the playground, Philip of his strict father. It could mean dolls: she had a Barbie set, complete with wigs, that he loved.

Or it could mean dress-up. Moira's mother was a milliner, and when she took her creations to the David Jones department store she often left the little girl with the ladies at the cosmetics counter. Moira would come home with samples of lipstick and blush, and Philip, the budding makeup artist, would try them out on her. Then she would try them on him. These sessions must have hit a deep chord, since Moira would grow up to be a makeup artist as well.

Philip also loved performing for Moira. When they were a bit older and both in grade school at St. Kieran's, he would take the belt from her dress, tie it around his hair, and slay her with impersonations of their elocution teachers. ("Greedy Goosey Gandah got grain greedily!") Moira's older cousin Noeleen Batley became an early-'60s Australian pop star, and they watched her TV appearances on *Bandstand*, wide-eyed and awed by her waxing hairdos.

At St. Kieran's, Philip found an even closer friend—a soulmate, really—in Peter McMahon. "Luckily," Doris told me many years later, "he was also a queen. Of course, we didn't know it at the time. We were both quite 'shy,' as it was called in those days." They formed a lifelong bond. Philip was the geeky one with the glasses—after he was unable to decipher the big ads hanging across the pool at a swim meet, his parents had taken him to an optometrist. (He talked his way out of playing football, which he hated, by complaining that he couldn't see the ball.) Later he wore contacts. Peter, in contrast, was black-locked and gorgeous. Though his ex-footballer father sneered at his effeminacy, his vivacious mother, Pammy, was so with-it that later she would be a nearly full-fledged member of their circle.

They were enterprising little sissies. When they were in their early teens, between the brick piers underneath Peter's house in North

Manly they put up false walls and hung rugs and laid more old rugs on the ground and brought in old paintings and furniture and big shaded lamps, all of it very '20s—the vogue for nostalgia was coming in. Philip's brother Andrew remembers it as a den out of *Ali Baba*, as fantastic as a stage set.

From grade school at St. Kieran's they had advanced to the dour St. Augustine's College in Brookvale, north of North Manly. Philip had little trouble adjusting—his report cards show above-average marks in most of his subjects, including Christian doctrine, and excellent ones in art—but Peter, swishy and apt to mouth off, nearly didn't graduate. After high school, the two best friends stuck together. Instead of a liberal-arts college they enrolled in the Julian Ashton Art School, in the downtown suburb known as the Rocks, the oldest and most traditional of the city's art schools. Philip's parents supported his choice, but their mutual friend, Jacqueline Hyde, who went to the rival National Art School—"the proper one," she calls it, because its students were experimenting with "action painting and hard-edge and op art and all that late-'60s, early-'70s stuff"—sniffs at the nineteenth-century academicism of Julian Ashton. But Philip never took much interest, then or later, in art-world trends. He was too busy at that time turning out '30s- and '40s-style portraits of himself and (occasionally) his friends, increasingly in drag: "very classical," according to Jackie, "although many years later she went on to doing them on black velvet." A commercial-art school might have been more useful, practically speaking; later Philip would be turned down for jobs in graphics because he didn't have the training. Still, he flourished at Julian Ashton, producing canvases and prints with an energy that combined his father's rigorous work ethic and his mother's frenzied exuberance.

He was still living at home on Horning Parade, where attitudes were changing with the times. As a young couple, Ace and Mildred had been active supporters of Democratic Labor, a bitterly anticommunist party peopled mainly by conservative Catholics. As you might expect of a Catholic-based group, it supported government spending on health, education, and social welfare, but it was intransigent on social issues like abortion and homosexuality. Over the years, as these issues moved into the glare of greater controversy, the party only stiffened. Tony Haid, who married Philip's older sister Marianne in 1971 and had the hippie values of the era, used to have shouting matches with Mildred—she called them "discussions"—and he would fume to Ace, "It's impossible to have a conversation with that woman! She doesn't listen to anything you say!" His ire delighted his father-in-law, who replied, "Oh yes, I've always known that about her." He was glad to feel he had an ally.

But despite their religious and political affiliations, Ace and Mildred never frowned on Philip's sexuality. When he came out to the family, at around eighteen, no one was remotely surprised, and if his parents were at all uneasy it was only out of concern for the difficulties they feared lay ahead of him. As far as religious interdiction, "there's the Catholic Church," Michael told me, "and then there's *Mildred's* Catholic Church. She disagreed completely with the church in relation to gay people." Ace shared her tolerance, which may have been why in time they began shifting slowly leftward; by the end of her life, Mildred, at least, was voting Labor.

Their kids were constantly cajoling them into the new era. When the boys started smoking marijuana, Ace and Mildred weren't shocked; their main concern was safety. "We'd rather you smoke it at home than end up in some bloody dealer's place," Ace said. Philip began cultivating a crop outside the front door. Mildred bought Andrew a hookah for his sixteenth birthday. And then one Christmas, around the family table, Ace and Mildred wound up taking a few hits themselves. Mildred was immediately blasted and began singing the jingle from the "Happy Little Vegemites" commercial. Thinking about it years later made Andrew pensive. "How did we get from getting the strap for laughing in the middle of saying the rosary to smoking a joint at the dining room table?"

There had been some money to expand the house after Mildred's mother died, and once Ace was admitted to the bar his salary went up as his jobs became increasingly distinguished. After Liz and Marianne married young and moved out, Philip got his own bedroom, which he transformed into a stylish artist's studio, painting the floors white and adorning it with his portraits and his psychedelic prints. When the once-swank Australia Hotel, a Victorian-cum-art-deco gem (and prominent cruising spot), shut down and sold off its furnishings, he and Moira Batley went down to pay homage to the grand old edifice. Philip took home an old British-style phone box, bright red and domed on top, and installed it in his bedroom. He claimed the aging Tasman hi-fi that the family used to gather around, singing "Rock Island Line" together. Soon the Beatles, Joan Baez, Joni Mitchell, Crosby, Stills & Nash, and above all Jefferson Airplane were blasting out of his room. He never got tired of painting Grace Slick; the druggy anthem "White Rabbit," mostly censored on the Australian airwaves, played over and over. He set up a press and began designing and silk-screening posters of his favorite bands—it was probably at this point that Day-Glo became permanently fixed in his aesthetic—as well as charming retro cards with flapper and art deco designs, all of which he took to the open-air Paddington Markets. They sold easily. The money went into clothes.

Men's clothes. Though by this time he and Peter had begun frequenting the drag bars and were dipping into drag themselves. At Julian Ashton, Philip went through his late-mod phase. Before he was stunning, he was groovy. He put on round tortoiseshell glasses, bought wide-lapelled jackets and bell bottoms at John and Merivale, the boutique that was Sydney's own small chunk of Carnaby Street, and let his hair grow. And it wasn't just the look. He developed an interest in the newly fashionable vegetarian cooking and chided Mildred about her meat-heavy dinners. He discovered Paul Bragg's *The Miracle of Fasting* and became a lifelong disciple. The Eastern spiritualism that had come west with the Beatles appealed to him. He was constantly out behind the house doing improbable yoga poses. He found that he liked being fit; he roller-skated, too, and often he and Moira, who had entered Julian Ashton the year after him, skated together across the Sydney Harbour Bridge to school.

During a 1971 Sydney bus strike, Philip made the trip on skates daily, a picture of hip insouciance with his *Sgt. Pepper's* tails and flares and flowing hair. The Australian evening news show *A Current Affair* found out and sent a crew to film him weaving deftly through the backed-up cars. A large photograph of him, headlined "Phil Got His Skates On," ran in the *Daily Telegraph*: "Art student Philip Mills . . . skated the ten miles from his home in Manly Vale into town, sailing through traffic jams and foul-ups with ease." A few days later, a follow-up story reported his arrest for violating a law that prohibited pedestrians "from proceeding longitudinally along the highway."

His sister Marianne, not one for the spotlight, was taken aback by all the coverage. "Phil," she said, mildly horrified, "everyone's *staring* at you."

Doris once told me that he and Mildred shared a "pathological need for attention." It was a phrase he often used. "That's what I *love*!" He beamed at her. "That's the *main reason*!"

2

SYLVIA AND THE SYNTHETICS

DORIS WAS BY NO MEANS THE FIRST PERSON TO CALL SYDNEY, as he described it to me, the drag capital of the world. Yet for a long time the city's rich tradition of cross-dressing flourished in the midst of a deep-rooted homophobia. Robert Hughes, in *The Fatal Shore*, his magisterial chronicle of Australia's penal origins, links this prejudice explicitly with the nation's historical shame. The gay sex that erupted when male prisoners were sequestered together, he writes, "was doubly damned: first, because it was a crime under law"—as it would remain into the late twentieth century—"and second, because it was mainly committed by those who were convicts already." The ongoing determination to extirpate the vice was thus viewed as a patriotic "act of cleansing—for homosexuality was one of the mute, stark, subliminal

Doris in his Synthetics phase, 1974. Photograph by Philip Morris.

elements in the 'convict stain' whose removal, from 1840 onward, so preoccupied Australian nationalists."

The louche freedoms of Paris and Berlin were alien to postcolonial Australia. But if you were in the know, there were places to go. Between the world wars, in addition to parks and "beats," as cruising spots were called, there were various lounges, such as the sleek Long Bar at the Australia Hotel (where Philip bought his phone box) or the working-class Belfields, on the corner of King Street and George Street—or Salt-Meat Alley, as the latter was nicknamed, since it was a prime place to pick up sailors—and there were restaurants, like the Shalimar, in the T&G Insurance Building, and the Latin Café, in the Royal Arcade, where you could cruise as long as you understood the codes and practiced them discreetly. None of these establishments were gay per se, but they had the kind of clientele—sophisticated, urban—that enjoyed a crackle of wickedness in the air.

As we now know, many gay men and women got their first taste of community in the armed services during World War II, which thus became a milestone in the development of a gay consciousness. But immediately afterward, the architects of the Cold War embraced the equation "perversion equals subversion," and the Australia of the period rivaled the States in both its bigotry and its ignorance. It was, in fact, even more repressive in matters of free expression: Gore Vidal's *The City and the Pillar*, a landmark of gay fiction published in the United States in 1948, was banned there until 1966.

The publication of *Sexual Behavior in the Human Male* (more familiarly known as the first Kinsey Report) in 1948, with its research disclosing that homosexual experience was widespread, brought extensive attention—along with shock and denial—to the subject of gay sexuality. The book, based on fifteen years of study with more than five thousand subjects, became an international bestseller. The churches, the medical profession, and especially the police all armed themselves for battle. In 1952, Colin Delaney, who that year became police commissioner for the state of New South Wales, pronounced homosexuality and communism the two biggest threats to the nation; in 1958 he again called homosexuality Australia's "greatest social menace." The upshot was, in the words of two Sydney historians, "a culture of blackmail, entrapment, arrest, exposure, infamy and disgrace."

And yet this violent repression had a hidden psychological benefit. As Garry Wotherspoon explains in his *Gay Sydney: A History*, "The way in which doctors, criminologists and politicians talked of 'the homosexual,' and the ways in which newspapers and magazines reported this, put this new conception into the public discourse. Taken together, it meant that vital components for the creation of a homosexual identity were in place."

Once the silence was shattered, a dam opened. As stories about homosexuals, however lurid, became fodder for the press, gay men and women realized that there were others like them:

> The very attempts to turn the machinery of state—and even society itself—against homosexuals led to unprecedented levels of publicity being given to homosexuals and homosexuality, to what they did and what they were. At one level and notwithstanding the . . . effects it might have on some individuals, this could be infinitely beneficial to other individuals who were suddenly informed that there was a vast homosexual world out there and that they—as individuals—were clearly not isolated and alone.

The discovery of community, however oblique, is one reason that, in the long run, this campaign to stamp out the unspeakable vice backfired. But even in the short run it met its match in the drag queens of Sydney.

The city had a tradition of elaborate balls, with an element of cross-dressing, that dated back at least to the 1920s. They generally took place at spacious halls in Kings Cross and other inner-city districts where the gay population was large and the tenor open-minded. These affairs were more bohemian than gay, attracting the kind of hipsters and free spirits who, a few decades later, would crowd into discos and punk clubs. But the ambience was queer enough to provoke constant hounding by the police, since cross-dressing was against the law. You could get away with it for these special occasions as long as you could show you had on men's underwear and you weren't in drag on the street for more than an hour before or after the event.

By the 1950s, the Artists Ball, the Arts Students Ball, and the Movie Ball (where you dressed up as your favorite star), all usually held at the Trocadero Ballroom on George Street, were major annual events. Some of the drag has become legendary. Karen Chant (as she's been known since she was a young man), having read that Marie Antoinette held the record for the most fabric used in a gown, came up with an outfit for the 1957 Artists Ball that incorporated seventeen hundred yards of tulle, much of it bunched into a gargantuan fishtail; it was so enormous that she had to be carted to the Trocadero in a moving van. The equally obsessive Claudia Wagner created an annual sensation by swooping through the doors in massive wigs that housed live birds. One year, a caged black chicken tied in place with a velvet ribbon to match her velvet dress attracted so much publicity—the Sydney *Daily Mirror* ran a story, with photographs, claiming that the bird had been abused—that she had to go on the lam. (She ultimately got off with a twenty-pound fine.)

Despite the notoriety of these events, the city had a lone drag bar, the Stork Club, out in the southern district of Sylvania. The club had to put up with continual police harassment. Then came the '60s. The drag clubs that began opening in 1961 were a phenomenon new to Sydney, but the clientele at most of them wasn't predominantly gay. The first was the Jewel Box, in Kings Cross, the project of a show-business entrepreneur whose showgirl wife had seen the "all-male" Jewel Box Revue in San Francisco and wanted to bring something like it to Sydney. Karen Chant—she of the seventeen hundred yards of tulle—soon became the compere (as emcees are called in Australia).

Like Finocchio's in San Francisco, which had been presenting female impersonators to tourists since 1936, the Jewel Box promoted itself as risqué entertainment for a sophisticated straight audience. So did Les Girls, a glittering spot, also in Kings Cross, that began its run in 1963 and kept going for several decades. In contrast, the Purple Onion, which opened that year a bit farther afield, in Kensington, aimed for the camp crowd. (Until well into the '70s, *camp* was the Australian word for *gay*; there was some regret when native terminology had to bow to international usage.) It was one among a spate of gay clubs and bars that would appear over the next two decades, even as sodomy remained a crime on the books. The Purple Onion—where Doris would perform with Sylvia and the Synthetics a decade later—was hipper and trendier than the straight clubs. By the end of the '60s, Rudolf Nureyev and Margot Fonteyn, the Beatles, the Rolling Stones, Dusty Springfield, and Dionne Warwick had all dropped in; Cecil Beaton wrote about it in his diary. Mostly the acts, here and elsewhere, involved elaborate costumes and lip-synching (miming, in Australian parlance) to show tunes and pop hits, though a few of the performers talked and sang in their own voices—among them Karen Chant, who was a prime mover and performer at the Purple Onion.

The shows were titillating and fantastically glamorous—as seen from the tables in the audience. For the performers, the reality was starkly different. They generally earned starvation wages, and legally they lived in a penumbral zone: if they showed up at the club already costumed, they could be arrested between the cab and the entrance. Still, new drag clubs continued to appear, although a suspiciously high number of them went up in flames, presumably because they hadn't paid the protection money that in that era both the mob and the police expected.

In the meantime, gay bars, another new phenomenon, were opening as well. Around the world, gay men and lesbians began colonizing sections of cities where they could be openly and comfortably themselves. In New York, the gay neighborhood coalesced around Christopher Street. In San Francisco, it was the Castro. In Sydney, the stretch of Oxford Street between Hyde Park and Paddington Town Hall became known as the Glitter Strip or the Golden Mile.

SUCH WAS SYDNEY IN THE '60s, WHEN THE YOUNG PHILIP MILLS began making his way to Doris Fish. "I've been in and out of dresses since as long as I can remember," he told me in 1986. He discovered the allure of Mildred's closet early on. "I remember being chastened for it, but not heavily. My mother and father did suspect that something was 'different.'"

He first put on a frock professionally, so to speak, when he was about twelve. At the end of every school year, one of the priests at the all-boys St. Augustine's would hire a theater, put half the boys in drag, and mount a big Broadway-style extravaganza, complete with strutting showgirls, cancan numbers, and kick lines. The begowned boys would sing in their own voices, which hadn't changed yet. In those years, when gender frontiers were comfortingly fixed, the families loved it. The first production that Philip was cast in featured selections from *Annie Get Your Gun* and other Wild West–themed songs, performed on a set that was supposed to represent a saloon in the Black Hills of Dakota. (Philip would become an adept set builder before he graduated.) Even though he was only a chorus girl, he told me, he had the highest kick in the kick line and "a really nice big dress." He and Peter McMahon, who were still best friends, "took it perhaps a little more seriously than some of the other boys did. I wouldn't say that we were the most beautiful, but we *were* the most dedicated."

Two or three years later, Peter discovered the drag bars, and soon he introduced Philip to the excitement of slumming. "It was fascinating," Doris continued. "That was '67, '68"—so he would have been fifteen or sixteen—"and the things people were wearing were just *fantastic*. Oh, the fashions. Everybody used to dress to the *tits*. Even now there are still zillions and zillions of drag queens there, but then it was thicker and they were more fantastic—hairdos that were three or four feet tall, jeweled . . . and this was just daytime wear! There were drag queens in Sydney who were like covers of *Vogue* magazine times ten. Drag queens usually are much more than just women. They're *aggressively* glamorous."

It wasn't long before the boys were dabbling in drag themselves. But although they weren't conscious of it at first, there was a generational divide between them and the older queens. Presumably in the preliberation era it took a compelling need for a man to risk an activity as aberrant, and illegal, as parading around in women's clothes. For Philip and Peter, it was a hoot. Getting arrested for the crime of drag must have struck them as a ridiculous idea. Anyway, they were part of a generation for whom getting arrested, whether for smoking pot or for protesting the Vietnam War, was becoming a badge of honor. And so they could pick and choose what they liked, baggage free, from this strange adult world of cross-dressers. Ultimately, they and their contemporaries would transform it.

By the time Philip came out to his family, at around eighteen, they were, as I said, hardly floored. For years they had watched him advising his older sisters on fashion and makeup and his mother on decor. Ace and Mildred, whose own ideas had broadened by the late '60s, were extremely tolerant. (Over the coming years they were going to have a lot to tolerate.) But Philip did more than merely inform them. As Jacqueline Hyde explained to me, "Doris felt she had to educate her family and get them involved. It was a *truth*, homosexuality. People had to be made aware of this thing and accept it."

Though that resolve was partly Doris being Doris, it was also one more sign of how radically the self-image of young homosexuals had changed by the time of Stonewall. "Well, we *did* think it was our birthright," Jackie said. "The generation before us had no idea. Even the bohemians had no idea. Homosexuality and transvestism—that was unspeakable to them." As for Doris: "She would not allow people to be horrified at her. She would not allow censorship."

The family worried, of course, and felt protective in an era when *poofter* was still a standard term in the national vocabulary.* Philip was mild, peaceable, and, though he was fit and strong, painfully vulnerable. Both of his younger brothers, who were "football-playing, surfing sorta toughies," in Andrew's words, are still proud of the way he handled an incident that took place on Horning Parade when he was

---

* As it remained in 1994, when one of the digital prints that Doris's friend the artist David McDiarmid included in his brightly hued *Rainbow Aphorisms* series read THAT'S MISS POOFTER TO YOU ASSHOLE.

sixteen or so. He was sitting on the veranda, drawing, when an across-the-street neighbor named Martin, "a bit of a dickhead," Andrew recalled, who must have known or at least sensed that Philip was gay, came over and began baiting him. Philip went on quietly drawing, but Martin—who was six feet tall to Philip's five eight—kept on goading him until, finally, Philip stood up and slugged him. The bully had a big shiner the next day, and he never bothered Philip again. As far as I know that punch was the sole time anyone saw Doris do anything violent. Except onstage.

Violence was a signature of Sylvia and the Synthetics, the "antidrag drag" group, as Doris called it, that inaugurated his theatrical career. The troupe was very much part of—or, perhaps more accurately, a cracked reflection of—the new era that was taking shape. In 1970 the Australian literary scholar Germaine Greer published *The Female Eunuch*, a founding text of '70s feminism. In 1971 Dennis Altman, who taught politics at the University of Sydney, published *Homosexual: Oppression and Liberation*, arguably *the* founding text of the modern gay-rights movement. Altman's book is especially striking, and touching, in its faith, which was then widely shared, that tremendous social upheavals were on the way. The deck was so stacked against gay people that no one imagined they could achieve their goals without broader changes to all society. (Altman's original readers would have been flabbergasted to learn that out of women's, Black, and gay liberation—the three movements for greater equality that he constantly cites—the push for gay rights would turn out to be the most successful in achieving its aims.)

And then, in 1972, after twenty-three years out of power, the Australian Labor Party under Gough Whitlam won the national elections—in large part because of its opposition to Australia's role in the disintegrating Vietnam War. The new Labor government initiated national health care and free university education and vastly increased support for its arts council, sending much of the funding to community projects. Among the young, especially, there was a heady mood of optimism and advancing freedom—a conviction that the revolution had begun.

In Sydney, all kinds of new groups were already flourishing, like the Roxy Collective, a team of hippie artists who'd gotten together in late 1969 to open a free studio and workshop at 7–9 Flinders Street, just off Taylor Square. Oxford Street's evolving strip of gay bars and clubs was just around the corner. The group sponsored whimsical '70s-style conceptual-art projects, like baking multitudes of pies for a giant anyone-can-join pie fight in Taylor Square. They put a huge sculptured nose above the Roxy's door and mounted eyelashes over the windows, and they adorned the facade with rocket ships and stars. Inside, they painted suds on the floor in a delicate pattern, with a little window on every bubble. "A lot of drugs went into that," Ron Smith—a member of the collective who would later work closely with Doris—told me. A giant pair of chubby legs strapped into high-heeled dancing shoes protruded, half fancifully, half ominously, from the ceiling. Over the Roxy's large awning they constructed a massive papier-mâché ice cream cone whose pop-art effrontery so offended the city fathers that, unannounced, they had it torn off the building, awning and all. "One morning," Ron recalled, "we woke up to this enormous crunching, grinding noise . . ."

The Roxy became the first home base of the boundary-breaking Sylvia and the Synthetics. There were as many as twenty bona fide Synthetics, plus quite a few peripheral ones, but a core group of eight or ten. It included a trio of gay friends, Morris Spinetti, Denis Norton, and Denis's boyfriend, Paul Hock; an actor, Andrew Sharp; a contortionist (now a well-reputed visual artist), Bruce Goold; the already-quoted Jacqueline (Jackie) Hyde, who during that distant era was known as Mel (officially Michael Anthony) Slattery; Mel's best friend, Clayton MacDonald; and Miss Abood, or Danny Abood, who was born Daniel Archer in Armidale, New South Wales, some three hundred miles north of Sydney, and whom Jackie describes as "the tall Lebanese one with the big nose that someone tried to pull off once, thinking it was fake." He and Jackie soon became two of Doris's closest friends and confidants. Jackie, a soignée brunette who has been living as a woman in Paris for decades now, developed her high-speed wit over months and years of emceeing drag shows with Doris. (Pronounced with the right Australian accent, her name becomes "Jekyll 'n' Hyde.") Time and alcohol have magnified her into the kind of sociable gorgon who could play Martha in *Who's Afraid of Virginia Woolf?*, a drama she is very fond of quoting. Miss Abood was the most scarily violent of the Synthetics, and his language remained full of violence and scorn. Doris had a set phrase for him: "She was her usual rude self and didn't care who knew it!"

Jackie—or, at that time, Mel—and Clayton, like Philip and Peter, had grown up in an outlying quarter of Sydney, in their case the western suburb of Fairfield. Mel, too, was Catholic, the eldest of thirteen children, and he, too, went to art school, taking much more interest in the avant-garde than Philip did. Clayton was as swishy and outrageous as Peter McMahon, already at fifteen adorning himself in cloaks and feathers, an adolescent Oscar Wilde. When the two of them sashayed past the local pub, Jackie remembers, the men inside would come to the door and scream at them. They were arty teenagers who made sculptures and sponsored poetry readings and spent their Saturday afternoons in Italian delicatessens, "drinking wine and eating salami. We turned it into a little Left Bank sort of thing."

After Jackie/Mel finished art school, he and Clayton moved together to Surry Hills, where they were soon immersed in the gay party scene. In the heady, druggy days of the early '70s, Jackie says, meeting people was everything. "You'd just meet them in the street. You could tell if they weren't really straight—they were either on roller skates or wearing velvet capes or had face paint in the middle of the day." That's how Morris Spinetti, Denis Norton, and Paul Hock wound up in their flat, according to Jackie. "You know, you have a few drinks and you get into drag—or you did in those days." The drag parties went on for a while, she recalls, and then someone had the idea of moving them to a larger space and charging admission—which is one version of how Sylvia and the Synthetics came into being.

Morris and Denis remember it somewhat differently (Paul Hock died years ago)—although, as Morris has written, given all the drugs they were doing "it's a wonder anyone remembers anything." In their version, the three of them and their friend the singer Wendy Saddington were in a cab on their way home from a bad drag show at Chez Ivy, a popular bar in Bondi Junction; Paul groused, "We could do much better than those tragic queens," and somehow the idea took hold. The trio's drag was crude. Morris rolled squares of cardboard into conical breasts and cut black paper into eyebrows that looked like tarantulas. Denis was hopeless with makeup, too, he says, whereas Jackie and Clayton were much more exacting about how they looked. "We'd all go to the Salvation Army headquarters—you could buy a big box of clothing for two bucks. They'd get matching calfskin shoes and handbags, this really Coco Chanel look, which was divine."

It was Paul who made a deal with the Roxy Collective to use the building for what could be described as either a performance or a party. Admission was two dollars, with half the proceeds going to the Roxy. Everybody entering got two free Mandraxes, the Australian and European brand name for the tranquilizers known in the States as Quaaludes, which were a familiar party drug in the '70s. They make you happy and they make you sloppy. It wasn't uncommon in those days to see people sliding off their barstools.

Sylvia and the Synthetics made their debut at the Roxy sometime in October 1972. According to Jackie, the entertainment was really nothing more than a ladder that you climbed up to show off your drag and wave to the crowd: "That was the show—a ladder against the wall."

I suspect there was *something* more, because the crowd was enthusiastic enough for a second show to be scheduled at the Roxy for Saturday, November 11. This one had a circus theme; Ron Smith, who was there, remembers Bruce Goold, the contortionist, scrabbling up a wall like a fly, as well as an act of fellatio on a trapeze. This was also the show in which Philip and Peter made their debut. They'd been among the partygoers the previous month and had made enough of an impression to be invited to join the troupe.

I've never heard anyone describe Peter—who soon began calling himself Jasper Havoc—as anything less than gorgeous, with his delicate features and his corkscrew curls, but Philip was a novice drag queen. He had matured into a handsome, square-jawed young man, but that jaw didn't make him a natural candidate for cross-dressing. Like Denis, he hadn't yet mastered makeup, and he was much more excited about being in drag—"some old shit wig," according to Ron Smith, and "dime-store dresses"—than about the drag itself. Denis calls it "old-lady drag." But the effort alone was enough to win Jackie over. "I would never have *spoken* to her if she hadn't been in drag," she says. "I felt sorry for the poor thing. She had little Japanese-war-bride glasses and this frumpy hat. I guess she was dressed as her mother."

When Doris offered his own account, it was far more glamorous. In a "Whatever Happened to . . .?" reminiscence he wrote about the group for the Sydney gay paper *Campaign* five years later, he recalled his debut: "I wore a red suit with blond hair. Later it all came off! Layers of underwear, including a pair of rhinestone-encrusted panties, cascaded to the floor. I became the first naked Synthetic!"

And thus, Doris Fish came into being. Jackie claims to have given him the name Doris because he was so dowdy. Doris told me a different story, which involved moving into a communal house and claiming a room full of '50s blond-wood furniture that everybody referred to as the Doris Day Suite. "And so the next day they started calling me Doris, just like that. There wasn't a moment's hesitation. And I took the name Fish from a cat named Lillian Fish. This was in Australia, and I was young, and I don't know if I was even aware of the double entendre of *fish* at that point.* It certainly wasn't a popular term in Australia."

Jackie contends that Doris knew perfectly well, and that he chose the surname purposely as a critique of the way straight men saw women. Nothing in Doris's own behavior, either then or later, suggested misogyny. Far from it—he had many close female friends, and there were female singers and actors (but no male ones I know of) that he worshipped. He did, however, like everyone else in the Synthetics, get a

---

* Esther Newton, in *Mother Camp*, offers the following taxonomy of misogynistic gay male responses to the question "Why don't you like X (a lesbian)?": "Because I don't like women, (or worse) 'broads,' (or even worse) 'fish.'"

charge out of pushing boundaries—the doctrinaire liberation movements of those years had stringent taboos—which meant sometimes going too far. The scorn becomes clearer, and so does its target, polite society, if you imagine that he'd gone all the way and called himself Doris Cunt. Giving offense was part of his aesthetic, and over time the ways in which he gave it got more intricate and assured. At this point, though, he was largely going on instinct.

"The Synthetics," Doris told me, "offered an outlet where you could be theatrical and really draggy in any way you wanted, because it was satire. You could be hideous if you wanted to be, or you could just throw yourself around onstage without having an act. It wasn't, strictly speaking, drag to be feminine. The look was just to get a look. Just—'*Look!*'"

There was another kind of satire going on as well: irreverence toward the glamorous professional drag queens at places like Chez Ivy and especially Les Girls, who worked hard on their look and delivered slick—and, by this time, celebrated—shows. It was a version of the scorn the young always feel for their elders, and the group's targets felt deeply insulted, especially since their pre-Stonewall audacity had played a big part in ushering in the new era of liberation. The Synthetics didn't refer to them by name, but if you knew the drag scene you could tell who was being mocked. For example, a certain Lockjaw Barbara performed a signature striptease with her back to the audience; at the end she'd turn around, full frontal but with her penis tucked between her legs, providing the illusion of female genitalia. Ron Smith recalls a takeoff of that number that Miss Abood used to do. His enormous penis was famous, and so tucking it gave him a tail. He would do the reveal in reverse, stripping front-on, with a hairy chest but just pubic hair, and then turn around. "And the audience would scream."

Though the Synthetics started independently, they were influenced by the Cockettes, a San Francisco troupe that had introduced the notion of gender-bending or, less politely, genderfuck only a couple of years earlier. "It was the same movement," Doris explained to me, "dresses and beards—though *we* didn't have any beards. They were ruled out straightaway." The Cockettes gave the first of their legendary midnight shows at San Francisco's Palace Theater on New Year's Eve 1969–70 and performed there regularly until October 1972, breaking up the very month that Sylvia and the Synthetics debuted at the Roxy. Like the Synthetics, they provided a kind of you-had-to-be-there event, and much of it was owing to the audience. Among the principal reasons for the delirious enthusiasm they drew was that, as the writer and director John Waters, who was frequently at the shows, has recounted, the experience was "something that you can never imagine today: going somewhere where every person on the stage and in the audience was on drugs." The performers—"hippie acid-head drag queens," as Waters describes them, accurately—weren't skilled, but their anarchic brand of musical theater was (thanks largely, no doubt, to the acid) immersive.

Drag had a long history in gay San Francisco, but genderfuck was an exhilarating new idea that had blossomed in what seemed to be a moment of total freedom. Both the Cockettes and the Synthetics saw themselves as the shock troops of the sexual revolution. Traditional drag, as they saw it, was the sad fruit of an outmoded psychology that viewed gay men as "inverts" or women manqué. The male Cockettes made no attempt to disguise their hairy chests and legs. They covered their beards with glitter. They covered *everything* with glitter ("You could always see which direction we traveled," one of them has written, "because, like a trail of bread crumbs, it sprinkled the sidewalks")— and with tulle, chiffon, lace, lamé, and Kabuki-level layers of face paint. Like the Synthetics after them, they were full of performers who loved to strip—if sex wasn't shameful, why keep your clothes on? And if sex roles were an artificial construct forced on us by a society of conformist androids, then why not put on a sequined evening gown? Their simultaneously raunchy and naive midnight musicals at the Palace, in which they sang in their own not-great voices, paid homage to the Broadway and Hollywood of the '20s, '30s, and '40s; they certainly hadn't abandoned old drag-queen notions of glamour. But the shows were barely rehearsed and, for that reason, wildly unpredictable—"a surprise to everyone, the cast included." They were a gift to writers and photojournalists looking to document the psychedelic frontiers of the sexual counterculture. If you were under thirty at the time and you tried to keep up with the scene by reading magazines, you knew about the Cockettes. I did, and Sylvia and the Synthetics certainly did.

That moment of total freedom arrived in Sydney a few years later than in San Francisco. Australia's first gay political organization, the Campaign Against Moral Persecution Inc., or CAMP Inc., held its first public meeting in 1971, the same year that Dennis Altman published his influential book. Liberation was in the air. Sylvia and the Synthetics weren't consciously political; "I didn't give anything a second thought," Doris told an interviewer in 1989. "It was just where can we get the dresses and the shoes to match." But of course for a movement whose progress depended on its members' coming out into the open, the Synthetics' insouciance toward gender conventions—their flaming *queerness*—was inherently political. All gay visibility was, and still is.

Like the Cockettes, the Synthetics included straight men. And there were women: a large one named Rona; a teenager who would change from her school uniform into something slutty and go on the prowl for sex; and Cherry Ripe, who, Doris wrote, "once inserted a banana into her feminine gender and it came out peeled!" ("Mashed," according to Jackie.)

But the most stunning must have been Carmel Strelein, who fell in with the Synthetics when she was twelve or thirteen, though she passed herself off as older. She was one of those individuals born to the avant-garde, with a wild originality that bordered on the savage. Carmel fashioned sweaters with extra arms, complete with hands and jewelry, and pants with extra legs; she yanked her dark hair back and pinned it in place with swastikas. Later she shaved it off completely and extended great batwings of black eyeliner all the way over her scalp. The portrait and fashion photographer Norman Parkinson was so captivated by her that he gave her a two-page spread in his 1978 book *Sisters Under the Skin*, in the company of such luminaries as Queen Elizabeth, Iman, and Miss Piggy. Carmel's fearlessness and her inventiveness were an inspiration to the Synthetics—especially to Doris, whom Carmel would follow to San Francisco in 1980.

To the Cockettes' outrageousness, Sylvia and the Synthetics added a new element: hostility. Or rather they brought it to the fore, since hostility lay just under the surface even of the love-and-glitter Cockettes. In 1970, for a guy to put on a frock wasn't merely an assertion of personal freedom: It was as defiant an act of public aggression as walking down the street naked. Miss Abood remembered that when he came to Sydney in 1971, "I wore '40s dresses over black pants, and I had really long hair and I wore little bits of makeup. I used to get around like that and just get abused, screamed at, but it didn't bother me. I quite liked it."

I quite liked it: Those words are key. The Synthetics liked it, and the Cockettes liked it, and their pleasure wasn't innocent; it lay in the malicious thrill of flouting norms they had contempt for. "We just knew that we were against everything that was considered normal, which we considered very corrupt," Jackie told me. The era of flowers in your hair was on the downswing. "We really didn't like hippies," she said, "although hippies basically made up our audience. Doris had a lot of hippie in her—she was herbal and all that sort of stuff. But we weren't. We wanted to destroy." Which makes sense: If you were in your twenties and gay in the early '70s, in Sydney or San Francisco or anywhere else, there was a lot to be angry about—the Vietnam War was still raging, and gay sex was still a crime. The Synthetics, as the visionary Carmel's swastika barrettes suggest, embodied the gathering discontent that would soon coalesce into the aesthetic of punk. It took only a few years for free love to give way to unleashed rage. Hence the violence, the noise, and the gauntlet thrown down to the audience at every show.

SYLVIA AND THE SYNTHETICS MADE THEIR THIRD [*] APPEARANCE ON Saturday, November 25, 1972. It's possible to describe this one more

---

* Or possibly their fourth: the show that was staged in a butcher shop (see p. 47) may have come before it.

precisely, because by now the group had gained enough notoriety to be written about. They had quickly outgrown the Roxy, or rather the loutishness of their audience had become too much for the Roxy Collective, which had recently painted a giant snakes-and-ladders game on the floor and didn't want the Synthetics crowd scratching it up. Their new show took place in the semivacant space that had formerly been the Purple Onion, the gay drag club, which was in the process of being turned into Ken's Karate Klub, a gay bathhouse that was, for the evening, christened Sylvia's Asylum. The old Purple Onion may not have been a very wise choice of venue, since the drag activities there had been, and remained, of vast interest to the city's vice squad; there are conflicting reports as to whether they shut down this performance. (They raided more than one.) A story on the Synthetics in an alternative newspaper described the disquieting thrill of the opening moments:

> Even before the main show begins, there are a couple of things to set the tone. The queen in the black dress on top of the ladder in the corner with one leg bent behind his head, standing upright on the other one staring into space leaves a surreal image floating in the mind, and the two who appear and rip down the red parachute that hung from the ceiling are in a frenzy of fury that's too real to leave you feeling easy. When one of them falls the twelve feet to the floor everyone believes he must be really hurt, and however cool you might be, real violence is disturbing.

Yes it is, and the Synthetics' shows were sprinkled with it. The twelve-foot plunge, however, was an unplanned coup de théâtre that resulted in a broken leg. In the audience, several young guys were wandering around naked. "Would you like to stroke it?" one of them asked a reporter. Doris remembered both the atmosphere and the audience as "electrifying." Andrew Sharp descended through a hole in the ceiling in a debutante gown, on the shoulders of a bodybuilder who had recently been named Mr. Queensland and who was, according to Doris, "wearing little more than a smile." The music began, with Sharp lip-synching Dodie Stevens's treacly 1959 ballad "Coming of Age." When he reached the lyric "My heart has never been lighter," he pulled out a sheep's heart and bit into it. Blood dribbled down his chin and onto his powder-blue gown. "Somebody," Doris reported, "walked out after that."

The high point was probably the number that came to be known as "A Housewife's Dream of Love." The mousy housewife, Connie Slab (as Denis Norton called himself), entered with a vacuum cleaner to deal with the mess from the preceding number. As she "hoovers away to the soul-soaring one-two-three of 'The Blue Danube,'" wrote a reporter, she becomes "increasingly fascinated by the sexual potential of the bits and pieces of the cleaner." Jackie enters in the role of a console TV, "complete with vase and daddy-in-the-war photo" and advertising cornflakes, which the TV soon begins hurling at the housewife, along with other products. As the music grows louder, more Synthetics enter with their own products (shaving cream, cookies) and do the same. "The vacuum's accessories are pulled to bits and everyone's away, simulating fucking each other and having themselves off with the extension tubes and winding suction hose. The mousy housewife sits in the midst of the hairy bottoms and sweaty groins, glassily enraptured with the immortal Strauss, quietly rubbing herself up and down on the main body of the machine."

"We didn't think it had any point to it," Doris told me, "but we got reviewed quite seriously in one of the art magazines as some kind of art-piece satire on the consumer society." Morris says that once the drugs took hold, "we just fell about the stage looking and acting like lunatics, slapping the audience with abuse. The crowd watching thought it was performance art."

The shows always began with a ritual announcement: "Unfortunately Sylvia won't be performing tonight. She was decapitated on the way to the theater." In truth there was never any Sylvia.[*] The Synthetics

---

[*] *Sylvia* was Morris's contribution, from a 1965 Carroll Baker melodrama. *Synthetics* referred to their fabric of choice.

were a leaderless collective. Their songs were generally lip-synched, to a set list that typically included a few 78 rpm records from the '30s and '40s, a couple of 45s from the '50s, and at least one current rock song, all played at punishingly high volume. ("The noise is tremendous and there's no escape," one journalist wrote, approvingly.) There might be anywhere from ten to forty people onstage. Once, they assembled twenty-six Marilyn Monroes—"twenty-six out-of-it, really bad Marilyns," Jackie says—who entered in five wedding gowns each to "Chapel of Love," only to shred them in the ensuing brawl. One outraged critic described the number as "a grotesque denigration of a heroine who is well loved by all, especially homosexuals." At other times, Jackie performed ballet vignettes to early music and "did a beautiful dance to a Stravinsky piano piece," Doris recalled, "dressed in crepe paper of many colors." Beautiful Jasper slithered into a '30s evening gown, lit a cigarette, and mimed to torch singers or sang in his own lovely voice. The troupe performed a dance to "Slaughter on Tenth Avenue" against a glittering New York skyline. "Anything went," Jackie says, "as long as it was weird and arty and offensive. There were lots of blood capsules and gore involved. The big thing was, we had to take drugs before we went onstage. We'd do these big pyramids of everyone on Quaaludes. You can imagine how well that worked."

And they threw things. When Miss Abood did "I'm Gonna Wash That Man Right Outa My Hair," Doris sent a tubful of water flying into the audience. As Snow Whip, Jackie spattered the crowd with whipped cream. For the Andrews Sisters' "Hold Tight," as soon as they reached the line "I get my favorite dish, fish," they began slapping one another with dead flatheads, then turned them on the spectators.

Miss Abood was the greatest champion of audience violence. Jackie says that he always carried a brick in his handbag and wasn't shy about using it. According to a report in a gay paper, "If you get too close to the stage, you're likely to be shoved back by a high-heeled shoe planted firmly on your chest." As one Synthetic explained, "People are used to the pretended violence in films—we give them the real thing. We actually *are* violent."

The violence, the nudity, the tackiness, the drugs—they all added up, weirdly, to a phenomenon that people, or at least some people—the insidery, mostly gay audience that embraced the art and fashion avant-garde—adored. The cultural moment was intoxicating worldwide. By 1972, the young urbanites who formed the Synthetics' audience had by and large shaken off the repression they'd grown up with, and they were inspired by the apparently limitless freedom of the psychos on the stage. Everything was permitted, including ineptitude. Even now, Miss Abood told me, "I'll be walking down the street and people will come up and say, 'Sylvia and the Synthetics! You changed my life!'"

DORIS'S FAMILY NEVER SAW HIM PERFORM WITH THE SYNTHETICS. In 1973 they were entering a period of crisis. After twenty-five years, Mildred and Ace's marriage had fallen into a state of decay. All those evenings he had spent cloistered over his law books had created a strain that didn't abate when the payoff came and he began his rise to increasingly prestigious and demanding government jobs. Mildred got more fanatical in her Catholicism, and her cheerfulness faltered. As Liz said: "Six kids with your husband locked away—why wouldn't you be neurotic?" In 1973 Mildred signed up for the *Australian Women's Weekly* World Discovery Tour, an annual magazine-sponsored expedition, which that year would besiege twenty-two countries between February and June. The older kids were out of the nest; only Andrew and Gina remained, and, at fifteen and thirteen, they could manage without her for a few months. Ace enjoyed the respite, Liz says. "We *think* he had a girlfriend. He didn't wash the sheets for three months. They were black by the time she got back!" And worse was on the way.

Disintegrating home life; accelerating notoriety. Such was the background against which Doris and Jackie and Clayton forged their philosophy of Romantic Cruelism. Jackie was the driving force behind it. Romantic Cruelism harked back to the Left Bank–flavored poetry readings that she and Clayton had sponsored as teenagers. It was a sequined version of existentialism, or that's how they liked to think of it; mainly it was an excuse for saying grim and cutting things, often at Doris's expense. "She was their kicking bag," Denis remembers, though he also remembers that "they loved her for it. Clare"—Clayton— "would start, and then Jackie would get that look, that little smile," and deliver the zinger. Doris was too sweet natured to let their cruelty get to him. But Doris was also a quick study, and he soon learned how to zing back. Mockery was a pleasure that sunny Philip hadn't much indulged in as he was growing up. Now he was constructing Doris and, in the process, discovering the legacy of camp bitchiness that, as a budding drag queen, was his to claim. He eventually became a master of the put-down, but it was a learned skill—a talent of Doris's, not of Philip's. His family never saw that side of him, to say nothing of the beast he sometimes turned into on the stage. In retrospect, the connection between this acting out and the collapse of his family, as well as the constant ragging he was getting from peers whose approval he craved, looks starkly obvious. "I think there was a mad streak in Doris somewhere," Jackie muses, without perceiving any responsibility for it.

As the months went on, Sylvia and the Synthetics found all kinds of places to wreak havoc, from the respectable Paddington Town Hall to an old butcher shop where they hung drag queens from meat hooks. Sometimes their friend the singer Wendy Saddington or an up-and-coming rock band would perform on the same bill, offering genuine talent. Anyone who was throwing a hip party wanted them there. ("I'm sure they were sorry," Jackie says, "because part of our act would be ruining their house.") Publicists hired them for openings. The record company EMI secured their services for a press event it was hosting in the Rothmans Theatrette at the Sydney Showground to promote a record release by a then-hot Australian singer named Ross Ryan. The troupe was supposed to come onstage dressed as bunnies and line up, each holding up a letter of his name, but that, of course, was a bust— you would be as likely to get a group of cats to line up properly. Then they performed, and the executives paled when the costumes came off and the blood started gushing. Finally somebody hit the lights. The damage from the fake gore to the hall's velvet curtains ran into the thousands of dollars. Afterward a headline proclaimed, "SEX, BLOOD AND CORNFLAKES: DRAG QUEENS TERRORISE SHOW."

They even got hired as fashion models. In 1973, the daredevil editor Richard Neville, who had been brought to trial for obscenity in both Sydney and London, was invited to guest edit a special issue of the trendy magazine *POL*. In "Anti-Fashion with Sylvia and the Synthetics," he got the photographer Grant Mudford to capture the "theatrical politicians," as he called them, in Platonic versions (Dior, Gucci) of the cast-off crap they spent their daylight hours rifling thrift shops for. Their makeup ranged from Bozo the Clown to *Night of the Living Dead*, though Doris was notably pretty among the freaks. For a second feature, Neville outfitted them in the inventive fashions of the young English designer Zandra Rhodes. They looked so demented, practically falling out the windows of the Roxy's midnight-blue facade in her flouncy blue and black sweaters, silks, and fun furs, that it's hard to imagine any reader wanting to buy the clothes. Neville evidently recognized the issue: he titled the spread "Zandra Rhodes May Never Speak to *POL* Again."

All this notoriety, however, didn't exactly equal success. Anarchy is no way to keep an enterprise afloat. The liberal consumption of Mandraxes meant that everyone was too out of it to pay attention to the box office. Instead of a cash box there was usually a paper bag, which often got lost or stolen. No one much cared. But without funds to pay off the police, raids were a constant problem. (Jackie again: "They needed to arrest *someone*, as they couldn't arrest the real criminals, because the real criminals were all working for someone who was paying them. So they would arrest us, for inciting people to debauchery. You could hardly deny that.")

Because of this hovering threat, they couldn't publicize their shows. They would leaflet the gay bars a couple of days before a performance, which was usually enough to get them a healthy crowd. Del Fricker, the head of the vice squad, was in attendance at least once; she collected four passed-out members of the audience and took them down to the station. Once, Clayton, who performed under the name Cockroach Clare, was hauled off to police headquarters and learned that the cops had been backstage in plain clothes, photographing everybody and all the drugs. They wanted names, which he supplied, he told the others when he returned—"And I asked if we could get copies, because they were great photographs!"

All these factors made the troupe even more labile than such groups are by nature. People drifted in and out constantly. Morris left early (in Melbourne he founded the short-lived Betty Spaghetti and the Raviolis), Denis and Paul not long after, and within a year or so the new core consisted of Doris and Jasper, Jackie and Clayton, and the formidable Miss Abood, with Doris eventually rising to the status of first among equals. Doris, Jackie says, was the ambitious one; the rest were only in it for fun. What drove Doris, as she sees it, was "the cult of the heterosexual" and the damage it did to gay men and women. Beyond personal ambition, he was out to change that worldview by force of will and the power of outrage, of outrageousness, of theater.

A turning point was what they called their "traveling porn show," which they presented at the local universities in collaboration with a well-known dominatrix named Madame Lash. The ninety-minute presentation truly was pornographic, so much so that it seems amazing they put it on more than once. A prelude consisted of clips from sex films. Madame Lash was towed onstage in a chariot by two maidens in bondage; she ripped off her skirt to reveal a large dildo, which she used to sodomize Doris and Miss Abood, both dressed in black conical bras and, at least until that point, leather skirts. But the student audience wasn't the same hip, druggy crowd that had gotten off on the group's freakishness in the clubs, and the excess was too extreme for it to handle. At one of the shows, Doris fellated a young man planted in the front row and spit his semen (or pretended to) at the spectators, which was enough to provoke the audience into throwing things and, finally, rushing the stage. Miss Abood, wielding one of the prop whips, rushed it back, and a melee ensued. Doris, playing to the cameras, went down on his back, fending off kicks with all fours in the air. The newspapers ate it up.

Nevertheless, the drift continued, and in the end Sylvia and the Synthetics were reduced to three: Doris, Jasper, and Miss Abood. They performed their final show on December 31, 1974. "Our skills were refined, our timing was perfected and our enthusiasm bubbling," Doris wrote in his reminiscence. "Danny did a Shirley Temple song, 'I Love to Walk in the Rain.' I provided lots of rain! We did a Supremes number; 'Slow Boat to China' was our '40s offering. But it *was* the end."

THE MILLS FAMILY, TOO, WAS COMING TO AN END, AT LEAST IN THE nuclear form the kids had known growing up. Soon after Mildred's return from her overseas tour, she took thirteen-year-old Gina to Bega, some 270 miles down the country's southeast coast, where Marianne and Tony had just moved. They were living on a farm, in those back-to-the-land years, and teaching high school. (They later settled in nearby Wolumla, where Doris would spend many Christmases.) Gina loved horses, and Marianne and Tony had found one for her to ride during the two weeks that she and Mildred were there.

On a Thursday not long after they got back to Manly Vale, Gina came down with what appeared to be the flu. She hadn't gotten better by Saturday. On Sunday she went into the hospital; an allergic reaction to penicillin sent her into intensive care. On Monday she deteriorated further. On Tuesday she died, from an illness that was never identified.

She wasn't just the youngest of the six Mills children; she'd had the special place of the little girl who arrives after a spate of boys. "She was dark and had a very pretty face," Marianne says, "and she loved animals, and she was very simple. Nothing was put on. She was the light of the family."

Her death was fatal to Mildred and Ace's marriage. They stayed together for another year and a half, with poor Andrew the one left at home to witness the arguments. He remembers his mother outside the house, hurling dishes at his father as he sat inside his car. The family as they knew it had disintegrated.

When I interviewed Doris for my newspaper story in 1986, he mentioned his parents' divorce and said it happened after he'd already left home. "Of course, it wouldn't have affected me anyway," he added. "I'm really hard and cold when it comes to things like that—though I would have been entertained by it. I'm sure it was very amusing." The facade had been fixed in place. By now the consummate Romantic Cruelist, in public he cultivated an air of invulnerability and indifference. This pose was part of his heritage as a drag queen, but it was also what most differentiated Doris Fish from Philip Mills, a distinction that in the presence of a journalist he coolly papered over.

He also brought up Gina's death: "I felt like I was watching a movie at the time. I didn't really feel personally involved. I suppose part of my personality is not to feel things deeply. I'm very shallow—in a deep way." All untrue, except the "deep."

3
WORKING GIRL

I T TOOK DORIS SOME TIME TO FIGURE OUT HOW HE WAS GOING
to support himself. For a while he held down various jobs, barely.
Though as an artist he was disciplined and committed—nothing like
the stereotype of the loopy drag queen—you wouldn't have guessed it
from his early employment record. Between high school and art school,
his father got him a public-service job at the telephone exchange, where
he was supposed to aid customers having phone problems. He did
the opposite. "We had no competition," he told me, "so people *had* to
deal with incompetents like myself." Later, when he was performing
with Sylvia and the Synthetics, he picked up some cash as a busboy

Philip the hunk. Photo by Michael Cook.

at a smart downtown hotel. His fingernail polish, which the troupe had made something of a mini-fad among its followers, put an end to that job. He went on the dole. "She thought she was wasting her time working," Jackie says. "Which is true—work *is* wasting your time." Any committed artist feels the same way.

After he joined the Synthetics, Jackie introduced him to Brian Barrow, a well-bred restorer of fine antiques who had an atelier in Randwick, in the Eastern Suburbs, where Jackie had gone to work. Trained in art, she showed a flair for the craft, and it became her career. Doris, too, picked up skills in gilding and faux-marbling from Brian, which served him well later when he was constructing sets and tarting up his living spaces.

A connoisseur of drag, as of much else, Brian Barrow admired Doris's wit, his visual artistry, and his good-natured refusal to let anyone ruffle him. He found Doris the most professional of the group— "the others were just trying to look bizarre." And so he offered him one of the spare rooms in his rather majestic home in Bondi in exchange for housework. A *little bit* of housework. But Doris couldn't be bothered with even that much. "He was a hopeless domestic," Brian says. Doris's lack of refinement ("Boiling up some frozen peas and macaroni and just sitting there eating it out of the saucepan—that was a meal!") also gave Brian pause, and his posh friends were condescending. Amused but also exasperated, Brian terminated the arrangement in a mock letter of nonrecommendation: "I can only foresee the stage, the street, the gutter, disease, and death for her."

In 1974, during the latter part of the Synthetics period, Doris worked in the wallpaper factory of Florence Broadhurst, a talented designer, by then in her seventies, who was both a legend and a dragon. The employees hated her, the wages were rotten, and Doris didn't stay long. But once again he picked up something important—in this case, the glittering metallic powders that went onto many of the wallpapers. He pilfered a generous supply and began mixing them into his makeup, the beginning of years of experimentation and innovation with cosmetics. Despite his increasingly rigorous strictures about his diet, he didn't think twice about spackling his face with toxins.

None of these jobs lasted; it would take several years for Doris to find a way of making money that suited him. "She was sort of puritanical," Jackie remembers, "living very frugally. She had a clear-minded path. She needed to go out and do her art—which was *her*," she says, echoing Brian Barrow's contention that Doris was a living work of art.

You could certainly think so on the evidence of the photographs in Barry Kay's 1976 book, *The Other Women*. (The American edition was titled *As a Woman*.) Kay was a Melbourne-born, London-based costume and set designer who was nurturing a new interest in photography when, on a visit to Sydney in 1972, he was struck by the large number and new openness of Sydney's cross-dressers. He began returning, camera in hand; the results went on display in a show that opened at the Australian Centre for Photography in Paddington in November 1976, and in his strikingly generous and appealing book. Kay didn't encourage his subjects to smile, and he downplayed their glamour, but their dignity emerges intact—probably, in some cases, enhanced. The photographs, which are in black-and-white (except for the one of Jackie on the cover), climax with a ravishing five-picture series of Doris, Jasper, and Miss Abood, including one of the latter in odalisque pose (leather harem pants, thick rouge and lipstick, hairy armpits and torso) with his usual air of defiance.* The last one is a group portrait outside the house at Point Piper where Jasper and Miss Abood had rooms: Jasper on the left, in a leopard-print New Look skirt with a matching pillbox hat nestled in his dark mop; Miss Abood on the right, in a satin skirt and a dark blouse, a thumb at the corner of his mouth, his gaze disconsolate; and Doris on the porch above and between them, the top of the triangle, clad in a short-sleeved floral-print dress and gazing into the camera, not in a friendly way. True to the essential Sylvia aesthetic, the friends look not like men aspiring to be women but like men at home in their glamorous women's clothes. Kay was wise to make

---

* The picture isn't nearly as scary as the 1982 *Australian Drag Queen*, by Joel-Peter Witkin, the American photographer of freaks and cadavers, which presents Abood in torn black fishnets and bustier, long gloves, and nothing else, his belly and pubes a shaggy jungle above his long cock.

them tone down their makeup, though Doris resented his insistence. Because they couldn't possibly pass for women and are making no attempt to, the portrait is drained of the pathos that unavoidably informs almost all the other pictures. These are not creatures who are searching for themselves—they very much know who they are, and their strength is what holds you. The picture ends the book on a powerful high note.

UNTIL HE LEFT AUSTRALIA FOR GOOD, DORIS MOVED AROUND A LOT. So did his friends. You might think it would have been more frugal of him to stay in one place, but it was the bohemian era of cheap rents: in a 1974 letter, Doris, who was living in a group house, informed Miss Abood, who had decamped to Darwin, that he could have his old room back for "$13 a week approximately depending on how broke anyone is at any one time."

Big houses encouraged big parties. The one I've heard most about took place in the mansion at Point Piper where Barry Kay took the photographs. Madame Lash, various Synthetics, and the drag queens from Les Girls were all there wandering around; so were both of Doris's brothers, who had brought along their surfing buddies, and Mildred, who never wanted to miss anything. Michael tortured a young friend of Andrew's by telling all the queens, behind his back, that he was staggeringly hung; they descended on him like flies. Mildred got excited by the pool. She hadn't brought along a swimsuit, but that didn't stop her. Her starlet figure had long since ballooned, and Michael winces at the memory of her lowering herself in naked. "Very delicate view, that was."

In between rentals, Doris, like his brothers, would return to the house on Horning Parade; their sisters had married and moved away. Doris's lifetime of accumulating had begun, and with every move there was more stuff. The mild-mannered brother who had once sat quietly drawing in a corner was now a budding star who had learned how to rustle up assistance when he needed it. The family station wagon would be requisitioned, and anybody who was around (including Ace, who remained on friendly terms with Mildred) would be dragooned into helping. As a neighbor watched Ace lugging a mannequin from the car to the house—it was a group mascot among Doris's crew, differently begowned and bewigged every day—the sheet around it fell away, revealing the large patch of pubic hair they had pasted on. "Fucking Doris," Ace is said to have muttered. He couldn't have been happy, either, about the six-foot-tall marijuana plants Doris had growing next to the front door. "Marigolds," Mildred explained to a neighbor, perhaps innocently.

Or perhaps not. Her life was so changed that it's hard to guess what she was thinking. A few years earlier she had been a middle-class wife and mother of six, and now she was a divorced woman whose oldest son was a new luminary in the gay counterculture. The depression that had set in after Ace's departure had turned chronic; Doris's presence was a lifesaver. They had always been close, and they grew closer. She became a well-known figure at his shows, if a somewhat annoying one to his friends. Doris always introduced Mildred to the audience, and he frequently brought her onstage: her ditziness and her gaffes became a permanent part of his shtick. She also loved chauffeuring him around; he never did learn to drive. There are even tales of Mildred driving Doris to cruising spots and waiting for him in the car—strange to contemplate, but not beyond belief. Doris clearly had an enormous libido to satisfy.

"She had to have sex at least once or twice a day or she would have died," recalled Miss Abood, who as Doris's housemate was in a position to know. Doris left little on the record about his youthful exploits, but the outlines aren't hard to make out for any gay man who remembers the unbridled carnality of the early '70s. There is no ambiguity about Doris's desire, about his attractiveness, or about his dearth of inhibition, onstage and off. "Sexual liberation was a major issue of all the early shows," he wrote in his Sylvia reminiscence, "and nudity was an expression of our emerging freedom." Here and there in his letters and writings he'll mention a boyfriend, but few of these relationships seem to have been serious or prolonged. Love was an appealing idea; sex was an imperative. And yet, for all the frenetic license of those years, gay sex was still illegal, and however popular the parks and the bushes were, they could be dangerous places to prowl.

In 1973, when Doris was twenty-one, he was beaten beyond recognition by two ostensibly straight guys he had been servicing in a schoolyard—not, apparently, to their satisfaction. They complained and he retorted, "Do each other." When Marianne and Tony got to the hospital, they walked right past his bed. His black-and-blue head was swollen to the size of a basketball and covered with gashes. His eyes were slits. He couldn't talk because his teeth were wired shut; his jaw had been smashed.

Ace was beside himself, and his distress turned to fury when the cops refused to take the beating of a poofter seriously. "Look at my son!" he demanded. "Look at what someone's done to him!" They shrugged. He telephoned repeatedly to find out if the assailants had been tracked down; nothing. The cops were useless, he complained. Eventually he became convinced that the perpetrators *were* cops. For the family it was a crash course in gay civil rights, or the lack of them.

Doris, in contrast, was serenely uncomplaining. "He had that amazing spirit," Marianne says. "He wasn't angry with anyone." Jackie sees less saintliness in his composure than resignation or cynicism: "The world was unjust, and we knew it." In his Sylvia reminiscence, Doris referred to the incident with light irony—"My smile was silver!" he wrote breezily. "It looked as though my teeth were silver plated for the night." He was lucky he hadn't lost any. Because they were wired together, he couldn't eat solid food, but since he was already fasting for his well-being on a regular basis, he wasn't unduly ruffled. Besides, Jackie says, they used to grate drugs through the wire.

Money remained a problem. In late 1974, as the excitement of the Synthetics wound down, Doris returned to the telephone exchange, this time as a night-shift operator. The work was boring except for his colleagues, a gaggle of gay men who stayed awake through the shift by popping diet pills. Doris was on a fruits-and-vegetables regimen (although he admitted to Miss Abood, "I believe in succumbing to temptation when it arises") and fasting at least one day a week. So he passed on the speed, and as a result he seemed less engaged than his colleagues, whose tweaked gabbling their bosses mistook for enthusiasm. He probably would have been sacked if he hadn't quit. But he stuck it out for eight months, and, since he was working nights and sleeping days and living back at Mildred's, he managed to save most of his earnings. He had a plan.

As outlandish as the counterculture was in Sydney, it was tiny, and the city was staid. In those days, if you were young and hip and alternative, you dreamed of escape. While most of Doris's crowd looked to London, Doris's Emerald City was San Francisco. It still glowed with the '60s allure of acid rock and the Summer of Love, it had hatched the Cockettes, and the breadth of its gay scene was renowned. In March 1975, Mildred having carefully sewn money into one of his pants pockets, Doris departed on his first trip to the city that would become his home.

"I can't begin to tell you how good this town is," he wrote Miss Abood shortly after his arrival. It had "a masterpiece of Victorian architecture on every corner. . . . Anything old is really cherished and preserved," as opposed to Sydney, whose colonial buildings were rapidly giving way to nondescript high-rises. He was delighted with the exchange rate. As for sex, "maybe next week." The real thrill was the secondhand shopping:

> I bought five pairs of shoes—gold, silver, black, Perspex*, crocodile skin and all beautiful. $1 ea. mainly smart late fifties. Three foxes joined together for $5 (perfect cond.) ($1 = 74¢ Australian!), the smartest black fifties cocktail frock, 2 other good frocks, a house coat, stockings, . . . ½ doz really good necklaces + bracelets + earrings (all about 50¢–$1 ea) and 6 starched petticoats . . . plus odd sundries. It was just a bliss day for $20.85 (including bus fare!) which equals about $15 Aust.

---

* British brand name for poly(methyl methacrylate), the clear plastic that Americans know as Lucite or Plexiglas.

"I'd never in my life *seen* Perspex shoes with rhinestone heels and fronts," he told me later. "I'd *heard* about such things—*museum* pieces, and I was finding them by the *ton.*" He bought them up whether they fit him or not; he could decide once he got home whether to keep them or sell them. He didn't do any performing. Most of his energy went into shopping—"That was my art life," he told me. Some of it, of course, soon went into men as well. He found an attractive if conventional interior decorator (Gucci shoes, designer jeans) with a lovely apartment on Telegraph Hill and moved in for the rest of his stay.

After a few months he joined Miss Abood in London, where he performed. Inspired by Carmel's experiments back in Sydney, he shaved his head bald and painted on black hairdos, "which even in London was pretty strange, though it was '75 and they'd seen everything by then." His new look got him quite a lot of attention in the clubs. Several Synthetics had settled in London, and Doris and Abood moved in with friends in Notting Hill Gate. One of their flatmates answered phones at Biba, the fashion superboutique that had famously been bombed by anarchists in 1971. With paranoia still conveniently simmering, a couple of times they arranged for her to announce that a bomb threat had been phoned in while they were in the shop. Having gathered all the merchandise they could carry, they were hurriedly cleared out with the rest of the crowd.

The secondhand shops along Portobello Road were less scintillating—three-inch heels as opposed to the five-inch ones you could get in San Francisco—though for years Doris regretted leaving behind a pair of rhinestone-encrusted thigh-high boots ("If you put them on you'd fall straight over") for which there was simply no room in his bags. He did spring for a pair of fishnets at Sex, Malcolm McLaren and Vivienne Westwood's celebrated boutique on King's Road. They cost a fortune but held up for eight years—"flexible chicken wire or something."

Bags even more crammed now, he returned to his lover in San Francisco, stopping first in Vancouver, where he spent October admiring the autumn foliage. In early December he made a side trip to perform in Seattle. By Christmas he was back in Sydney for the beginning of summer.

No doubt his bags were stuffed with Christmas presents—his shopping skills included an endearing flair for choosing just the right gift for the right person. The family still gathered for the holiday in Manly Vale; apart from some mild sniping, there was no real animosity between Mildred and Ace, who often dropped by. One Saturday Doris rented a stall at the Paddington Markets, where years earlier he had hawked his cards and posters, and sold all the drag he had amassed on his trip. He charged what felt like extortionate prices and took home $300—real money in the mid-'70s. Immediately he began planning his return to San Francisco, with an extended stay in mind.

Until then, he moved with Miss Abood into a small house in Darlinghurst, near Green Park, one of the city's cruisiest beats. They both spent a lot of time there. The capricious Miss Abood would sometimes pick up a trick late at night, lose interest by the time they got home, and send him into Doris's room. Doris would wake with a horny stranger sitting on his bed. No one left disappointed.

One night Doris went home with an American who was living in Glebe, a few suburbs west of Darlinghurst. There was a massage table in his bedroom, and Doris was curious: "What do you use that for?" Massage was only a pretext. He turned tricks, and by the next week Doris was in his employ. And thus arrived the solution to the money puzzle: for the rest of his working life, Doris would bring in his steadiest income as a prostitute. With his healthy good looks and his voracious sexual appetite, he was a natural.

And a bargain. He seldom charged more than ten or fifteen dollars a trick—"five dollars for this, five dollars more for that," he told me—but he had the stamina to turn as many as a dozen a day. "You'd get there at nine in the morning and work to five or six at night. By late afternoon you'd just be exhausted, take the phone off the hook." Even with his more-than-reasonable rates, almost at once he was making several hundred dollars a week.

Soon Miss Abood was working out of the house in Glebe, too. They were thrilled, and a little bewildered, by how easy it was. But they were innovative and enterprising, becoming the first male prostitutes to put massage ads in the gay papers. The only dark cloud was the cops, who occasionally gave them a bad scare—they were hauled down to the station in Sydney and, later, to jail (briefly) in San Francisco. But the threat of charges never put a serious dent in their business. Both of them would continue earning money as prostitutes for years, though, as Miss Abood emphatically pointed out to me, "Doris was cheap. I most definitely was not."

Doris had low standards all around. Even before they started, Miss Abood told me, when Doris wanted sex he would take his contacts out so he wouldn't be choosy. Once they did start, it became a point of pride for Doris to send home even his unsightliest clients—"cussies," he called his customers—"satiated. At least relieved. A lot of the clients told me that I was the only one they'd been to who would, you know, give out." He didn't feel demeaned by the sex he was paid for. He enjoyed it, which made it doubly enjoyable for the cussie.

"Oh, she used to have sex with the most hideous people," Jackie recalled with a shudder, "just so she could point them out and say, 'I had sex with *them*.'" Miss Abood recounted coming home one day to find Doris servicing an obese horror they both knew and being informed afterward that he'd charged him only seven dollars. "Doris, that's disgusting!" Miss Abood snapped. "Oh, it's all right, love." Doris was placid. "I made him come twice!" But there were beauties, too. "God, did I get some good-looking guys," Doris told me wistfully. "I had a great time. I didn't know you weren't supposed to enjoy your work, so I was really enjoying it. I was in seventh heaven."

Actual prostitution felt less compromising to Doris than his legitimate jobs had. It was almost a vocation; he used to claim it as a branch of social work. He gave retiree discounts and said, "I hope people will treat me like that when I'm old." Gay sex was so easy to come by in those years before the advent of AIDS that you had to have special reasons for paying for it. You might be in the closet—Doris joked about the clergymen and the lawyers and the judges he serviced. Or you might be one of the troubled, the unlovable, the sexually untouchable. Among Doris's effects in my possession is an undated note:

Phil,

You've already met my brother, a few months ago. He's speaking, somewhat, and is house sitting for me. Your visit will be therapeutic for him as it was before.

He's still a bit quiet and shy so take it easy. I want him to relax and enjoy himself.

Try to be understanding, if he's slow or asks a lot of questions.

Thanks,
[signature]

P.S. He's a bit insecure and nervous. Reassurance is helpful. I told him you were a friend so your come on is yours. This is a surprise for him.

I don't know whether I find that message touching or unsettling or both. It wouldn't have unsettled Doris. He told me about clients without limbs, clients with colostomy bags—all part of the work he embraced.

Being an object of desire also satisfied that need for attention he was always talking about in interviews and in his stage patter. Despite his good looks, he'd been an awkward child—especially next to Jasper, whose beauty impressed everyone. Miss X, later on one of Doris's closest friends and colleagues, saw a similar factor at work. "I was always looking for a really handsome man," he said. "But Doris was like, 'No, I want to be the handsome one. I want to be worshipped.'" He learned how to get the attention he craved by slipping into drag and then, in a different way, by taking it off. Glamorous Doris and studly Philip were both parts of his personality, even if they were roles he assumed.

Prostitution was also, of course, a way of keeping sex from getting in the way of his ambition. Doris had boyfriends, but few of the non-paying ones lasted for long—possibly because of his day job (Miss X's theory), but more likely because romance took a back seat to his career. "He had a family and a core of friends," Miss Abood observed, "but he saw people, he cultivated people as potential fans. He was very serious about Doris Fish."

Professionally, he kept a sharp divide between the prostitute and the drag queen. Centuries of history link prostitution and drag, and in late-'60s Sydney, as Doris pointed out, "you could get the best men if you were a drag queen, because you'd get the straight footballer types that were too closeted to go with another man but would be happy to be seen with someone who at least looked like a woman and could make them feel more masculine." Whether he was referring to his own early sexual experiences is a matter of conjecture, but later on he rejected this aspect of drag almost completely. The men for whom donning drag is an aphrodisiac, he said, "don't generally do it as a career-oriented thing." Doris himself had no interest in combining cross-dressing with sex. "I could pick up gorgeous men while I'm in drag," he said, "but then they'd mess your makeup, tear your blouse—I mean, it's just dreadful. And you know, if you're having sex with someone while you're in drag, that's a private theatrical performance."

For Doris, drag was always a form of theater. He never wanted to be a woman—he never even wanted to *seem* like a woman. He could fool people into thinking he was, he said, but then "when you walk down the street no one looks twice at you, because you're so convincing that you just pass. And that doesn't get me the attention I desire." Even in his portraits of himself and his friends in drag, he scrupulously painted in what he called the "madam's apple."

"She always thought that anyone who wanted to have sex with her in drag was *sick*," Jackie recalls. "Sometimes, if she caught them looking at her tits, she'd lean across and say, 'Would you like to caress my brother's socks?'" Doris urged Jackie to take up turning tricks herself, but Jackie wasn't interested. "You've got to be a hustler," she says. "Doris worked hard to promote herself—in every way."

That meant talking himself up, writing for newspapers, and advertising—both shows and services. When he was staying with Mildred, he even ran massage ads in the *Manly Daily*. He would not allow anyone, as Jackie said, to be horrified, including his family; writing them from San Francisco in 1981, he reports, "I'm working as a real life whore again and doing quite well. I'm going out with a young attractive millionaire tomorrow night to see some show. He often gives me $100 and lots of gifts whenever I see him which is usually once a week."

Prostitution is a thorny subject. Its gay version seems somewhat less thorny, at least to me, because the power differential that's all but intrinsic between a paying man and a working woman is so much less fraught between two men. There is, of course, plenty of room for exploitation in the world of gay prostitution. But Doris wasn't exploited—I know a lot of people who have been more abused and humiliated in their legitimate jobs than he ever was as a prostitute. Granted, the world of commercial sex is cruel (like the world of commercial anything), and few of the personal accounts of prostitution I've read try to defend it as a path to ego gratification. But Doris was an extraordinary person. He wasn't bullied or cajoled into turning tricks by a pimp or a strong-willed boyfriend. He wasn't desperate. He came out of a solid middle-class background, understood that he had other options, chose the work freely, and liked it immediately.

Bernard Fitzgerald, who was one of Doris's cussies before he became one of the loves of his life, finds it beautiful and moving: "Whores are the most fabulous people. They give away this gift that they have for a very short time in their life, when they're magic gods. They don't think they're giving it away, because they take money for it. But they're giving it away—they're sharing this amazing thing. And only in gay whore life does that happen. Straight whore life is a nightmare of horror and using and cruelty and vileness, but I find gay whoredom really magical. They're *all* social workers. They're all people who give love. It may be restricted in its range, the love, but what they give is themselves, naked, to another man." That was how Doris understood it, too, and he was proud of his work: proud of the pleasure and the attention it brought him, proud that it paid the rent, and also, certainly, proud of the strong political statement it made about sexual freedom. He practically glowed when he talked about it.

The new openness of the '60s had changed the debate, insofar as there had ever been one, about the morality of prostitution. In San Francisco, in 1973, Margo St. James founded the visionary organization COYOTE to defend the rights of sex workers. Not everyone, of course, was convinced, and that debate became (and remains) so polarizing that—as Jennifer Blowdryer, a friend from Doris's San Francisco years who's written about her own experience hooking, points out—"people felt they had to be all the way against sex work or all the way for it." Doris's zeal leaves her a little bit skeptical: once you stake out a position, she says, whether pro or con, you become an advocate—"and once you become an advocate you cease to tell the truth."

No matter how much Doris loved whoring, surely he had shitty days at work. Everybody does. There must have been cussies who depressed or repelled him and afternoons when he just didn't feel like it; there must have been clients who paid him and treated him like a whore— who paid him so they *could* treat him like a whore. Doris was in control of the situation only up to a point. Pent-up sexual energy, once it's released, is anarchic and sometimes violent. He can't have evaded some disquieting encounters. Doris believed in having a positive attitude— bad experiences, like his beating in the park, were something you didn't dwell on. That doesn't mean he didn't have them.

There was also the specter of illness. "I said right from the beginning," Jackie told me, "'Doris, you should be really careful if you're going to be a male prostitute, because there are so many diseases around.' We didn't even know about the gay cancer. She said, 'I can get rid of them by fasting and water.' And I said, 'Don't talk rubbish! Syphilis is big-time.' I was always terrified of syphilis, but at the time everyone went down and just got drugs or a shot. But she didn't believe in any of that. She had that hippie thing about her. That was our only really big fight. It turned into a screaming match."

All these factors notwithstanding, I don't have qualms myself about the morality of prostitution, only about the way so many prostitutes are treated. As far as it being illegal, that's hardly a condemnation—when Doris started turning tricks, gay sex itself was illegal. I want to tincture his enthusiasm with a shade of nuance, but I don't want to suggest it wasn't real. Prostitution was right for him. It gave him the funds, and therefore the freedom, to be Doris. Its only real downside was that it probably killed him.

4

THE TUBES

IN JUNE 1976 DORIS'S YOUNGER BROTHER MICHAEL THREW A
party for his twenty-first birthday at Mildred's house in Manly
Vale. Doris's friends outnumbered Michael's and Andrew's, many of
whom were flustered at the sight of young men necking on the couch.
But when Doris pulled the kitchen table into the middle of the crowd,
climbed onto it in a slinky white gown, and performed as Marilyn
Monroe, he was such a sensation that Andrew got him to perform at
his own twenty-first birthday party three years later.

Doris had spent the first half of that year turning tricks, saving up,
and plotting his return to the States. By June he had socked away what

Doris performing with the Tubes, 1976. Photo by Daniel Nicoletta.

was for him a small fortune. He'd also been busted by the Sydney cops; sex work was illegal, gay sex was illegal, and so gay sex work was off-the-charts illegal. The run-in humiliated and terrified him and put an end, for a while, to his prostitution. He managed to get off with a "good behaviour bond," under whose terms he would avoid penalties if he stayed out of trouble for two years.

Soon after Michael's party he called up his decorator paramour and flew to San Francisco for what this time would be a much longer stay. But he'd never felt any more at home in the world of homosexual good taste there than he had among the antique queens of Sydney, and whatever remained of their chemistry soon shriveled before Doris's outrageousness: "Glamour was in my blood, and I started buying up showgirl costumes instead of groceries." Doris's boyfriend was displeased by his extravagance and openly scornful of his lust for celebrity. Heavy drinking compounded his unpleasantness. And so, as Doris put it, "I broke my first heart."

He tracked down Paul Tudman, a broad-shouldered, big-mustached, strawberry-blond Brisbanite he'd met at a party in Sydney a few weeks earlier, and Paul invited him to share his roomy apartment at 2347 Market Street, a half block away from Castro Street, for which they paid a combined monthly rent of $200. Their personalities clicked, and soon they were calling each other Debbie and Cheryl ("Shurl" in Australian), though Paul wasn't a cross-dresser. Doris remembered him, in one of his *Sentinel* columns many years later, as a "gorilla of party animals" who once claimed he'd "had 'true love' twenty-two times in one afternoon at the Mardi Gras in New Orleans."

It was the era of cocaine, and Paul was heavily into both using and selling. He was also, as it turned out, one of the canaries in the San Francisco coal mine. "It was a running gag that if you felt ill you could call Cheryl and find out what the latest exotic flu or infection was, because she always got it first. She just mixed antibiotics with her speed, and it seemed to work for a while." And then it didn't. "She's dead now, of course—one of the early ones."

Soon Doris had a new boyfriend, a bodybuilding carpenter who worked for his ex and who, like Paul, encouraged his ambitions. Specifically, they urged him to enter the upcoming Tubes' Talent Hunt. Posters plastered all over the city held out the promise, in bright-red letters under a rendering of what appeared to be conjoined-twin aliens playing an accordion, that "WINNERS WILL PERFORM WITH THE TUBES AT BIMBO'S," a large nightclub on Columbus Avenue in North Beach. Underneath, smaller print admonished that "only the unusual and bizarre need apply."

The Tubes embodied the goofy, unmalevolent side of '70s San Francisco lunacy and excess. Though they were "a bunch of straight guys, mostly"—as Michael Cotten, who played synthesizer for the band until 1986 and remains the unofficial keeper of its archives, told me—they were alert to the drag culture of their town. At some point in their shows, their outré lead singer, Fee Waybill, would smear on makeup, don a wig, squeeze into an obscene metallic jumpsuit, and lurch on-stage in platform boots as an androgynous lout named Quay Lewd.* The band also featured a gorgeous female singer, Re Styles, and several barely clad dancers, one of whom, the towering Jane Dornacker—a clever songwriter who had cowritten the Tubes' lewdly funny "Don't Touch Me There"—would later do shows with Doris. The band's contempt for flower-child virtues made them, like Sylvia and the Synthetics, forerunners of punk, and their aesthetic was similarly satirical and maximalist, although, unlike the Synthetics, they were talented, ambitious musicians. For their finale, which was usually a jeering send-up of their audience called "White Punks on Dope," there might be twenty-five people onstage. In 1976, when Doris was twenty-four, they were looking for oddballs to add to their San Francisco shows.

The competition took place on a Sunday afternoon at the Boarding House, a popular club on Bush Street. It was a professional operation, and the band, which was taping it, slipped a few of its own acts into

---

* As he's still doing, by the way.

the mix—notably Re Styles and the dancer Cindy Osborne performing "Rock and Roll Weirdos" in the glabrous conjoined-twin costume featured on the poster, with Jane Dornacker, who'd written the song the night before, joining in from the piano.

When Doris had noted the poster's call for the bizarre, he'd thought, *No, there's going to be a lot of weird things. I'll just go as a normal kind of drag queen.* His look had gradually been softening anyway. He put on a strapless pink '50s tulle-and-satin party dress that ballooned with petticoats, a badly disheveled pinkish-blonde wig, and a modicum (for Doris) of necklaces and bracelets, accented with a silver clutch. He shaved his chest—he was now going to the gym, working out with heavy weights so that when he put on a padded push-up bra he would have cleavage. The ratty wig, the low-cut dress, and the plastic jewelry combined to make him look gloriously cheap. But most of his planning had gone into his drag. As he sat there watching the contenders before him repeatedly get the hook well before their three-minute time limit was up, he still hadn't settled on what he was going to do.

When he finally got called onstage—he was number thirty-three—the slutty get-up drew appreciative titters. He leaned into the mike and began talking in a Blanche DuBois purr with no hint of Sydney: "You know, girls, it's hard to find a guy that really turns you on, and you just dig everything he does. . . . Well, I had a guy like that." Doris, or rather the floozy he's playing, goes on to tell the story of their breakup ("and I've been as *evil* as a wet hen ever since") and their chance meeting at a bus stop: "I turned around, and there he was—lookin' *good*, oh!"

Habitués of drag bars may recognize the lengthy lead-in to the potent 1970 version of "Maybe" by the Philadelphia girl group the Three Degrees. I can't say that I did when I saw the tape, and most of the audience thought Doris was just doing a funny character. The routine seems almost off the cuff—which is how it should seem, since Doris had probably lip-synched the song hundreds of times by then.

From the beginning, Doris is in control: It's clear that the crowd is reacting to him not as a weirdo but as a clown. What begins as tittering swells to laughter. When he reaches the line, "So we stopped at a *cozy* little place, and I guess the shock of seeing him made me order a martini, because that's something that *I'd* never done before"—which isn't funny or is maybe just slightly absurd on the record—they completely break up.

Doris started getting nervous as he neared the end. All the other performers had been booted well before this point in their acts. The monologue rises tensely—"I couldn't let go, not this time. Not this time. So I took his hand, I looked straight into his eye"—to the first shattering notes of the song. Doris certainly wasn't going to break into song, since he couldn't sing. So he improvised a quick throwaway: "And that's as far as I can remember what happened!" It brought the house down.

By now he had discovered, or constructed, his comic persona. The contrast of his trampy look with his modest, trying-to-be-ladylike delivery is very funny. "It's a complex level of things," he said much later, trying to explain the mechanism as much to himself as to me. "This Doris Fish character thinks she's a real woman, or she thinks she's fooling everybody. That's an underlying gag that I have with myself onstage, even though intellectually I know that I'm not fooling anybody. And the audience laughs at the delusions of the character." But these delusions have no pathos; Doris the Romantic Cruelist abhorred pathos. They're just funny—as the Tubes recognized when they invited Doris to perform with them at Bimbo's.

They also chose a second winner, a dark-locked twenty-one-year-old named Pearl E. Gates—really. Pearl had moved from Germany (her father was in the military) to San Francisco, alone, in 1973—the Tubes were the first band she saw there—and nourished dreams of breaking into the rock-and-roll scene. For the Talent Hunt she wore satin boxing shorts and boxing gloves and a cape that announced "PEARL" in glitter; she'd painted on a black eye and bandaged her forehead, and she tap-danced and shadowboxed to music from Phil Manzanera's *Diamond Head*, an album she knew the Tubes loved. They loved her, too, and the Talent Hunt marked the beginning of a career that would make her a local rock-and-roll celebrity. After the audition, she and Doris hugged excitedly, and soon they were thrift-shopping for costumes together as the show at Bimbo's approached.* On the first night the dressing room was intimidating, with guitarists slapping on makeup and busty dancers slipping into G-strings and everybody laughing and joking and getting high, but Doris nodded confidently at Pearl, who followed his lead as they laid out their outfits for the evening. "Be as glamorous as them and do exactly what they're doing," he told her, "and we'll fit right in." She hadn't put on nearly enough makeup to suit Doris, so he asked her, "Who would you like to look like?" She gave it some thought and replied, "Sophia Loren!" Then he went to work.

Doris's facility with cosmetics was by now well developed. He would use base and powder to neutralize a face and then treat it as a blank canvas. For Pearl, he would add eyeliner and shade in her cheekbones and enlarge her lips and extend her eyebrows. It took time, but the result was consistently stunning—and beyond that, Pearl says, transformative: "I knew that when I had that face on I wasn't me anymore—I was this glamorous creature. And I started acting like that creature! I felt so confident."

Every night Doris gave Pearl a different look, and it didn't take long for the band to pick up on Doris's expertise. "Doris knew more about makeup than anyone," Michael confirms. He was especially helpful to the men, whose approach until then had been to just trowel it on. Fee Waybill would also watch him for hints on swishiness. Not that Doris was flamboyant. Michael remembers him much more as "this cool-cat hipster kind of character"—not like a straight guy, but not like a drag queen, either, until he was in drag.

Show business cliques are notoriously hard to crack; you have to earn your way in. Doris and Pearl kept their heads down, listened more than they talked, and concentrated on delivering. The band did two shows a night. Pearl was in more numbers than Doris, since she could sing and dance. Doris came out at the beginning of the second part

---

* One of the contestants who didn't win—surprisingly, since his routine was funny and weird—was the twenty-five-year-old Robin Williams, singing a sex-change song called 'The Hormone Blues." He performed the same routine on TV the next year, on a revival of the comedy-variety show *Laugh-In*.

with a monologue introducing Quay Lewd and joking about his love affairs with the boys in the band, and everyone was onstage for "White Punks on Dope" at the end.

For both Doris and Pearl, the run was three weeks of show business heaven. A parade of celebrities came backstage to hang out. Boz Scaggs was there almost every night. Doris got to meet Julie Christie, Holly Woodlawn, and his hero, Grace Slick. There was free-flowing alcohol and, it being the '70s, cocaine, of which Doris partook only moderately. Doris always wanted to stay alert, Pearl told me, and Michael noted the same control: "He wasn't someone who seemed to come to drag and performance through some desperate need—none of the psychological baloney. I always thought, *This is a person who's not gonna die first.*"

Careerwise, the three weeks at Bimbo's gave both Doris and Pearl the push they needed. Pearl and Jane Dornacker recognized each other as kindred spirits, and, with a male drummer and several Tubes dancers, they formed Leila and the Snakes, a band even more cracked than the Tubes. "Don't Touch Me There" and "Rock and Roll Weirdos" were on their set list. The band had a cultish success for a couple of years, but eventually Jane and Pearl headed in the opposite directions of comedy and rock. Pearl changed her stage name, and in 1978 Pearl Harbor and the Explosions became one of San Francisco's defining New Wave bands. In 1980 she decamped to England, where she married the Clash's bassist and added a "u" to her surname.

IT WAS AROUND THE TIME OF THE TUBES SHOWS THAT DORIS MADE the acquaintance of a colorful drag queen who called himself Ambi Sextrous. Rumor had it that Ambi came from Texas oil money and his family paid him a thousand dollars a month to stay away. The truth was only slightly more prosaic: born Robert Lee Graham in 1953 in the town of Pauls Valley, Oklahoma, where his father was a prominent cattle breeder and civic leader, he had fled (to his parents' dismay, not relief) in 1970 and eventually settled in San Francisco, where he lived on a trust fund established by his grandparents. That meant that Ambi, unlike everybody else in Doris's circle, had money. He[*] went around in eye-popping combinations of orange and green dresses and pink and purple boas (rumor also had it that he was color-blind), and, unlike most of the other post-Cockettes drag queens, he featured a beard, which was often heavily encrusted with glitter or glued over with colored fun fur. Doris abhorred the beard—he always disliked facial hair on drag queens—and he mostly abhorred Ambi, too, as a 1977 letter to Miss Abood attests:

> Last Sunday Ambi Sextrous had a party for Garbo's birthday. It was really hideous but sort of fun. She did a cabaret set. She sings in a dull baritone, very seriously and very badly. The first number was "Cry Me a River." I knew we couldn't expect that to be the only one so I insisted on another. "I Could Have Danced All Night" was No. 2. I politely threw superlatives around and went back to the crackers & dips. She went to change for the next set. We got out before it.

That disdain notwithstanding, Ambi fluttered on the margins of Doris's circle and performed with him from time to time, though never, after their first show together, as a headliner.

That show took place in late October 1976, with Doris and one Mary Anne Drogenous as supporting players in Ambi's *Halloween Harlots* revue—"A Night of Real Glamour! with Fake Women!"—at the SIR Center downtown. SIR, the San Francisco Society for Individual Rights, was an early gay-rights organization—it dated from 1964—and its community center on Sixth Street was the first in the country. The show is notable in Doris's story mainly because Tippi was working the lights.

---

[*] He preferred the masculine pronoun, he told Jennifer Blowdryer for her "Transvestite of the Month" column in *Ego* magazine, "simply because of my genetic sex. . . . It's a pity there is no androgynous pronoun, other than 'it,' which unfortunately can refer to a kitchen appliance as well as a person. Let's face it, the English language is a gender-identified disaster."

So, TIPPI.

"A glass of champagne—bubbly, bubbly, bubbly!" "A little exclamation point." "A tiger in high heels." "A hummingbird, beating its wings away." Tippi elicited many such accolades from friends and admirers. Silvana and I wrote a tribute in which we called her "a knowing waif, a bird with a broken wing, a living Barbie doll, the patron saint of small, unprotected creatures, the oldest living child star in captivity, and the most resplendent ponytail-in-bondage ever to grace the stage."

Tippi was born in Cleveland on June 6, 1952; Brian Douglas Mead is the name on her birth certificate. Her parents were small of stature and so was she—a tiny thing, and a blue-eyed blonde in a family of brunets. At the age of three she informed them, "I'm a girl. And you should treat me like a girl." Kindly though Dwayne and Mary Mead seem to have been, they were no more prepared than any other decent middle-American couple of the Eisenhower era to deal with a trans child. Unlike Doris, who never gave anyone any trouble, Tippi was a handful. Her older brother and only sibling, Dwayne Jr., was assigned to keep an eye on her (I'm going to stick with feminine pronouns, though they came later) when the family went shopping; one of her favorite tricks was to conceal herself in a round clothing rack as the three of them circled around fretting. Or she would vanish into the Barbie aisle—Barbie was a lifelong icon. Having seen Tippi dance, I would never have believed she'd had no formal training if her brother hadn't told me. She started her informal training at nine. Dwayne Jr. had mandatory Friday-evening dance lessons at his junior high school; on Saturday mornings, in lieu of cartoons, he would show Brian what he had learned, everything from the foxtrot to the twist, and Brian picked the steps up much faster than he did. She also painted, sculpted, made jewelry, and took photographs, and in high school she acted. She was the only member of the family who could sing and, when she was young at least, the only extrovert.

Dwayne Sr.'s job as a technology troubleshooter for Western Union kept the family moving constantly. Brian attended a dozen or more schools, always the new boy and always the sissy. She would arrive, and the bullies would swarm. The damage was lasting. When she reached adolescence she learned how to mollify them by putting out. Those abusive encounters were damaging, too. There was at least one suicide attempt. Although she had a superb verbal memory and did well in class discussions and on oral tests, she was a terrible reader, and exams were a disaster. Only near the end of high school was her dyslexia diagnosed, explaining her difficulties too late to shore up her confidence. During her senior year she announced that her name was now Erik—her imagination hadn't widened to girlier possibilities—which is the name on official documents from her later life. After graduation, she lived in Chicago, New York, and Los Angeles. She was once asked how long it took her, after she was on her own, to get into drag. She snapped her fingers and said, "Like *that*."

The full story was more complicated. Around 1971 she hooked up with a potbellied hippie who called himself Mr. Natural, and they lived in his van, selling roach clips on Telegraph Avenue in Berkeley. They stayed together for at least a couple of years, eventually winding up in an apartment on Market Street in San Francisco. How exactly she subsisted before and after him I can only guess. Hippies scrounging around the Bay Area in those years came up with resourceful ways of procuring cheap or free food and services, and—no guesswork here—at times she turned tricks. "I loved the work!" she said later, in her bright-eyed way. What she couldn't handle, and what eventually drove her out of prostitution, was what she called the "interpersonal relationships." She had a rabbitlike wariness, and the least hint of attachment frightened her. Even repeat customers made her uneasy.

She met Tom Faulkenbery around 1973 or 1974 at the home of a mutual acquaintance on Guerrero Street in San Francisco. At the time Erik was featuring a goatee and a mustache, in order, Tom explained, to clear up the inevitable questions. "'Cause people would wonder. They'd stare at him and wonder."

I asked him if Tippi had trouble with that.

"*He* didn't have trouble. He had trouble with *them* having trouble—to the point where he would hide. I was hiding, and he would hide with me. When he met me, we were two hiders." Soul mates.

Tom was born in 1941 in Jackson, Tennessee. As a boy he traveled with carnivals, which was where he found out about marijuana. "I was a pot-smokin' hippie since twelve years old, before hippies or pot was ever heard of by most people."* In late adolescence he was incarcerated at a Mississippi reform school (though in structure it was more like a prison farm); he escaped a few months before his eighteenth birthday. "When I ran from that farm in Mississippi, I kept runnin', mentally. Anything, anything at all, could trigger me off, and I would just walk off with nothing but the clothes on my back, and hitchhike away from there and never go back. I did that probably hundreds of times. 'Cause I was uptight. It took me many years to get out of the closet. I didn't have the courage to be as open as everyone that I was admiring. So I was hiding from them, too."

That first encounter with Tippi on Guerrero Street was electric. "Within probably five minutes after meeting, we kissed. Of course, I found out later that that wasn't so special, because he kissed everybody! But I fell in love immediately. I couldn't take my eyes off of him, or"— these words through tears—"my hands, once he gave me permission. We were together from that point on. All my life I was running and hiding from life. And so was he. And he met me and we fell in love and we hid together. We didn't run."

They lived in a series of dives, among them a storage closet just big enough to hold a mattress in the basement of a Fisherman's Wharf art gallery. Out on the wharf, Tom, who was and still is an accomplished artisan, crafted flowers and butterflies out of bent wire. He was a handsome, strapping guy with wavy auburn hair and a full beard and a big smile, and he wore a stovepipe hat he'd stitched together out of denim patches. Circles of girls would surround him, and he'd give them his flowers in exchange for tips. "It took me one minute to make a flower. And I was makin' 'em two, three, four hours a day, and earning thirty, forty, fifty dollars in tips." After a while the gallery owners discovered that he and Tippi were living illegally in the basement room and kicked

---

* While I've corrected other people's grammar, I've tried to retain the flavor of Tom's southern country diction, though, as elsewhere, I've compressed and elided and, in places, rearranged.

them out. They wound up in an apartment above Hamburger Mary's, a zany gay burger joint that was a central hangout in the '70s (Miss X waited tables there for a while), with their much-loved border collie and a domesticated rat that had belonged to a previous tenant and lived under the refrigerator.

"We stayed inside a lot. We'd smoke one joint and then smoke another, and then smoke a joint after those. We went places that we needed to go and to visit people we knew. But we didn't know many people." They spent long hours making love, although, in the ethic of the era, they also went to the bathhouses "and other places that you wouldn't even want to know about. It always freaked me out to see Tippi having sex with anybody, but I never told him that. I did whatever he wanted me to do. I figured I was an old man compared to him"—he was eleven years older—"and I had absolutely nothing. All my life I had nothing."

Tippi dressed ambiguously; it wasn't drag per se but something less classifiable. *Androgyny* was a popular term in those days. David Bowie, Lou Reed, and the New York Dolls, among others, had given the concept pop-culture cachet, and it wasn't just gay young men whose gender you couldn't determine from a glance on the street. But for Tippi, who was petite, blonde (so her facial hair didn't stand out even when she wore it), and utterly girlish in her comportment, androgyny went much deeper than style—even if at that point, according to Tom, she still thought of herself as male. "He had no desire to cut his dick off. Some people who go in drag want to turn into women. If he did, he never said it to me or anybody else.

"When I first met him, he had a dream of being onstage." Tippi had, in fact, acted with the San Francisco Free Theater during her early years in the Bay Area. Among her roles was, appropriately enough, a mouse in *Aesop's Fables*. "I tried to get him to take dancing lessons, because I figured if he started going to a dance studio he would meet all kinda people that would open him up to whatever he wanted to do. But that would have required him to go on his own." In time, Tippi did begin to make the acquaintance of drag queens. Ambi Sextrous was one of them; another, a pretty airhead who called herself Freda Lay, became a close friend.

Ambi and Freda urged her to go further. She was ready for the encouragement. She began putting on more makeup. She taught herself to walk in heels, wearing them doggedly around the house. "If he couldn't do somethin' in high heels," Tom said, "he would just keep doin' it till he could." I have a vivid memory of Tippi at the Miss Solar System pageant in 1984, gliding up and down a long staircase in her stilettos with a grace that would have done credit to Cyd Charisse.

"When he would go in drag," Tom told me, "he'd look like a woman. And a *pretty* woman. And then, when he met Doris Fish and Miss X, they opened him up. All of a sudden he turned into a drag queen."

Tippi met Doris shortly before Ambi's *Halloween Harlots* show, at a party south of Market, on Natoma Street. "I couldn't believe how marvelously original this person was," Tippi told me. "Everywhere you could think of to put something, there was something. And she featured a natural chest—well, it *was* the '70s. To this day, I'm surprised how I could just walk up to someone like that." Evidently she made up her mind about Doris as quickly as she had about Tom— like *that*.

Much of what Tom recalled he told me through the tears that still flow easily when he talks about Tippi. "For three or four years we were in a honeymoon state. But then he grew bored with me when he started hanging out with that crowd and doing shows and plays and things, and after a while he broke off with me because I was—after thinking about it for years—I was probably a pull-down to him, mentally." There was no bitterness; he even had a picture of Doris on his wall. "But I know that if it hadn't been for him, Tippi wouldn't have left me. And I know that Tippi was better off to leave me. They only showed him the door to get through so he could be who he was. He stopped hiding and came out."

Tippi's transition was rapid once it got underway. Her friendship with Doris developed more slowly. It would take another year or so for them to assume a central role in each other's lives.

Doris's minute-and-a-half monologue introducing Quay Lewd during the Tubes show must have been something. It stuck with Jane Dornacker's manager, Eddie Troia, so vividly that he would call a few years later with an idea for a new show. More immediately, an enterprising producer-director named James Moss saw the Tubes' extravaganza while he was making preparations to shoot an underground movie. As he watched Doris command the stage, he decided he had found his star.

Moss had been born in LA in 1941 and spent his childhood as a busy actor, with roles (as Jimmy Moss) in some thirty movies and twenty-five TV dramas. Later he studied at Columbia, published some short stories, and in 1973 wrote and codirected a now-lost underground movie, *Dragula*, starring the legendary porn star Casey Donovan in a tale about a vampire whose bite turns his victims into drag queens. By 1976 he was in California again, ensconced in San Francisco's gay scene and planning to cover it in *Magazine Movie*, a satirical anthology in the anything-goes spirit of the mid-'70s: drugs, drag, and kinky sex. It was either never finished or never shown, but filming it took up several happy months of Doris's life, and a few tantalizing stills survive.

Soon after Moss introduced himself to Doris in 1976, they filmed the first two episodes at a local studio. "Hanky Panky" dealt with the elaborate handkerchief code that was then in vogue in the bars—back left pocket signified you were a top, light blue that you were into fellatio, and so on. The second segment, "Cheap Thrills," addressed the effects of amyl nitrite, whose intense rush had made it a popular club and sex drug; as Nurse Fish, Doris took part in a "cautionary" demonstration of a heart-rate acceleration that goes out of control.

Moss was an experienced publicity hound. He managed to get an arresting headshot of a lipsticked Doris wearing some kind of rhinestone chain-mail helmet—the look was very deco, which was also then in vogue—on the front of *Kalendar*, a free bar rag whose covers typically featured naked hunks. He also got the paper to run a press release ("Zany and satirical, *Magazine Movie* is a *Sesame Street* for hip adults"), his bio ("Mr. James Moss is now thirty-six years old, lives in San

Francisco with his parrot Butch and collects teenagers as a hobby"),
and a still of Doris surrounded by the kind of naked hunks who were
missing from that week's cover.

Jasper—Doris's childhood friend Peter McMahon—arrived for a
visit in mid-December 1976, and from that point on the two of them
were, as Doris wrote Miss Abood in early January, "almost constantly
in drag. New Year's Eve was fantastic. I was in an electric-blue glitter
fabric two piece go-go girl outfit with an excess of gorgeous jewels and
accessories, including hot pink high high stilettos with peep toes! Jazz
was in tiger, off the shoulder, split to the waist and steaming hot! What
a pair of gutter girls! We danced on tables, beds, chairs, each other and
ate cakes."

Jasper quickly got drawn into the movie. In one new sequence, he
and Doris played maids to a dominatrix who forced a groveling client into women's clothes. In another, Jane Dornacker (now going by
Leila T. Snake) appeared as a femme fatale with a shoe fetish; the two
drag queens supplied the props, seventy-seven pairs of stiletto heels
from their own collection. But the real excitement was around what
was being billed as the International Quaalude Eating Contest. Doris
was once again going to be cast as Nurse Fish, "in charge of drug distribution," he told Miss Abood, "and general care of the dying"—a crack
that would seem less amusing a couple of years down the road. "We're
planning a stomach pumping scene, too." Jasper would play the popular
favorite, "the Australian Quaalude (Mandrax) Champion."

It was a title he had some claim to. "Darling," Jasper once said,
"there's a lot of drugs coursing through my veins, and they're all having
a wonderful time!" He is reported to have crawled into cabs on various continents and directed their drivers to destinations in Sydney.
He toured the world "not remembering a thing," Jacqueline Hyde says.
"She might as well have stayed at home." His friends laughed about
it. Some months later, when Jasper was back in Sydney, Jackie wrote
Doris about a birthday party she'd attended: "Jasper was the hostess.
I arrived to find her beautifully dressed but unconscious on the floor
(obviously having a great time)." But eventually the humor thinned.

Jasper's drug intake, it became apparent, wasn't mere recklessness or rebelliousness. Your twenties are typically a time of finding yourself, as Doris and Jackie and Tippi were all doing. But they can also be a time of losing yourself. Whether Jasper was downing so many pills in response to some deep unhappiness or was just one of those addictive personalities who can't get off the hurtling roller coaster, we don't know.

Doris's own drug use in those days was mainly confined to pot. On New Year's Eve he and Jasper tried angel dust; "I'm still recovering," he complained to Miss Abood, adding that he'd since found out that it was very dangerous. "I believe it. Not again." Doris wasn't quite abstinent, but in later years he described his attitude as "Once you put on makeup, you don't need any other drug."

The International Quaalude Eating Contest for *Magazine Movie* was staged in late January 1977. Real pills were supplied "for added 'cinema vérité' impact." Jasper chose leopard-print harem pants and opera-length gloves for the occasion. Although he claimed not to have had a Quaalude for three weeks, he got so wired on the evening of the shoot that he swallowed several before he arrived. As a result, he came in second, because even though he put away as many pills as the winning contestant (fourteen, according to one count) and was more glamorous than anyone, he collapsed, dramatically and photogenically. Ambi Sextrous also competed, but he was disqualified for taking speed.

By now Doris had fallen truly in love with San Francisco. "Victoriana and butch men by the ton," he rhapsodized in a letter to Jackie. "Big dicks and pendulous balls abound and everyone is so friendly and eager. Australian girls well treated here!" There was just one downside. "All goes well except that I'm so poor. I'm nearly $1000 in debt but not disturbed by it." Among various moneymaking schemes (including stardom), he had been designing rugs and carpets, but they didn't bring in much. The inevitable solution was to return to Sydney for a while and go back to being a "mattress actress." "I remember saving nearly $1000 a month when I was working before," he wrote Miss

Abood. "But I'm terrified of getting busted again, as I'm on a two-year good behaviour bond. Whatever happened to the proposed abolition of victimless crimes? Us pros get a pretty rough deal. I know I *really* earned my money."

He kept postponing his trip home. Although on December 1 he informed his brother Andrew that he'd be home on Christmas morning—"my Xmas present to you all!"—he didn't touch down in Sydney until February 2, 1977.

He stayed until the following September, whoring and saving up for his return to San Francisco. For a time he managed a male brothel. He also performed in various clubs with Jackie; they were still outrageous and sometimes aggressive in their shows. Notoriously, he would take a swig from an audience member's drink and spew it at her (his victims were typically female) or at her whole table. For a black-light number one night, wearing a multihued nylon caftan ("a really talented dress under UV lights"), he put sparklers in his wig, and as he was spinning around onstage the wig caught fire. Before he knew what was happening a stagehand had run out and yanked it off. Doris was furious—he hated Finocchio's-style drag acts that ended with the reassuring destruction of the illusion. ("I would rather have burnt to *death*," he said, "than have my wig pulled off onstage.") He and Jackie preferred making the audience squirm.

The biggest news concerned Jackie herself—or Mel, as she was still known, though in honor of her developing breasts Doris and Miss Abood took to calling her Melons. Jackie says that the hormones were not originally her idea. "I was in bed and Clayton came in and said, 'Look what I've got, hormones! They're going to make us look beautiful.'" Everything was less regulated and easier to obtain in those days, and in Australia, which was even more youth obsessed than the rest of the world, hormones had become something of a fad because they seemed to hold off the aging process. "They would give you beautiful skin," Jackie says, "and help your hair if you went on them for a few weeks"—but you had to stop before the effects became more pronounced. "Nobody wanted the tits." Or almost nobody.

Clayton simply wanted to stop aging. "He was terrified of becoming a man, although he didn't want to be woman, either. He just wanted to be an ephebe, an adolescent—a very pretty adolescent. He was *so* beautiful." Even when they were teenagers, outraging the pub goers in Fairfield as they swished down the walk, people often took him for a girl. He dressed androgynously and preened at the admiration he got. He was drawn to middle-aged men but recoiled at the thought of becoming one himself. "He couldn't deal with body hair and getting old. He went into deep depression when he started to become an adult." Like Jasper, he self-medicated with alcohol and drugs.

Jackie's attitude toward hormones was different. "I didn't mind the tits! I decided that I wanted to stop being bashed for being a poof and have those men who bashed me want to have sex with me instead. Which is what happened." For all her volubility, Jackie is not very forthcoming about herself. Something deeper was obviously at work in her decision to live as a woman; this was a time, after all, when the notion of gender fluidity elicited dumb incomprehension. What does seem clear is that the decision, and the transformation, made her happy. While Doris was in Sydney, Jackie underwent breast augmentation surgery. In a letter written soon after his departure, she alluded fondly to his last sight of her, "sitting up in a hozzie[*] bed with newly bound up tits. What a wonderful transsexual haze to look beautiful through!"

Prostitution went well for Doris, and—only this once, as far as I'm aware—it took a romantic turn. Bernard Fitzgerald was a psychiatric nurse; bearded and dark, with broad shoulders and piercing eyes, he had no reason to seek out prostitutes other than, in his words, "a predilection for paying for it." He used to patrol the massage ads in the local papers. "I can't remember what Doris was offering, but it clicked. He was straightforward, natural, and no bullshit. I was attracted just speaking to him on the phone. And this never happens—it's too dangerous—but we met and we had sex that was reasonably fabulous, and we started a relationship."

---

[*] Hospital. Australians are attached to diminutives—cf. Doris's "cussie," "prossie," etc.

It was by no means an exclusive one. During the same period in 1977, Bernard was seeing the artist David McDiarmid and the manager of a string of saunas whose name was Bruce. Who would ever have expected Doris the prossie to cock an eyebrow at that kind of polyamory, so typical of the gay '70s? But once he fell for Bernard he found that he couldn't be nonchalant.

THE PERFORMANCE HIGHLIGHT OF DORIS'S STAY IN SYDNEY WAS A reunion of Sylvia and the Synthetics for a "Queen's Birthday Extravaganza" at their old stomping ground, Paddington Town Hall. It got a scathing review in the gay paper *Campaign*, whose critic griped at the "slipshod" staging: "things fall over, microphones don't work or the 'stars' don't know where to hold them; . . . the 'stars' themselves—mandied or coked into near insensibility—stumble about the stage, fall over ladders, lose their wigs, step on each other's gowns, mime badly and sing too far away from the mike." In other words, nothing had changed—including the audience, which, he fumed, "drinking, ingesting, and flirting to its heart's content, roared its approval." The old anarchy reigned again.

A clueless critic is one of the unavoidable pitfalls of show business, but this review sounded an ominous note that, in the coming years, was going to swell. As gay liberation gathered steam—quickly, almost dizzyingly—and social acceptance seemed within sight, an angry debate arose over the community's image in the press and the harm that drag queens were doing it. At the same time, some feminists had begun to complain that drag queens promoted the constricting, oppressive notions of female glamour that they were trying to battle. As *Campaign's* reviewer grumbled, "I see no reason why Miss Fish should perpetuate the worst sort of macho misconceptions and 'gay' stereotypes. . . . I really can't see how such events advance the cause of male love or homosexual dignity one iota."

5

ROMANTIC CRUELISM

T HAT SAN FRANCISCO WAS KNOWN AS THE GAYEST CITY IN the world was a big part of its allure for Doris. The reasons for that reputation go back to the city's early history. It was just a town of some eight hundred souls on January 24, 1848, the day gold was discovered at Sutter's Mill, 130 miles away. Two years later that number had shot up to 35,000; by 1900 its population was close to 343,000 and it was the eighth-largest city in the nation. The deluge of prospectors, speculators, laborers, and merchants was initially 90 percent male— the distribution of sexes didn't even out until the end of the nineteenth century—turning the city into a kind of test tube for the male libido released from the restraining influence of women, as the Castro would

Doris and Jackie compering at Cabaret Conspiracy, 1979. Photo by Maryse Thorby.

become more than a century later. (The overwhelming maleness of San Francisco's early years is a common denominator with Sydney.) Drinking, whoring, and gambling amounted to municipal industries, and early on the variety of the city's offerings was rich enough to earn it the nickname Sodom by the Sea. The Dash, the first in the city's long line of expressly gay bars, opened in 1908 at 574 Pacific Street. It was a scuzzy place where drag queens entertained on a small stage and, for a dollar, would put out in curtained booths on either side of the room.

During Prohibition, San Francisco was probably the easiest city in the country to get a drink in. After repeal, in December 1933, a gay culture that had been fermenting in the speakeasies and that always included a drag component flourished in a knot of openly gay bars, mainly in North Beach. The first and most enduringly famous was Finocchio's, whose marquee attraction was its floor show of female impersonators. In the '30s it had some of the wildness of the Dash—the "girls" did more than dress up—but by the 1970s it had declined into a pallidly naughty nightclub that, as Bob Dameron's popular gay-bar guide warned, was "strictly for tourists." (When Doris and Tippi and Silvana and I made a foray there in 1986, we were impressed by the seriousness of the drag even as we had a sense of being the only gay people in the audience.) Other gay bars opened regularly, despite periods of crackdown, notably the late '50s. And even those bad stretches, as the historian Nan Alamilla Boyd points out in her *Wide-Open Town: A History of Queer San Francisco to 1965*, can be interpreted as panicked reactions to increasing gay visibility just as easily as signs of the gay population's weakness or oppression.

During the Second World War and the Korean War, San Francisco was a strategic military base as well as a major port of departure for men and women in the armed forces. Many of the soldiers and sailors who first discovered or acted on their sexual desires in the same-sex context of the military remembered the city's beauty and its wealth of gay bars. The thousands of them who had the bad luck to be outed and cashiered—during the '50s their numbers climbed to as many as two thousand a year—were not only deprived of veterans' benefits; they were also saddled with less-than-honorable discharges that couldn't be hidden from prospective employers, not to mention families. Tolerant San Francisco looked like a sane place for them to try to put their lives back together. To cite one revealing census figure, between 1950 and 1960 the number of single-person households in the city doubled to comprise well over a third of its residence units.

And then there were the paradoxically positive effects of persecution. As in Sydney, the virulently antigay press reports of the McCarthy years informed isolated gay men and women that they weren't alone. Meanwhile, the numbers of police raids on bars, entrapments in restrooms, and convictions for gay-related offenses like lewd conduct and the ill-defined "vagrancy" continued to climb. The situation finally prodded the still-inchoate community into fighting back, with a drag queen who waited tables at the Black Cat Café playing the movement's Patrick Henry.

The Black Cat had opened in the Tenderloin just after the 1906 earthquake and had moved to 710 Montgomery Street, near the foot of Columbus Avenue, after repeal. But its modern history began in 1945, when an Austrian Holocaust survivor named Sol Stoumen bought it. The bar had long-established bohemian credentials; gays made up only a part of its clientele of artists, intellectuals, and general nonconformists. But it became increasingly gay after Stoumen hired the exuberant José Sarria in 1947. Sarria, a native San Franciscan of Colombian-Nicaraguan descent, had been cross-dressing from an early age. He began at the Black Cat as a cocktail waiter who would occasionally sing, but the force of his personality was such that before long he was donning drag and doing his own one-man parodies of operas every Sunday. He got so popular that, in his own immodest but accurate estimate, "I became the Black Cat."

When state authorities identified the bar as "a hangout for persons of homosexual tendencies" and suspended its liquor license, Stoumen, who was straight, took them all the way to the California Supreme Court—which in 1951, in *Stoumen v. Reilly*, handed down the (to many flabbergasting) decision that affirmed the right of even so depraved a population as homosexuals to gather in public places as long as they weren't engaging in "illegal or immoral conduct." It turned out to be a qualified victory, since the police then decided that illegal or immoral conduct (for homosexuals) included such bland behavior as hand-holding, dancing, and, of course, kissing, to say nothing of solicitation. The harassment continued.

Meanwhile, Sarria's activism became more conscious and more pointed. Somehow he'd been spared the burden of guilt and shame that shadowed the lives of so many gay men and women of his generation. From the small stage of the Black Cat he warned the crowd about which parks and restrooms the cops had under surveillance. He urged them to demand a trial by jury when they were arrested for lewd acts instead of meekly copping a plea. Most famously, he made everybody join hands at the end of the evening and, in an early act of solidarity, defiance, and pride, sing "God Save Us Nelly Queens." "United we stand," he told his audience again and again; "divided they arrest us one by one."

In 1961 he took the preposterous step (or so it was then considered) of entering the race for the city's board of supervisors, making him the first openly gay American to run for public office. Though he was, as expected, trounced, he garnered an eye-opening six thousand votes—a number significant enough to convince at least some local politicians that there was a gay bloc worth courting. (Dianne Feinstein, to her credit and to her benefit, was among the first to woo it.) Sarria's quixotic campaign marked the beginning of direct gay participation in the city's political process, which would culminate, on November 8, 1977, in Harvey Milk's election to the board of supervisors. By then Doris had made San Francisco his home.

But 1977 also marked a sudden downturn in the fight for gay rights, and in the turmoil of that year, drag queens—who up till then had lived on the periphery of gay life and had been practically invisible beyond it—were at the center of the storm.

Since Stonewall, gay men and lesbians had seemed to be riding a steady wave of progress toward acceptance and equality. Gay culture had reached widespread new visibility with the emergence of disco, which not only claimed a huge gay audience and played in gay dance clubs across the world (in a reversal, you now heard complaints from gay men about straight couples invading their spaces) but also had its very own diva in Sylvester, who'd formerly been a member of the Cockettes. By 1977, some forty local governments in the United States had passed ordinances protecting gay men and lesbians from discrimination. No one was expecting the virulence of the backlash.

The county commissioners in Dade County, Florida, which includes Miami and Miami Beach, had voted their own antidiscrimination measure in with the new year. Predictably, fundamentalist Christians opposed it, and they found a rousing torchbearer in the person of a local congregant: the wholesome singer Anita Bryant, a sparkly thirty-seven-year-old former Miss Oklahoma who was familiar to everybody from the TV commercials she did for the Florida orange juice industry. ("Breakfast without orange juice is like a day without sunshine!") Bryant became the newest luminary in the long history of American bigotry with declarations like "Homosexuals cannot reproduce so they must recruit." Her organization, Save Our Children, went national, and in 1977 and 1978 it flourished, sponsoring referendums that successfully repealed the ordinance in Dade County as well as similar ones in St. Paul, Minnesota; Wichita, Kansas; and Eugene, Oregon.

Those repeals, usually by two-to-one margins or worse, were a shock to the gay men and women who up until then had thought the world was getting ready to welcome them. Progress all but stopped, on the surface; it would be years before laws would shift again in favor of gay political protections. But as we can see in hindsight, Bryant's campaign was really a gift to the gay community—partly because it fired up political organizing but also, and probably even more significantly, because, like the earlier police crackdowns and their accompanying press, it exponentially increased visibility.

Still, at the time it was hard for homosexuals to feel optimistic. The central issue now became one of strategy: how to win the hearts and minds of the public, to convince it that gay men and lesbians were just like everybody else, that we were *normal*. Drag queens, who constituted a tiny minority of gay people, were anything but normal. Yet the news cameras loved them (as they still do). Was it fair, or even sane, to allow them to represent gay people? The angry debate splintered the community.

Luckily for Doris, it came when his own self-assurance was at a high point. By now he had a handle on all the compartments of his personality. The ease with which he could slip on his various masks kept him from being wounded by the abuse drags were getting from both outside the community and within it.

In 1973 the feminist poet and rabble-rouser Robin Morgan was already calling male transvestism an obscenity. "*We know what's at work when whites wear blackface,*" she fulminated (in italics); "*the same thing is at work when men wear drag.*" Of course, attacks on their political correctness weren't something to dismay Doris and Jackie, who savored offending their audience. Given that this was a time when the overwhelming majority of gay people were still in the closet and most straight people thought they didn't know any homosexuals (and they certainly didn't know any drag queens—most gay people didn't, either), no one who had crossed that Rubicon would have been likely to cave before critics they considered prigs. "Feminists would storm out!" Jackie recalls with amusement. "They kept calling out, 'Dress as men! Stop mocking women!' We *weren't* dressing as they were dressed. They were in jeans and T-shirts."

But a lot of gay men were fuming, too. "The scorn directed against drags," Edmund White noted in his chapter on San Francisco in *States of Desire: Travels in Gay America* (1980), "is especially virulent; they have become the outcasts of gay life, the 'queers' of homosexuality." The debate over assimilation—over just how straight it was going to be necessary for gay people to act in order to win social acceptance—would bedevil the gay community into the age of AIDS, when life-and-death concerns took over.*

For most of the twentieth century, effeminacy had been the mark of the male homosexual. Many gay men, especially those with a toe outside the closet, embraced it, because it reflected their understanding of who they were. It gave them a sense of identity, and it also signaled their availability to other men. But the ideology of gay pride encouraged them to become what they found attractive—to reclaim their masculinity, often in exaggerated ways. A new gay style evolved among the horny young population of the Castro: short hair, mustaches, tight jeans, flannel shirts, hooded sweatshirts, leather jackets, and work boots or sneakers. The fashion quickly moved east, becoming so orthodox that people started calling its exponents "clones."

For many gay men it inspired a new swagger, and the bars they frequented turned into intimidating caverns of sweaty machismo. Those who weren't butch and didn't aspire to be could easily feel as if the demons that had blighted their adolescence were now invading their safe havens. But Doris thrived in this hairy-chested world. Although he didn't dress like a clone—when he went out as a boy, he liked color and bold patterns—he wasn't hitting the gym so zealously just to enhance his cleavage. He cruised the parks and the sex clubs and had

---

* The controversy over permissible gay styles reaches back at least as far as the early decades of the twentieth century. As George Chauncey relates in *Gay New York: Gender, Urban Culture, and the Making of the Gay Male World, 1890–1940*, many straight-acting American queers in the 1920s and earlier bristled at the "fairies," the swishy young men who affected makeup and (to a greater or lesser extent) drag, "for they believed it was the flagrant behavior of the fairies on the streets that had given the public its negative impression of all homosexuals." Interestingly, this debate extended into other communities: "In their censure, they were not unlike the many German-American Jews who believed that the 'foreignness' (or reluctance to assimilate) of the eastern European Orthodox Jews who immigrated to the United States in large numbers at the turn of the century had provoked American anti-Semitism, or the many middle-class African-American residents of Northern cities who blamed the resurgence of Northern white racism on the 'backwardness' of the uneducated rural black Southerners who migrated north a few years later. Some gay men drew the parallel explicitly."

the success you would expect of a compact hunk with a ripped torso. As Jackie noted, with a touch of bitterness, "Doris went off into the boy thing because *gay* went off into the boy thing." The kind of bars he was at home in "we weren't allowed into anymore—*I* wasn't allowed into anymore."

The ongoing debate over styles was so fraught precisely because it was serious: It took place against the threatening background of the backlash. Yet even at this bleak moment, the community didn't lose its sense of humor or the conviction that it *was* a community. Across the spectrum from clones to drag queens, the recognition that it was under siege gave it a sense of common purpose and even, amid the sniping and the bickering, unity. Queers who had considered themselves alienated from politics suddenly understood their stake in the battle—for example, Tippi, or, as she was calling herself in the summer of 1977, Miss Leading.

Hanging out with Ambi and Doris and Freda Lay had brought Tippi to a new level of self-confidence vis-à-vis drag. Doris's director, James Moss, was taken with her (everybody was), and soon after meeting her he put her in a magazine he was editing, posed in a varsity jacket at a Castro Street phone booth next to a flyer headlined "AFRAID YOU'RE NOT BUTCH ENOUGH?" It was Moss who talked her into entering the Anita Bryant Look-Alike Contest being held at the Boarding House (the same club that had hosted the Tubes' Talent Hunt the previous year) on May 28, ten days before the crucial vote in Dade County, while Doris was still in Sydney.

Magazine Movie was sponsoring the event, and the judges included Harvey Milk—already a local political celebrity but not yet the elected official he would become in November—and Margo St. James, the prostitution-rights activist. Though the contest was tongue-in-cheek, it wasn't a joke: Its beneficiary was the Dade County Defense Fund, which was raising money to fight the repeal. Officials including Police Chief Charles Gain, Sheriff Richard Hongisto, and Supervisor Dianne Feinstein sent in letters of support that were read from the stage. Leila and the Snakes performed, and Leila herself, Jane Dornacker, served as emcee. The *San Francisco Examiner* reported, "A dress, petticoats and a pair of 1950s sunglasses was what it took for Erik Mead, who uses the stage name 'Miss Leading,' to win." More specifically, Tippi was outfitted in pearls, a pink pinafore and a cardigan, cat's-eye sunglasses, white spike heels, and a beribboned black wig. Jane asked her where she'd found the pinafore.

"In a trash can!" she replied brightly. Her victory earned her dinner for two in a restaurant and a bouquet of paper roses. The runner-up, in a purple swimsuit over silver-sequined tights, was Ambi Sextrous.

The contest was widely covered—Bryant had become an obsessive media topic—and Tippi enjoyed a few weeks in the public eye. In late June she appeared again as Anita Bryant in the annual Gay Freedom Day parade (attendance was estimated at 250,000), and after the repeal of the Dade County ordinance she helped raise funds for the Miami Gay Support Committee, which was sponsoring a boycott to pressure the Florida Citrus Commission into severing its ties with Bryant. (The pressure eventually worked: in 1980 it declined to renew her contract.) Tippi even wrote a speech* for one of the fundraisers, telling the crowd,

> Recently Anita Bryant referred to homosexuals as "human garbage." Well, I do get my possessions from garbage cans. But then Anita Bryant's estimated income is $350,000 a year from appearances, mostly at county fairs. She will not entertain anywhere that serves alcohol. However, I'm available, and I could sure use the money. My sole income is $276 a month from SSI.† I receive this money from the government because I have been defined as unemployable due to my physical form. In or out of drag, society is incapable of relating to me.

---

* I would have liked to reproduce the eccentric orthography of Tippi's handwritten pages, but in type it looked so weird that it made her seem even less "edjumacated" than she contended. Doris wrote (perhaps a little patronizingly) to Jackie, "You'd love her. She's really very bright."

† Supplementary Security Income, a Social Security program for the low-income elderly, blind, and disabled that during that era doubled as a government grant to San Francisco artists, who became adept at convincing bureaucrats that they were mentally incompetent. SSI thus benefited the city culturally.

Doris returned to San Francisco in September 1977, moving into James Moss's house on Pearl Street. Between September and December he mailed off a series of increasingly importunate letters to Miss Abood in Sydney: "So glad you're coming"; "We're all anxiously awaiting your arrival . . . I think you'll be very successful here both as man & woman"; "You've gotta get here! No 'ifs' or 'buts,' darlink"; "What the fuck are you doing still there anyway?" For one thing, he was eager to start cracking it again. "All we'll need is a house & phone. . . . The police are really cool"—not that cool, as it turned out—"only street boys get hassled. So you'll have no money problems. And they pay more here!"

Meanwhile, he threw himself into Moss's new project, a dollar magazine named, lumberingly, *San Francisco Gay Life—Where It's At*. (It had links to a similarly named magazine in New York.) The '70s had seen an explosion in gay publications nationwide—by mid-decade there were some three hundred. They rode in on a wave of advertising dollars from gay-oriented businesses, starting with bars and bathhouses, and, reflecting the economic reality, they catered overwhelmingly to men. The scrappy new publications provided a forum for talking about everything from the arts to the gym to the bedroom. Every community seemed to have its own newspaper, or more than one; in San Francisco, the *Bay Area Reporter* had launched in 1971, the *Sentinel* in '74. In addition to the regular ads, there were often many pages of (lucrative) classifieds, from guys seeking sex and from hookers offering it.

Moss's new magazine, Doris wrote Jackie, looked like a moneymaker even though in his mind it was just "a nice bland publication designed to offend no one." It certainly would have offended Anita Bryant. In its amateurishly laid-out black-and-white pages you could find both drag queens and leather queens, which was Doris's point: It sought to attract the widest possible gay audience (and advertising) by avoiding any real controversy. Nothing could have been further from Doris's aesthetic. Still, he enjoyed putting his art skills to use, and he liked being able to cover his living expenses. But the most exciting thing about the publication was the opportunities it afforded for self-promotion. In the premier issue an ad for "Halloween Makeup by Doris Fish" ran next to the table of contents, and Doris appeared in a French maid's outfit, serving refreshments, in the photos accompanying an interview with the disco diva Sylvester. For later issues he wrote profiles and restaurant reviews, illustrated ads and comic strips, and even did a cover portrait of Patti LaBelle.

At the launch party, on October 15, 1977, some five hundred men and half a dozen drag queens danced to disco as more than two hundred slides from *Magazine Movie*, mainly of Doris, flashed on the wall. He had returned from Sydney with a new look: after milking the '30s, the '40s, and the '50s, the next step was inevitable. For their shows the previous summer, he and Jackie had inaugurated, with the aid of the fluorescent powders he'd lifted from Florence Broadhurst's wallpaper factory some years earlier, what they called the Day-Glo Revival. Now, he wrote Miss Abood—acknowledging the "tremendous impact on my drag style" of Carmel Strelein, the teenager who had brought such protopunk creativity to Sylvia and the Synthetics—he was into pale lips, gargantuan eyelashes, and extreme eyeliner: "I wore every chain & necklace I own draped all over an orange felt fringed top with cut-off shorts, a fluorescent striped shawl around my waist, fishnets and bright red boots. Various bits disappeared as the party hotted up."

Late '60s was a style he would work, literally, to death. At this point he was still close enough to Sylvia and the Synthetics to relish the glamour of degradation: "Paul [Tudman] spat on me so I took off all my clothes except the shoes pantyhose and bra and jewels and jewels [sic], then he threw drinks over me. I rolled on the filthy floor. My makeup was streaked all over, my face & my wig were sopping wet. What a mess! I looked fabulous!"

Curiously missing from all these letters—and an indication of the narrowness of his focus at the time—is any mention of politics, including Harvey Milk's momentous election in November and his assassination the following year. To the end of his life, Doris was politically engaged only in the larger sense of promoting gay visibility. He doesn't seem to have attended many protests or taken much interest in elections, though you couldn't be a gay man in the San Francisco of that era without understanding the good—or, more often, the harm—that politicians could do you.

A new subject does appear, though. "I'm really missing Bernard," he wrote Miss Abood. "That's not like me, love." They had agreed in Sydney that Bernard would come to San Francisco that year for an extended visit. "I'm terrified that when he eventually gets here I'll have changed. I don't think I will, cause this time it's the real thing!"

When Miss Abood arrived—finally—in mid-December 1977, he joined the staff of *San Francisco Gay Life—Where It's At* as an editorial assistant and got his picture in the magazine, too—black gloves, heavy makeup, and copious body hair, under the headline "Photo Creature Feature." He and Doris found a one-bedroom flat on Haight near Octavia. Doris took the bedroom and Miss Abood the parlor; they had a phone installed and were soon back in the profitable business of prostitution. It was, as Doris had promised, easy. They went thrift-shopping every day, and within weeks there was barely enough room to contain all their shoes.

It was a happy time, madcap and intimate. Miss Abood might come home to find the seven-foot-tall gardener who was one of Doris's regular cussies (he paid in vegetables) staggering around the apartment with Doris's legs wrapped around him. One night as they were brushing their teeth before bed, Doris nude at the bathroom sink and Miss Abood perched on the toilet, Miss Abood took his toothbrush and slid it straight up Doris's bum—"The whole lot of it! I just let it go and I said, 'Doris! Gimme back my toothbrush!'"

EARLY IN 1978 MISS ABOOD FLEW TO NEW YORK TO MEET RENATA, a friend from their Synthetics days in Sydney. She got off the plane from London wearing swastikas in her ears and pants strapped together at the knees—she'd outfitted herself at Malcolm McLaren and Vivienne Westwood's punk boutique, Sex, where Doris had once bought fishnets. During a wonderful week in New York, Miss Abood decided he had to live there. Then they were robbed. He and Renata were reduced to making their way back across the country via Greyhound bus with barely enough cash for sandwiches.

They made it, though, and Renata became the third of the happy hookers of Haight Street, servicing the straight guys. Then one night—as Miss Abood recounted in a letter to Jackie—he and Doris "were sitting in the lounge making a floor-length mink out of bathmats and glittering shoes for Doris's outfit for the Betty Grable Look-Alike Contest" when a couple of cops, "hideous, obviously watch *Starsky & Hutch* religiously," burst in and found Renata in the bedroom with a cussie. "We all got handcuffed and dragged off to the station. We were booked with being keepers of a house of ill repute & Ren with soliciting etc." They were held until friends from their building showed up with bail. The next morning they all slunk to court terrified of deportation, but to their relief the case was dismissed, and within twenty-four hours everything was back to normal. Doris always feared the police, but his few run-ins with them didn't slow him down for long, and eventually they backed off from sex workers who operated with a modicum of discretion.

There was more excitement: Bernard Fitzgerald announced he'd be arriving late that summer. His visit must have taken out some of the sting when Renata departed and Miss Abood decamped to New York. Doris went on turning tricks while Bernard was there—which, given Doris's outsize libido, doesn't appear to have put a crimp in their sex life. Prostitution was not, however, his only way of making ends meet, which he needed to do since, as he admitted to Mildred, "This honeymoon will cost a bit." He was still working for James Moss's magazine. He sold some paintings, including one of Tippi and Tom Faulkenbery for which Tom paid him fifty dollars. He painted signs and made posters for a new bar and continued with his carpet designs. To help with the rent, Tippi took Miss Abood's place in the apartment.

Bernard was fascinated by the wild mix of characters—Tippi, Tom ("Such a nice guy, and such a redneck!"), Freda, Ambi, and Pearl, who had just walked away from Leila and the Snakes (peeving Jane) to form Pearl Harbor and the Explosions, which immediately became a force on the local rock scene. Bernard and Doris went to one of their shows; they also attended a Joni Mitchell concert, with Doris in Joni drag. In general, though, Doris "was on his best male behavior," Bernard recalls. "We were both very aware that I was in love with *Philip*"—which was what Bernard called him—"and Philip was in love with me." Neither of Doris's serious partners (there would be another) was particularly taken with his drag persona. They were amused, but that wasn't their attraction—which isn't surprising, since Doris himself, unlike Jackie and Tippi, felt no link between drag and sex. The "fake woman" that his posters advertised never followed him out of costume, and certainly not into the bedroom.

As autumn approached, they planned a cross-country road trip. Via an ad on a notice board they hooked up with "2 discomaniacs from New York" (as Doris described them to Mildred) who were looking for passengers to share the cost of fuel. By the time they got to Albuquerque, Bernard says, "we were cramped and unhappy, and we were bored shitless by them." They made their escape on a bus to Dallas, where Doris, an assassination aficionado, was eager to visit the Texas School Book Depository. They then procured a drive-away car (drive-away services, which connect drivers with car owners who want their vehicles delivered to distant locales, were widespread in those years), and with Bernard behind the wheel, they traveled through Little Rock, Memphis, and Nashville, then up through Kentucky and Ohio to Pittsburgh, staying in spooky old motels ("because Doris just loved them") and satisfying their hunger for, as Bernard puts it, "that experience of broadness and richness and eccentricity" that was the America they'd seen in the movies. Meanwhile, their romance blossomed.

From Pittsburgh they flew to New York, where their lodgings were spooky in a different way. Miss Abood had found squalid quarters on 43rd Street in Hell's Kitchen, long before there was anything chic about the neighborhood. During daylight hours the couple played tourist, but once the sun set the drag came out. Doris and Miss Abood donned their most glittering frocks for Edith Massey's debut at CBGB.* ("Good in small doses," Abood opined.) The crowd was trashy-fabulous and the photographs numerous; one of them became the basis for a self-portrait that remained a favorite of Doris's among his paintings.

Bernard wasn't as enthusiastic. "I used to go out in Hell's Kitchen with them dressed like that and me dressed like a normal fag, and I was fucking terrified." But it was more than terror. "I couldn't understand why Philip was increasingly disappearing behind Doris, when I thought Philip was so fabulous." Still, when he left in October this dissonance was only background noise. Doris would be joining him in Sydney when he returned for another long visit in December. By now the balance between the two cities had shifted: San Francisco was Doris's home. He'd been away from Australia for well over a year.

A second off note was Jasper. In a letter written jointly with Miss Abood to Jackie and Carmel, Doris reported an early-morning call Jasper had made to New York in which "he sounded well and seemed quite together," but the next day the friend who'd put the call through— Doris still had connections at the telephone exchange—"couldn't get Jas to crawl to the phone."

Back in San Francisco, Doris did a Halloween show at Bimbo's with the revamped Leila and the Snakes, Freda Lay, and his new roommate, Tippi. Their bond quickly strengthened. Doris encouraged Tippi to supplement her SSI checks by getting back into prostitution, though, as I said, Tippi's deep-seated fear of people limited her prospects as a sex worker. But the two of them had fun together, and Tippi, for all her neuroses, must have seemed easy after the prickly Miss Abood. They planned a We're Dreaming of a Pink Christmas party—"Everyone has to wear pink or else"—for the day of Doris's departure, December 10. In late November Jane's manager, Eddie Troia, who'd been so impressed with Doris during the Tubes shows, called up with a proposal for a new revue starring Doris, Tippi, and Freda. "Just as I'm about to

---

* Edith Massey (1918–1984) was the extremely game eccentric who had won a cult following in John Waters's movies, most famously as Edie the Egg Lady in the 1972 *Pink Flamingos*. Circa 1978 she put together an unlikely punk band, Edie and the Eggs.

leave!" Doris moaned to Jackie. "But I know it would take months to materialize so I'm not worried." (It did materialize the next year, as *Sluts a-Go-Go*.)

Doris asked Jackie, who always did the writing for their shows—"Everyone thinks you're better than Lily Tomlin!"—to get some scripts together for his trip home and proposed a few numbers he'd worked up. Jackie had news of her own, about the always-outrageous Carmel, who earlier that year had started a punk band, the Screaming Abdabs; Jackie had been renting her a small room since the summer. "Carmel is 8 months pregnant & is giving the 'happening' away but she's been wearing some great 43" waisted silver mini's to the Italo-Australian club where she's been tangoing and twisting."

By the time Doris touched down in Sydney, on December 12, Jackie had the welcome-back-Doris show worked out. ("We'll be inviting all the worst people," she had promised.) She held it in her "factory," the large workspace where she was becoming increasingly skillful at decorating and restoring furniture, and in addition to the numbers they had planned, she interviewed Doris about his overseas "tour": His returns were starting to take on a glow of visiting celebrity. A couple of weeks later she threw another party at the factory: "An absolute riot," Doris wrote Miss Abood, where she "served Kentucky Fried Chicken which ended up on the floor. I was greeted by a glass of wine in the face by Mel"—as Jackie was still known—"herself. That set the tone of the evening with people hiding in corners terrified for their clothes and maybe their lives."

The note of hysteria was in jest; Doris and Jackie were never out of control. But some of their closest friends were. As in the States, the consciousness-altering-drug culture that had flowered during the 1960s was rotting at the edges. Jasper wasn't the only former Synthetic on the skids. Jackie's old friend Clayton, Doris reported to Miss Abood, "is sleeping in parks"—it was summer in Australia—"and carries her possessions with her. She lost the use of one arm thru the abuse of drugs tsk." That "tsk" was typical: Doris gazed with dry eyes on anyone in the grip of vice. Clayton had been spiraling downward for some time.

Jackie claims he was responsible for fourteen fires at the various houses they shared—"You can't be in drag *and* smoke *and* get out of it."

The scuttlebutt on Carmel was more upbeat. The baby had been born and adopted, and she had dyed her hair black and greased it back. "That girl looks incredible, nothing like a real person," Doris told Miss Abood. As for Jasper, he was laid up in Sydney Hospital, miserable, his right leg fractured in two places after falling down the stairs at a drag event: "Needless to say she was mandied but she looked great—better than Kim Novak. I did her makeup." Doris hadn't written off his oldest friend the way he had Clayton and others. In this case his disapproval melted in the warmth of denial: "Otherwise Jas is fabulous and I'm convinced '79 will be a good year for him."

A bigger bummer was Doris's discovery that Bernard had drawn back from his ardor. Or that was how Doris saw it. "We split up last week," he wrote Miss Abood gloomily in early January. "I decided that he wasn't madly in love with me, and it was frustrating, because I want to be the one in control—the loved one." He'd had it, he declared. "I hope I never fall in love again!" They resumed seeing each other almost at once. But not for long: One evening at dinner, Bernard told him he'd been out with the artist David McDiarmid the night before. "I was very thin-lipped," Doris wrote Abood. "Obviously I was No. 2. Of course the problem is me, I need attention and have to be No. 1 so today I told him our on/off relationship is off (again!). I'm so annoyed to have to do a rerun of 'Breaking Up Is Hard to Do,' especially when I'd done it so well the first time."

Although Doris claimed that Bernard thought he was "pathologically over-sexed," I'm pretty sure Bernard had a libido that was up to the challenge. He is a reflective man, still darkly attractive, who looks back on their time together with rueful affection. When Doris came back to Sydney, he told me, "I was living the life I wanted to live. I'd been inspired by him, the way he lived his life in San Francisco, doing whatever he wanted." What Bernard wanted was passion. "I had three people that I was committed to. I scheduled dates. Everyone got a night, and it was sort of rigid for a while. Doris didn't like that, of course. Doris was a star!"

Doris's insistence on having his name above the title in Bernard's story wound up costing him any role at all. Given the unruliness of Doris's own sex life, this yearning may look paradoxical, but Bernard sees it as consistent with what he calls the "screaming-slash-weeping" '40s-movie-star persona of the classic drag queen: "You're either Joan Crawford being totally aggressive and glamorous, or you're broken-hearted by a man." Looking back now, he regrets being pushed into the role of the heartbreaker. At the same time, he concedes, "I *was* neglecting him. All my other relationships at that time were terrific fun. With Doris it felt heavy, recriminations and disappointment." Moreover, there was his detachment from the world of drag: Doris had always made it clear that his career came first.

Doris dealt with his chagrin via a combination of exercise and sex, both professional and otherwise. He worked days at what he called a brothel—a gay gym designed for hookups, I assume. He also got a job redecorating the old Roxy, whose latest incarnation was the Barracks, a "fuck/suck bar" (as he delicately put it) in the sweaty-leather mode of the late '70s. He did Tom of Finland–style murals—"dicks & bums & graffiti"—and spray-painted "WHO THE FUCK IS DORIS FISH" on one wall and "MACHO SISSY" next to a self-portrait on another. After the venue opened in late January, he found it "great for getting fucks," straightforward and efficient.

One afternoon he dragged Jackie down to the old Roxy to show her his handiwork, telling her, "Stand here! This is where we first met. It's the *same spot!*" He didn't get the reaction he anticipated. No doubt he was foolish to open himself up with a burst sentiment to the defending champion of Romantic Cruelism, but no matter how diamond-hard Doris made his surface, gentle Philip was never far beneath, as Jackie knew—or thought she did. She took full advantage of his unguard-edness by openly recoiling. (Years later, when she told me the story, the memory of the place—"where people were giving each other AIDS before we knew that's what was going on"—still repelled her.) It wasn't just the malicious pleasure of mocking Doris she had once shared with Clayton, though. Jackie, unlike Doris, was an outcast from this over-heated new world of gay machismo in which Doris moved so fluidly, and that sense of ostracism doubtless sharpened her cruelty. Doris certainly felt the put-down—he had learned Romantic Cruelism at her feet. All too well, as he would soon show.

When Jasper got out of the hospital, Doris moved in with him. The setup was, in some ways, perfect: a two-bedroom flat (bedrooms upstairs) where there was already a phone, so he could make appointments for out calls (mostly), service a few regulars at home, and work on his paintings in between. He put ads in the gay papers and business percolated. What wasn't perfect was Jasper. Doris tried to be positive. "She seems to be improving," he wrote Miss Abood; the binges were becoming less frequent. "I'm not really trying to stop her but hopefully she'll realize she can't handle her dope."

In February 1979 he did another three-night weekend in drag. On Friday evening there was a Linda Ronstadt concert at the Sydney Showground; it took him hours to get ready. As a final touch he applied the dazzling white tooth paint that had become a regular feature of his makeup. It was a theatrical product, designed for the stage, and the effect up close was alarming. His tickets were for seats down near the front, and he waited, strategically, until the show was just about to start to make his entrance on his brother Michael's arm, squeezed into low-cut leopard-print ski pajamas girdled with an orange Day-Glo belt over a foam-rubber ass and tits to match, with two big black wigs and the usual excess of jewelry. The crowd, already impatient, "went crazy," he wrote Miss Abood. "They all stood up on their seats to see me. I waved regally and signed autographs, posed for countless (five) photos and generally stole the show." He added, "Linda sang well."

The next night he performed for his brother Andrew's twenty-first birthday. Andrew, who was beginning his career in construction and contracting, had recently bought a house with a friend in Collaroy, on the Northern Beaches. They were anointing it with a more elaborate recap of Michael's twenty-first birthday party three years earlier.

The following evening—Sunday, February 18, 1979—marked the debut of Cabaret Conspiracy, the brainchild of a young impresario named Johnny Allen, who had been brooding over how many talented performers there were in Sydney and how few venues they had to perform in. The weekly showcase opened at Garibaldi's, an Italian restaurant in Darlinghurst with a large hall in the back; the performers, like the audience, were a mixture of straight and gay. Doris and Jackie—billing herself as Sandra Lamont—were the comperes. Over the years they'd developed an easy, caustic give-and-take onstage; after shredding each other, they would turn their talons on the performers. They specialized in prying out backstage confidences (like who was sleeping with whom) and then sharing them with the audience—who loved it. The shows became a hit, and soon the crowd was dotted with local celebrities.

For the second Sunday they asked Jasper to perform. He'd always had an excellent (if not particularly female) singing voice; he didn't need to lip-synch. The opportunity lifted him out of his stupor, and he spent the week rehearsing "Falling in Love Again" with a pianist friend every night. On Sunday he decked himself out in vampish Dietrich drag and, though it took him an unsettlingly long time to find his way onto the stage, he delivered a beautiful rendition of the song. "I was so proud of her," Doris wrote Miss Abood. They invited him back; he planned "That Old Black Magic," à la Marilyn Monroe in *Bus Stop*, for the following week.

Since the weekend had been exhausting as well as exhilarating, Doris took the next day off and spent it working on his self-portrait at CBGB. He'd started to hope he might accomplish enough painting on this trip to mount a show of his work. Jasper was on a cloud. He went out to see his (very cooperative) doctor in order to pick up some Mandraxes that Miss Abood had asked him to mail to New York, and when he got home that evening he must have taken a few out of the bottle. He and Doris talked about the painting and chatted for a while, and then Jasper went upstairs to make some order in his overstuffed room. It was a rat's nest of treasures, so crammed with drag and his art deco collections that he could open his door only just enough to squeeze in and out.

"I was thin-lipped as I heard her stumbling around her room," Doris later wrote Miss Abood, "constantly coming in to ask me if we should keep this or that. I said no a few times—basically she was being constructively out of it but getting more so every time we spoke. Around 12, I helped her [get] more things off her bed so she could go to sleep. I took her boots off"—Jasper was still suffering the aftereffects of the double fracture—"and tucked her in and turned out her light. I went to the bathroom & the kitchen. She came stumbling down the stairs. I didn't talk to her & went into the lounge room but turned back to see her popping another Mx. I tried to find them but couldn't."

Jasper's voice had slowed to a drawl, which afterward Doris used to imitate. "Dorisssss . . . have you seen my caaaaardigan?"

"What do you want it for!" he snapped. "It's so hot!"

"Vaaaarious reasons," Jasper slurred, vexed at being grilled.

"Well, what's *one* of the reasons?"

"It's got my match-es."

"I *don't* think you want a *cigarette*," Doris said. He was seething. "You should go to bed. It's two o'clock in the morning and we've got to get up early"—Jasper had a teaching job, and Doris had to be at the brothel. He told Miss Abood that he was almost ready to hit him. Jasper replied with a grande dame scowl and half crawled back up the stairs to his room. Doris went up to his own room, shut the door, and undressed. As he closed his eyes he could hear Jasper stumbling around.

Early the next morning Doris arrived at Jackie's place, flummoxed and smelling of smoke. "Jasper's burnt the house down!" he told her, aggrieved, as he perched on the side of her bed. "Or at least her bedroom." Doris had been awakened at 3 a.m. by molten nails falling from the ceiling above him and by Jasper's shouts. For a panicked moment he couldn't open his door; when he managed to, he was blasted by the flames coming from Jasper's room. He pushed on Jasper's door—the knob itself was white-hot—but of course it stuck against something. He tried throwing in water, but soon the door itself was in flames. As he was running to telephone the fire department he heard the sirens, and the engines rolled up. He wrapped himself in a towel and stood outside, watching flames shoot off the balcony as the firemen fought the blaze.

"Now I'll have to move out!" he complained. "And the place was so nicely fixed up. And now the phone is out and I've *just* had a photo ad put in *Campaign*." He griped on, ignoring Jackie's questions, ranting about all the headaches this new mess was going to cause him and what a nuisance it was going to be to find a new place and have a new telephone installed, until finally Jackie raised her voice enough to get him to pause: "How's Jasper?"

Doris looked at her blankly. "Well, she's *dead*, love."

As Jackie said drily, some years later: Doris had a sense of theater.

"Well, that's good," Jackie snapped back, as if they were in a routine onstage. "I never really liked her anyway." Which, as they both knew, was far from true.

Doris said, "She loved *you*."

"And that," Jackie said afterward, "was the end of that conversation. It was such a bitchy thing, to take advantage of my retort."

All that was left of Jasper's room was bricks and ashes and a few hanging fixtures. The body was burned so completely that it took the firemen some time to locate it. Except for the smell of smoke, Doris's things—including the new painting—were salvageable.

Many years later, when Doris was dead himself, his friend Connie Champagne sat down with Jackie in Paris to interview her about Doris and asked her, among other things, what her favorite memory of him was. She reflected and said, "I suppose my favorite memory is my most horrendous memory, which is when she tells me that Jasper's dead. It's the cruelness of her talking for ages and ages and not telling me. Because I knew that he was devastated."

She told me much the same thing when I asked her what she thought Doris had been feeling. "Oh, extreme sadness. Because this was his best, best, *best*, longest friend. He really loved Jasper. But we were not into expressing emotions—never, never a pinch of emotion." Just the opposite: "Doris was painfully frank. When Jasper's mother, Pammy, asked Doris to assure her that he hadn't suffered, Doris looked at her and said, 'He was screaming a lot.'"

Doris's flipness appalled Miss Abood, and it caused a rift between them for a time. Even though he acknowledged to me that it was his friend's way of coping with the tragedy, it also convinced him there was something vital lacking in Doris. "Doris didn't have some of those emotions. And you just had to accept that in the end."

I don't accept it. I don't believe that Doris's hard facade was a shell covering a void. He never showed his family—even the exasperating Mildred—anything but love and warmth. He was capable of profound kindness, as he would demonstrate in nurturing Tippi, who became his lifelong charge. And he would later face annihilating pain with heroic stoicism. But in the space of a few weeks Doris had lost Bernard and now Jasper, two people who'd been central to his life. Shock must have played a part in his reaction before it calcified into a routine. He was still young—he would turn twenty-seven that August—and the young don't know what to do with endings. In Sylvia and the Synthetics he'd been drawn into the ethos of transgressing everything, and it had worked for him so far. Piety over Jasper's death might have seemed false, even ridiculous, an endorsement of the sanctimonious morality young people were rebelling against. The Synthetics had channeled the beginnings of punk, whose aesthetic of anger had saved many in our generation from self-pity and would serve even more when our friends and contemporaries started dying of AIDS and no one much cared. For now, though, it was an armor that Doris was fitting to the contours of his own personality, not always adeptly.

Was there a trace of something less generous? Possibly. Doris and Jasper had been in competition since they were five years old. Jasper was the pretty one. Jasper painted as well as Doris did, perhaps better. Jasper had an exquisite voice; Doris couldn't carry a tune. But Doris was stronger, and he had discipline. With Jackie, the tension was different. Doris had been in awe of Jackie since day one. Jackie had taken him under her wing and taught him how to apply makeup, how to shop, how to dress; she had put him in touch with glamour and pointed him down the path they'd both traveled so far on in their different ways. Jackie was the intellectual; Jackie was the wit. She wrote the scripts. Sometimes, just to torture Doris, she would claim she was winging it. "I'd always say, 'We'll think of something when we get onstage'— but the point was, I'd *already* thought of something. I just didn't want to tell Doris." She enjoyed watching him squirm. It was Jackie who'd read the French existentialists and, with Clayton, invented the ethic and the aesthetic of Romantic Cruelism. Doris was their student and, not infrequently, their victim. Now he was showing that he had mastered these concepts with a sureness they would never match. None of them had his ambition or his lust for celebrity. Over the years, their friendship had been changing little by little. Now, in the space of a few hours, the tables had turned.

Jasper's funeral was held a few days later at St. Kieran's, the little parish church in Manly Vale where the Millses had worshipped and where Doris and Jasper—Philip and Peter—had gone to grade school. Doris and Jackie dressed as Italian movie stars in mourning, their drag somber, their sunglasses enormous, parasols raised to protect them from the Sydney sun. Carmel's short account in the punk zine *Spurt!* captured the ambience: "Jasper Havoc 1953–1979 . . . Burnt to a cinder in a room full of exotic drag. All they found was a tooth. They performed last rites on that slender piece of ivory at St. Kieran's, Manly Vale." And in a reference to the near-comatose haze in which he had wandered so often, she quoted the priest's "As we are in this life, so we are in death" and concluded her report, "In Jasper's case he wasn't far from the truth."

Shortly afterward, Clayton died, from a heart attack brought on by an overdose of chloral hydrate (a popular sedative before the advent of more reliable ones like Ambien), in a gutter in Darlinghurst.

6

SLUTS A-GO-GO

J ASPER'S DEATH HAUNTED DORIS. BUT HE MASKED HIS SORROW.
"I still wake up some nights and relive that night," he wrote Miss
Abood later the same month, March 1979. "But at least she was stunning before she went, and she'd said she didn't want to live past thirty
anyway, so I don't really grieve for Jas but I do miss her now and again."
He dined out on the story for the rest of his life, turning it into a half-
comic Romantic Cruelist set piece.

In the weeks following the fire, he threw himself into work. He
rented a flat on the ninth floor of the St. James Apartments, centrally
located a block away from Hyde Park on Stanley Street, "with lovely

Doris in *Blonde Sin*, 1980. Photo by Daniel Nicoletta.

views," he wrote Miss Abood, "of Darlinghurst toilets and brothels." In eight days he took in $1,375, a record, and it all went into the bank. Then one day a client showed up who, he told Abood, was "just too fabulously gorgeous to be a cussie." When the stud asked him, "Do you do extras?," he cautiously replied, "I don't do extras," mentally adding, "officer." The cop was having none of it. He pulled out his badge and called in his partner, who "would've fooled me for sure. In his fifties in a brown leisure suit, he was a typical cussie." Though they didn't arrest him, they told him, "No more." "Yessir," he answered meekly. "And now," he grumbled to Abood, "I'm an almost out of work prossie."

The breather didn't last long: by early April he was turning tricks again, though only out calls, which meant staying at home and waiting for the phone to ring. He used the time to paint, working on a new self-portrait and a series of watercolors. But since he was planning to return to San Francisco in July he soon realized he had too little time to organize the show he'd had in mind—most of the galleries were already booked. "Wouldn't get it together anyway," he wrote Miss Abood glumly. "I just have too much time and not enough motivation. . . . Maybe my problems are intensified by the loss of a lover and the death of Jas"—a rare moment of openly expressed sadness. "I just feel there's very little purpose in striving, except that it makes you forget how purposeless it is!"

But Doris was constitutionally optimistic, and soon he once again had reason to be. Cabaret Conspiracy had taken off, and his local fame was growing. Dennis Altman wrote about the series for his column in *Campaign*, singling Doris out and applauding Cab Con, as it soon became known, as "part of what gay politics is all about" (though he acknowledged it was not "specifically gay"), "namely the creation of new forms of community awareness." In the late '70s, gay politics couldn't really be about anything else, since there were so few gay politicians. Although queer communities were fermenting in cities around the world, politics couldn't penetrate the electoral realm until the community awareness Altman was talking about had produced the conditions for that massive coming out of the closet that it was then in the process of creating. The most political thing you could do as a gay man or lesbian, at that time, was be open about it.

Jackie kept changing her stage name—Sandra La Mont, Sandra La Moan, Helen Bed—because, unlike Doris, she was conflicted about the notoriety. Doris, meanwhile, ramped up his '60s look with a beehive, short, thick lashes, and very pale mod-style lips. The two of them compered together, slagging the acts they were introducing and doing their own broad sketches, like a Good Friday passion play with Doris as Mary Magdalene and Jackie as the Virgin squabbling at the foot of the cross. ("You bitch, you killed my son!") The popularity of the shows kept increasing, but Doris had a return ticket to San Francisco for early July. "I keep worrying that I'm leaving when my showbiz career here is about to blossom," he told Miss Abood, "but I fear that if I stay it won't!" He took his final bow on May 27, "and the place was crammed to the tits!" he wrote Abood. "And almost every act was a tribute to Doris Fish!" The evening peaked with the audience singing from cue cards to the tune of "Bye Bye Blackbird":

> Pack up all your drag and blow,
> Off you go, singing low,
> Bye bye Doris.

He was speechless with delight.

His prospects as a performer really did seem to be multiplying. He'd quit Cab Con a month in advance of his departure in order to act in *As Time Goes By*, described on a flyer as "an agitprop theatre history of gay oppression and liberation." The six cast members played multiple roles, and Doris appeared as both a transvestite and ("using trick makeup," he wrote) a "real" man. The play took place in three time periods, moving from 1890s London to 1930s Berlin and on to the first Sydney Gay Mardi Gras, in 1978. That occasion, the year before, had been a milestone owing to a police-provoked melee that electrified the country's gay-rights movement.* As Time Goes By was, in fact, part of a series of events leading up to the second, 1979 Mardi Gras. That year Doris's participation was limited to his role in the play, but in the '80s he would become a Mardi Gras star.

BY THE TIME HE RETURNED TO SAN FRANCISCO, ON JULY 4, HE'D saved up $4,000. Only a week later he flew to New York to spend three weeks with Miss Abood, who had settled in much more happily, found friends, and started a long stint of increasingly high-end prostitution. While Doris was there, they performed at a nightclub uptown and at the Anvil, a then-notorious 14th Street dance bar that featured drag queens and go-go boys upstairs and a labyrinth of warrens for trysts below street level. "I ended up swinging from a trapeze by my platformed little feet to the Beach Boys' 'California Girls,'" Doris wrote Johnny Allen, the founder of Cab Con. "The queens loved it." New York, he added, "is the centre of the universe! Next time I'll go live there for a while."

He never did, though. His star was on the rise in San Francisco, too. With Tippi and Freda he started planning a new revue held together by a thin plot about a group of showgirl-hookers, tough broads typical of the '30s and '40s movies they all loved. Tippi had a movie-crazy friend named Brad Chandler who she thought could help with the script—"He's literate!" she said. Ambi Sextrous was throwing a twenty-seventh-birthday party on September 16, and Tippi used the occasion to introduce Brad to Doris.

DALTON BRADLEY CHANDLER II. THE GENTEEL NAME WAS deceptive. A college dropout, a drifter who had done time, an omni-sexual satyr, a louche mooch with a taste for controlled substances. A dark, skinny John Waters look-alike (as he has been described) who,

---

* See Chapter 9.

under Doris's tutelage, morphed, much to his own surprise, into a glamorous witch with a basilisk stare.

He was born in Cincinnati on October 28, 1951, making him a year older than Doris and Tippi. His parents church-hopped, and he always sang in the choir. He wrote his first play in the second grade and cast himself in the central role. His high school classes didn't interest him, but reading and psychedelics did. The itch to perform led him to community theater, which he stayed with into his college years, of which there were only two before the University of Cincinnati suggested that he continue his studies elsewhere. It was in a theater group that he met a young man whose eye had been drawn to San Francisco by its intersection of gay freedom and flower power. Brad was game. He was the definition of game.

But they got stranded in Los Angeles first. Somewhere in the desert a clueless gas station attendant wrecked the engine of Brad's VW Bug by pouring motor oil into the port for the transmission fluid. The car limped into LA. That was August 1971. For two years Brad dabbled at odd jobs to earn the money to fix it. The oddest, and the best, was as a projectionist at a gay porn cinema just off Hollywood Boulevard, where pretty much all he had to do was occasionally change the gargantuan reels of spliced-together 16 mm loops; otherwise he was free to smoke, read, embroider, and shoot the breeze with a fellow employee, a pretty Hollywood High dropout who was into drag, had a boyfriend in San Francisco, and went by the name Freda Lay.

Inertia and penury kept the two friends in LA until, after a year, they got so discouraged they decided to pack it in and go home. In Kingman, Arizona, the Peter Max–style flowers all over the Bug and the flowing hair of the driver and his passenger attracted the attention of the cops. Brad's friend hadn't mentioned the roll of amphetamines he'd purchased from the cute boy at the gas pump when they'd stopped to fill up. The upshot was a month and a half in the Mohave County Jail, which they like to refer to as "the spa."

Furious at his family for refusing to front him bail (their sentiment was "It will do him good"), Brad scratched the idea of returning to

Ohio. When he finally made the move north, Freda's San Francisco boyfriend invited him to crash for his first few days in his spacious Market Street apartment in the Castro, where he lived with a portly, bearded pothead everybody called Mr. Natural—the same Mr. Natural Erik Mead had shared a van with. And so when Brad rang the doorbell on that early-autumn day in 1973, it was Erik, still in her wispy-goatee phase—she hadn't yet evolved into Miss Leading, let alone Tippi—who answered the door, making her the first person Brad met when he arrived in the city.

Brad was charmed by Tippi's vulnerability and—something not everyone who knew her later from her ditzy stage persona recognized—her intelligence, especially around movies. They were both glamour addicts and stockpiles of Hollywood trivia. They would while away hours at the Times Theatre in North Beach, where you could sit for as long as you liked, smoking whatever you liked, through the daily ninety-nine-cent double and triple bills.

Brad spent the next several years, as he tells it, going to parties, getting wasted, screwing—it was the '70s, the great decade of sexual excess—and sponging off people. San Francisco was cheap then. He lived in a series of rooms for which he paid a pittance in rent. When necessary, he waited tables; at Hamburger Mary's he got to know a fellow waitress named Mary and moved into her apartment around the corner on Isis Street. The city's best dance bar, the Stud, was nearby. There he and Mary honed the art of getting people to buy them drinks.

"Was Mary a friend or a girlfriend?" I asked, and Brad answered, "Well—yes!" Although up till then he had never thought of himself as anything but gay, he found he liked sleeping with women, too. "Why cut out half the population?" he says. "If you like sex, have sex! Broaden your horizons! Give yourself a chance! You might end up having sex three times in an evening instead of only one—with three different people! I did fuck a lot of people. They've got an awful lot of coffee in Brazil!"

At first he didn't see Tippi that often. They moved in different circles, insofar as the reclusive Tippi moved in any circle at all. But they never fell out of touch, and over the years Brad became one of the few people Tippi trusted. Sometimes they would sit around with Freda, who had also moved north, and put on makeup and dress up and watch old movies on TV. Brad's love of costume went back to his days in community theater. He'd done drag for costume balls, and through other friends he had connections to former Cockettes, who would doll him up when he went out with them. Still, he didn't think of himself as a drag queen. Yet.

But he was a taboo breaker ("What's the worst possible thing I could do? OK, let's do that!")—much like Doris, who returned from Sydney to his apartment on Haight Street in July 1979. Tippi had taken Miss Abood's place as his roommate and was doing drag much more intensely by then. It was Tippi who arranged for Doris and Brad to meet at Ambi Sextrous's birthday party that September. The theme was "Come as Your Favorite Fellini Character." As Sylva, the gossamer-gowned sister in *Juliet of the Spirits*, Brad wore a strapless dress under a plastic rain slicker he'd borrowed from Freda, which wasn't nearly warm enough. "I thought, *Oh, good God! No wonder drag queens are portrayed as such bitter people! Look at what you've got to go through!* Little did I know what the next ten years were going to hold for me."

Brad and Tippi arrived early. Hours passed with no sign of Doris. "Of course I now know what she was doing," Brad says. "Doris loved getting made up more than anything, except maybe eating, and she loved to take as much time as possible. Getting there was anticlimactic—which is why she was late to everything." By the time Doris finally swept in, practically all the other guests had left and Ambi had gone to bed. So much the better, since the three of them could skip the party chitchat. Doris hadn't bothered to outfit himself as a Fellini character—he was just Doris, Brad recalled, in a Pucci-esque op-art dress, a blonde wig, "the heavy heavy *heavy* tanned no-makeup Dusty Springfield look, and *the whitest teeth I'd ever seen.*"

The teeth were what Brad fixed on. "I hated the color of my teeth. I was always a smoker, and when you put on a pale makeup base, it makes your teeth look terrible. 'Wow!' I said. 'What's that?'" Doris explained tooth paint. "Doris always said, 'I'd paint my eyeballs if I could!' She had tons of great stories and was very interested in me. I now realize that Tippi must have been building me up. She hung on every word. She entertained me. God, she was great. And we became best friends."

Soon afterward Brad dropped by their apartment for a visit. Tippi turned to Doris and suggested they get him to help with the script they were working on. The show they dreamed up would go through a dozen metamorphoses over the next couple of years. But their characters were set from the start: Dorice Poisson (Doris), proprietress of the Fishnet Club, where the showgirls turn tricks in between numbers; Lois Standard (Tippi), her long-lost daughter, born in the alley behind Finocchio's; the spectacularly dim Candy (Freda); and Helen Damnation, runaway heiress to the Helen Damnation funeral parlor and fast-food chain, in hiding and incognito as the mysterious Miss X. Which is what everyone I know has always called Bradley Chandler—that or just X—and so that's how I'll refer to him from now on.

They called the show SLUTS A-GO-GO and, envisioning it as a one-shot, put it on for a Sunday night Halloween party at the Pride Center on Grove Street. The date was October 28, 1979, Miss X's twenty-eighth birthday. The energy was high, the drag was over the top, and the lighting was professional, paid for (as so much would be) with a chunk of Doris's savings. He wrote Jackie* that it was a "comedy smash hit" and gave much of the credit to Miss X: "She's a clever queen, luv, and was a great help in the dialogue department. She's only just started doing drag but is advancing quickly."

Doris's plan was to return to Sydney by Christmas for the Australian summer. After the success of *Sluts a-Go-Go*, he had an inspiration: Why not bring the show with him? He would bankroll Tippi, who could never have come up with the money; X and Freda would pay

---

* No more Mel. In the greeting line he used the name Sandra—I assume for Sandra La Mont—which soon thereafter became, definitively, Jacqueline Hyde.

Ace and Mildred Mills, 1968. Courtesy of Andrew Mills.

Miss Abood and Doris in mufti, early '70s. Courtesy of Johnny Allen.

Doris and Miss Abood at the Sylvia and the Synthetics reunion for the Queen's Birthday Extravaganza, 1977. Photo by William Yang.

Jasper, Doris, and Morris Spinetti onstage, 1974. Photo by Philip Morris.

"Jasper, Doris and Danny" from Barry Kay's *The Other Women/As a Woman*, 1976. Courtesy of the Barry Kay Archive, ©Hubertus Janssen-Werner.

Jasper Havoc, 1975.
Photo by William Yang.

Carmel Strelein by Norman Parkinson, from *Sisters Under the Skin*, 1978.
Norman Parkinson/Iconic Images.

Jane Dornacker, Miss X, and Doris in *Blonde Sin*, 1980. Photo by Daniel Nicoletta.

Doris, Tippi, and Miss X at Doris's wedding reception, 1981. Photo by Daniel Nicoletta.

Miss X and Doris at the Castro Street Fair, 1983. Photo by Daniel Nicoletta.

Poster for the premiere of *Vegas in Space*, 1991. Courtesy of Phillip R. Ford.

Sandelle and Tippi in *The All-New Happy Hour Xmas Special*, 1985. Photo by Greg Foss.

Tippi and Tom Faulkenbery at the Haight Street Fair, 1980. Courtesy of Peggy Darm.

Sandelle escorted by X and Doris in formal boy drag, 1985. Photo by Greg Foss.

Tommy Pace as Imelda Marcos and Doris as Marie Antoinette in *Dragon Ladies and Their Fashions*, 1986. Photo by Daniel Nicoletta.

Doris with the Showbags, 1987. Left to right: Twistie, Miss 3D, Doris, Cindy Pastel. Photo by William Yang.

their own way. It sounded crazy, but Doris assured them they could get enough nightclub work to, at the worst, break even. He made a quick trip to New York to see Miss Abood, then returned to San Francisco to pick up Tippi and head out. X got the travel money together with help from his family (they were more openhanded than they'd been about bail), but poor Freda couldn't swing it.

As much fun as it was for X to think about, though, it felt like a fantasy: He didn't truly see himself as an entertainer. Maybe that's why he missed his plane—that, congenital lateness, and the dark mood that had settled over him. He was always the night sky to Doris's moonglow. He came home from the airport plunged in bleakness and telephoned Doris. "Look, is it even worth it?"

"I can't fucking believe it!" Doris shouted into the phone. "They've been touting it in the papers: Doris Fish's triumphant return to Sydney! Everybody's talking about it! You can't buy this kind of publicity! Get on a plane and get here!"

And so he did. A car picked him up at the airport and whisked him straight to a club, where suddenly he was perched on a piano and singing "Over the Rainbow"—or as much of it as he could remember—to an exuberant crowd. It was revelatory, transformative. "All my life people had been telling me, 'You're not really that good, you can't really sing, you're not that pretty, you'll never be a blonde, blah blah blah.' I bleached my hair as soon as I got over there! And I performed—we all did, all the time—and I got my chops."

Audiences loved them. They covered the city, often hitting two or three clubs in a single evening and finishing with a midnight show at their favorite venue, Stranded. Nestled in the basement of the Strand Arcade, an elaborate Victorian galleria downtown that dated from 1892, Stranded was a baroque fantasia of gilt and marble and red velvet hangings with Corinthian columns and frescoed ceilings. Much like Cab Con, it drew its crowd from the art and fashion and media worlds, mixing gays and straights and trendsetters and drag queens. And it paid: a twenty-minute show on Friday and Saturday nights together netted them $500.

Everybody wanted to meet the American queens. As Doris said, "Being in a new town, you could pretend to be really talented and out-going. You could leave all your inner phobias and paranoias behind, because no one knew you were supposed to have them." Miss X fell into a highly convenient romance with a pianist, who played for their shows. Tippi also found a lover: he drove a Mr. Whippy ice cream truck, and, typically, no one ever laid eyes on him.

They revised *Sluts a-Go-Go* to make room for Sydney drag queens. The story line now involved a troupe of American go-go girls who, after getting separated from the 1968 Bob Hope USO tour in Viet-nam, team up with their Australian counterparts. The shows depended much more on live singing than on the lip-synching of the past. Tippi had a nice if somewhat reedy voice—"Not a belter by any means," X says, "but they had me to cover the Ethel Merman aspect"—and even Doris managed to bray out a few numbers.

Jackie performed with them, though not a lot, since her furniture business took up most of her time and her hunger for the spotlight was no match for theirs. But X's ear for dialogue made him, in a sense, the new Jackie, as his singing made him the new Jasper. I asked X if Jackie resented his ascendancy. "Who could tell with Jackie?" he replied. X and Tippi certainly saw her a lot, especially during the daytime, when Doris needed the apartment to turn tricks. He had a new ad in *Campaign*, and this time, apparently, the police gave him no trouble. But business hardly satisfied his libido. One night he and X went to Les Girls to check out the highly professional drag show there and brought home two body-building hunks. Doris got the bedroom, and X got the roof.

Lyrics were Miss X's Achilles' heel—on that very first evening, he'd blanked out on "Over the Rainbow"—but no one seemed to mind. At Cab Con, the audience sang along to help him through "Falling in Love Again" when he forgot the words. For a longtime votary of Hollywood glamour, drag queen drama came naturally. In a typical entrance at Stranded, he crawled across the marble floor and up the leg of the pi-ano, and, once on top, whipped around and started to sing. He was indeed advancing quickly.

There was also a Beat show, *Tight, like a Ponytail in Bondage*, and an *Amazing Sexploits and Cunning Stunts* evening at a club named Syd's. They hosted a slave auction at the Barracks, the sex club that had once been the Roxy. An antidrag heckler got physical and pushed Doris ("resplendent in black fishnet stockings, plastic vagina with teeth, and sensible shoes," according to *Campaign*) off the pool table/stage, but the audience caught him and swung him back up; Doris then pushed his antagonist off the table and the audience parted to let him slam to the floor. Despite losing his wig in the melee that followed, Doris regarded the evening as another triumph, though he wondered, "How do you follow an act like that?"

The South Pacific Nightclub Tour, as they always called it afterward, lasted four glorious months, and it bonded them permanently. In Sydney Doris would continue to reign as Doris, but in San Francisco the Sluts a-Go-Go—they took their name from the show—became a trio (with no malice toward Freda, who went on performing with them but eventually drifted off in her own hazy direction). There was never any question about who the queen bee was, but Miss X and Tippi commanded an all-but-equal share of notoriety. Doris made sure that they did.

THEY GOT BACK TO SAN FRANCISCO ON MARCH 18, 1980, AND marked the new decade with new living arrangements. Tippi moved into X's large apartment in the Castro, at Market and Sanchez, which X had initially shared with a cousin; somewhat later, so did Freda, and it became known as Slut Central. Doris went back to living with Paul Tudman—Cheryl—a block and a half away, at Market and Castro. He'd returned with an agreement to continue the monthly column he had started writing (with occasional help from Miss X) for *Campaign* in Sydney. In April he got a call from Martin Ryter, a photographer who'd had an idea for a cable TV show. A friend had taken Martin to *Sluts a Go-Go*, and he was, he says, completely enamored: "They were so bad it was unbelievably great."

It was early in the era of cable, when video equipment was becoming increasingly available to consumers. Martin managed to get some funding from the gay biweekly *The Advocate* for a magazine-style show they named *Click TV*—the idea was to click the viewer's brain switch on—and for the next year he and Doris taped a weekly segment. (It never aired.) "She got it," he says. "She was built for television."

That was partly because Doris was so brazen about cornering his subjects. When the winner of the Mr. Castro pageant was crowned at the Castro Theatre, Doris bounded onto the stage, grabbed him, dipped him, and planted a long kiss. At the premiere of *Can't Stop the Music*, the (famously terrible) movie starring the campy disco band the Village People, he collared Felipe Rose, the American Indian in the costumed troupe, as he emerged from his limousine; the other Village People were so unnerved (unbelievable as it now seems, they were officially in the closet) that they drove off and sneaked in a back entrance. "Luckily," Doris wrote in *Campaign*, "I didn't have to sit through the movie." He and Martin barged into a charity fundraiser where Doris managed to ensnare one of his heroes, Joan Baez ("We chatted briefly about my stunning outfit"), as well as a less-than-enthusiastic Lily Tomlin. In August they went to Nevada to cover the National Reno Gay Rodeo. Doris paraded around in outlandish outfits, but he found the rodeo events less engaging than the action under the bleachers.

They also did *Tonight Show*–style interviews, using Martin's Jackson Street home as a studio, with Doris in a stewardess outfit he'd bought at a thrift store. They invited local celebrities like the writer Armistead Maupin and the drag nuns who called themselves the Sisters of Perpetual Indulgence. Occasionally, especially when they knew it might jangle their guests, they adorned the set with nude boys.

After a year *The Advocate* pulled the plug—probably, Martin thinks, because of the controversy surrounding drag queens in the increasingly defensive gay community post–Anita Bryant. But *Click TV* helped Doris develop his instincts as a provocateur, if they needed any further developing. His outfit for the taping of the Gay Freedom Day parade in June 1980 featured plastic bosoms with "wet-look nipples painted with pink glitter nail polish," he wrote Jackie. Toward the end of the day it got hot, "so I jumped into a fountain (all on video, of course). I did lots of rude gestures for the straight tourists and families—busy giving gays a bad name."

SLUT CENTRAL WAS THE SITE OF THEIR FIRST MEETING WITH EDDIE Troia, Jane Dornacker's manager, who had phoned the previous November, when Doris was just on the verge of leaving for Australia, with an idea for a show. He called again as soon as they all got back from Sydney. "I'm bringing over a minor genius who's going to help with the music," he told them. The minor genius was a Philadelphia-born scene-maker named Timmy Spence, who played keyboards in Jennifer Blowdryer's punk band, the Blowdryers—he was then going by Timmy Blowdryer—and in a pretty-boy band called Times Five. X's first impression was not favorable: "He was so 'I'm Timmy Blowdryer and you're not. And I'm on every guest list of every bar and club in the city and you aren't.'" But he was also tall, fair, and beguiling—Doris described him in his *Campaign* column as "six-foot one-inch of masculine genius"—and, however obnoxious his preening was, it didn't keep either Doris or X from developing a crush on him.

Another of Timmy's fans was Carmel Strelein—the former underage Synthetic and Norman Parkinson model—who by now had made her way to San Francisco and become a Slut Central regular. Coming out of the Sydney punk scene, she was naturally drawn to Timmy, and it was mutual—"She was funny and she was so extreme"—though sometimes her brazenness unnerved him: "One time I was taking a shower over there, and Carmel hopped right in. I was really shocked!" The two of them put together a band that lasted for two performances.

Eddie Troia's coke spoon was his trademark. Their meetings began, almost ritually, with a snort before they got down to work. Over a few weeks they turned the crude *Sluts a-Go-Go* show into a less crude "play with music" under the same title. Rehearsals began in early May, and on June 27 the first preview took place at the Hotel Utah, a South of Market tavern dating from 1908 with a carved wooden bar and a postage-stamp stage. The dressing room—for six people with more than a dozen costume changes each—was the ladies' toilet. Under Eddie Troia's manic enthusiasm, they kept reworking, developing, shifting things around. By August, *Sluts a-Go-Go* was in its sixth re-write and had settled in at the Hotel Utah for a run that would continue, on and off, for close to two years.

Eddie Troia hadn't exaggerated: Timmy's songs were smart and funny, and his musicianship gave the production a new gloss of professionalism. In exchange for his contribution, the four drag queens performed with his band. Over the next year or so, Timmy and the Sluts, as they called themselves, became regulars on the club scene. They even released a New Wave single, an energetic piece of organ-driven bubble gum called "Brand New Dance"; Carmel helped out.

Mostly, though, they did '60s music, with the Sluts providing backup vocals and go-go dancing. Doris got the spotlight on a couple of numbers, which he spoke-sang his way through. "Doris couldn't carry a tune in a *bucket*," X says. "And she hated that. When you looked through her record collection, it was *nothing* but female vocalists, and why? Because she wanted to *be* a female vocalist, and it was the one thing she couldn't do. You always want what you can't have."

In October, Eddie Troia talked Jane Dornacker into joining the cast. Jane was a ballsy comic, a good singer, and a witty songwriter, and her six-foot height had the special benefit of making everyone else in the show look less crook. (Audience members would take bets as to who in the cast was a biological female; Jane was the only one.) She came with some of her own songs, including her man-size-girl's lament about walking along innocently, "the picture of charm and poise," when out of the blue a catcall comes

> *From the open window of a passing car*
> *Or the shadowy doorway of some dark bar*
> *As if to be nasty and mean:*
> *"Drag queen! Drag queen! Drag queen!"*

By Doris's own admission, the show was full of dreadful lines. "A lot of times there'd be five minutes of plot just to get to one joke." There were some classics, too, as when Tippi, whipping an envelope from her bra, would say, "I have my costumes here," and then, struggling to lift a heavy suitcase, "and my makeup and hairspray here!"

With Jane, the show gained a new title, *Blonde Sin*—"the sin they left out of the Bible"—and a more complicated plot, though it still involved Dorice Poisson's attempts to get a group of showgirls together for the Bob Hope USO tour. Jane was a "Russian defective" fleeing the Communists to study go-go dancing under the world-renowned Dorice. Miss X became the runaway daughter of a munitions maker and the heiress to the Brand X fortune.[*] At the end of one version, a white-fur-clad Dorice departed for the Bolshoi to star in a go-go production of *Swan Lake*.

Subtle it wasn't. Practically every show that Doris and crew would mount over the next decade, with the exception of two or three forays into legitimate theater, would be this kind of daffy throwaway vehicle. At bottom, Doris wasn't a theatrical artist (though in time he became one) but a visual artist who used theater as a means to an end—the raison d'être for *Blonde Sin* was the costume changes. While everybody made contributions, it was Doris's vision that reigned. He had a strong aesthetic and an even stronger will.

Since the run was discontinuous, they found ways to fill the gaps. In August they appeared at a party at the Mabuhay Gardens, the city's premier punk club; the theme was Hell, and Tippi and Matt, a sweetly accommodating hunk who appeared in the show for a while, were striking as a nearly nude Adam and Eve, with Matt's pet boa constrictor as the serpent. In late September they did a *Slumber Party* show ("lots of nighties & underwear") at a club on Polk Street. In late October the Tubes' Michael Cotten invited them to go-go dance at a party the band was throwing for Talking Heads. Doris described a November 1

---

[*] In 2000 he offered a reporter another explanation: "He lifted the name from Dear Abby columns because, he says, he was intrigued by the atrocious behavior of 'a friend I'll call "Miss X"' whom readers were constantly griping about."

performance at the San Francisco Art Institute for his column in *Campaign*: "One brave girl throws a tomato at me. It misses. I pick it up and silently walk to where she is sitting. Her boyfriend looks on as I mash it into mousy brown hair and smear it all over everything." Meanwhile, audiences kept coming to *Blonde Sin*.

But if they were getting mildly famous, they weren't getting rich. "I'm absolutely broke," Doris wrote Jackie late in 1980, "but not too disheartened as I'm sure it's only temporary." In September he had reported that they were earning twenty dollars a night for the show, "which is enough to survive on, especially considering we've been starving for months." Martin Ryter says, "Those girls were in poverty, and they didn't care. They were workers. They were doing it for the love of show business." But they did care. In June 1981 Doris apologized to Mildred for his silence, telling her that he had started to write her but "there was no good news last month—I couldn't even afford the stamp to send the letter." By the time he did write, his usual good cheer had returned. "I'm working as a prossie again, so I can start repaying my $1,000 in debts." And there was bigger news. "Did I tell you I'm married?"

The bride was a lesbian he'd known for about a year.[*] Doris described her to Mildred as "Swedish/Norwegian in origin, very intelligent and incredibly funny." There was an engagement party, with champagne and cocaine, at Doris and Cheryl's apartment; the wedding itself, a low-key affair, took place on April 9 at City Hall, with Doris dressed in a suit and tie and Cheryl and X acting as witnesses.

Ten days later, the newlyweds held a reception at 422 Oak Street, the home of Greg Foss, a place and a person that were about to assume major importance in the lives of the Sluts. Doris had on a Chantilly lace wedding gown dotted with pearls from X's wardrobe, which he wore backward and unzipped in order to display his plastic boobs, and a faux-pearl tiara that he augmented with a great deal of veiling. He, Tippi (the flower girl, in off-the-shoulder powder blue), and Miss X

---

[*] Since she didn't wish to be interviewed, I'll refrain from naming her.

(in very-low-cut black lace)—brunette, blonde, and redhead—featured matching purple eye shadow, and it's hard to say whose look was the sluttiest. Ambi sang; there were flowers, champagne, and a three-tiered wedding cake; and, astonishingly, no one misbehaved.

"I still have to save up money for the lawyer," Doris continued in his June letter to Mildred, "so I can get my green card." The immigration interview didn't take place until December, as he wrote in a Christmas card to his parents. The two of them managed to convince the authorities that they really were a couple, "*but* I have to stay in the U.S.A. until it's all finalized, which will be 3–6 months—no suntan this year." Or the next year, either, or the next.

Doris's wasn't the only green-card marriage that season. Carmel managed to land a spouse, too. The bridegroom was Miss X.

7

VEGAS IN SPACE

M ORE ROMANTIC CRUELISM: IN JANUARY 1982 DORIS, MISS
X, and Miss Leading (soon to be known as Tippi) agreed to appear at the On Broadway, a punk club, at a memorial benefit for Coco
Vega, a famously skanky drag queen whose appetite for drugs had rivaled Jasper's. He had passed out on heroin and choked to death on
his vomit. Coco was before my time in San Francisco, but I've heard
many renditions of his Latin-accented signature line: "You know what
the saddest thing is, girl? The saddest thing is when your beard starts
showing through your makeup!" He had been enamored of Doris,
who didn't reciprocate and would dart into heavy traffic, if necessary,

Doris as Captain Tracey Daniels in *Vegas in Space*, 1984. Photo by Daniel Nicoletta.

to avoid him. At the memorial, Doris mustered as much feeling as he could feign to cry out, "Why Coco? She had so much to live for—next week's check! And there must have been some drug she hadn't tried yet." Miss X added, "I'm sure she's happier now. I know *I* am." They urged the audience to give generously "for the five Pres-to-Logs needed for the cremation," and Doris finished with a poem:

> *There was a hairy queen named Coco,*
> *And everyone said she was loco.*
> *One night she OD'd*
> *On alcohol, Librium, Quaaludes, heroin, and speed,*
> *And tomorrow she'll go up in smoko.*

Jackie responded to Doris's "charmingly sensitive" report of the obsequies with news of several other acquaintances who had also recently been "called to the arms of Jesus." Jackie's mind was elsewhere, though. The previous August she had mentioned a new French boyfriend, and by now the relationship was serious. Thierry Voeltzel had relocated from Paris to Sydney two years earlier, in 1980, and had quickly made an impression on the scene. "We don't wish to announce that he's turned to women," ran a snarky little item on one of Jackie's soirées in *Campaign*, "but wasn't that THIERRY VOELTZEL we saw with Jackie at the end of the night?" It was. In March 1982 he took her back with him to Paris, where they opened a business restoring antique furniture and creating high-end furniture in the same style.

It was also around this time that Miss Leading adopted the name Tippi. She later explained to me that Miss Leading had been "such a '70s name, and I was really bored with being limited to that personality. You get famous and you're limited by your fame, which is why I do not seek fame. I have not adjusted at all well to what fame I have." As for the new name, "most people think it comes from Tippi Hedren"—the demure yet frosty blonde star of Hitchcock's *The Birds* and *Marnie*—"and in a way it does. That's sort of a minor personality of mine. But it really came from Tippi Magnin, Cyril Magnin's dog." (Cyril Magnin was a socially prominent San Francisco retail magnate.) "I wanted a name that screamed 'local pet,' something cute and lovable, something people could instantly become intimate with. But not *too* intimate."

THERE WERE FANS WHO WENT TO *SLUTS A-GO-GO* AND *BLONDE SIN* over and over. One of them was Greg Foss, who'd hosted Doris's wedding reception the previous spring. A Santa Fe native who worked as a baker at a popular soup-and-sandwich restaurant named Salmagundi's, Greg was drawn to drag. He had gotten his feet wet back in high school—the mother of a friend had a collection (literally: a small locked warehouse) of high-fashion dresses dating back to the '50s. The two boys would sneak in, pick out a couple of pretty ones, flounce around in them for a while, and then rip them off each other, literally, and hide the shreds—a very Sylvia and the Synthetics approach to drag. The first time Greg saw the Sluts perform, around 1980, the show struck a dormant nerve. He kept going back, bringing friends; naturally, the Sluts noticed. After he found out what hand-to-mouth lives they were leading, he began inviting them home after performances. When Doris listed the highlights of 1980 for his column in *Campaign*, he included Thanksgiving at the "gorgeous house" of his "generous fans" Greg and his roommate, Matt: "We drink, stuff our faces, bellies, doggie bags, break glasses, lamps, and insult everyone. They love us."

The gorgeous house was a typical pregentrification Victorian at 422 Oak Street, in the lower Haight. Matt had recently taken up massage as a profession but didn't know much about the business side. Doris did, and he suggested ways for Matt, who was attractive, to increase his profits considerably. Since they also needed more rent money, it occurred to Doris that he might use 422 Oak Street for his daytime activities—he was still living with Cheryl on Market Street and storing most of his drag down the block at Slut Central—and thus neatly compartmentalize his life. Renting to prostitutes made Greg nervous at first, but—"OK, what the hell"—the arrangement flourished, and so did their friendship.

For a Halloween performance of *Blonde Sin*, Greg went as Ginger Grant, the redheaded bombshell that Tina Louise played on the '60s sitcom *Gilligan's Island*. He had ruined his synthetic wig by using a hair dryer on it—"I didn't know anything about drag. But it was all I had, so I wore it. And Doris loved it!" A tattered wig would have complemented Doris's aesthetic at the time. From then on Greg Foss was Ginger to everyone. He came up with a last name, Quest, from *Johnny Quest*, an old cartoon show.

In late 1981 the Sluts were planning a rehash of old routines they called *Fish for Christmas*; Doris painted a six-foot-square self-portrait in fluorescent hues and hung it as a billboard above a card store at Market and Church. When, unexpectedly, Freda dropped out, they went to work on Ginger: "You could do it! You know all the moves and words!" Ginger wasn't so sure. "I was scared to death, but they talked me into it." Alcohol helped. "What did they use to say about me? You would have to *drag* Ginger onto the stage, but once you got her on there you would have to *drag* her off."

Before long Doris began wondering why he was paying rent to both Ginger and Cheryl, especially since Cheryl had added angel dust to his roster of drugs and was getting more erratic in his behavior. Doris had seen that spiral before. The move to 422 Oak Street was the next-to-last one Doris would make. The decor wasn't much at that point—"piss-yellow walls with shit-brown trim" is how Ginger remembers it—and so it provided an ideal canvas. "I *do* have a tendency to take over when I move in," Doris told me later. The faux-marble craze had arrived, and Ginger revealed an artisanal bent; like so many of Doris's protégés, all he needed was encouragement.

A second person the Sluts befriended around this time was Phillip R. Ford (as he has always billed himself professionally, presumably on the model of Cecil B. DeMille and David O. Selznick). The "R" is for "Raymond." Phillip was ten years younger than Doris—he was born on May 31, 1961—and grew up across the Golden Gate Bridge from San Francisco in the prosperous Marin County enclave of San Rafael, though his doting parents were lower middle class; his father was a mailman. He was, as he describes it—and Phillip has an uncanny facility for recounting his past without sentiment or bitterness, either—a fat sissy who had his head in a book when he wasn't watching a movie. At twelve he discovered Hitchcock. He started making short films when he was fifteen. In high school he took up theater and drugs. His doctor gave him pills to control his obesity; he lost sixty pounds and commenced a twenty-year speed habit. Out of the flab emerged a handsome extrovert with luxuriant hair, a quick smile with the hint of a sneer, and an easy physical grace. He smoked marijuana, became a bravura drinker, and continued on to cocaine and psychedelics, all the while remaining highly functional. His short movies kept getting better, and after entering the film program at San Francisco State University, he was admitted into the Core, a challenging course of study and praxis for the department's most gifted students.

He met Doris in October 1981, when he was twenty, at the home of a friend who had invited several young filmmakers to show their work. Phillip's entry was a twenty-five-minute Super 8 sound film called *Trouble in Paradise*, a John Waters–esque satire in which some inebriated Marin kids boil to death in a hot tub. Doris was there, out of drag, and he was amused. They met again when Phillip was shooting *Recipe for Terror*, a five-minute short in which a big-haired housewife is attacked by her appliances. His actress was a friend of Ginger's who had suggested they film in the kitchen at 422 Oak Street. Doris hadn't moved in yet, but he must have already been entertaining clients there, because he was watching with interest as Phillip tied fishing wire to the toast that was going to fly out of the toaster. "I know what she was thinking," Phillip says: "*He makes movies.*"

In December Phillip went to see *Fish for Christmas* "and laughed and laughed and laughed and laughed and laughed." He remembers Miss X singing "Fry me a liver, I fried my liver over you." He enlisted Doris as an extra for his next project, a fifteen-minute homage to *Reefer Madness* that he called *Rollercoaster to Hell.*[*]

422 Oak Street was great for parties. In 1981 Greg and Matt threw a Las Vegas–themed one, with lots of showgirl drag, and the Sluts performed. Later they referred to it, affectionately, as *Vegas in a Toilet*, to distinguish it from the much wackier blowout they threw in April 1982. The Vegas theme had been so congenial that they decided to repeat it, enhanced with an extraterrestrial overlay in keeping with Ginger's long-standing interest in UFOs. Doris's business was thriving as the planning moved into high gear. On a visit to New York to see Miss Abood, he went down to Canal Street and spent a thousand dollars on fabric—Mylar, vinyl, and bolts of fun fur in hot fluorescent colors. Then he came home and they covered the house with it. For the alien look he ordered vats of pigment from the Day-Glo Color Corp. "You mix it with oils to make lipsticks," he explained, "and with powders to make powders, or you can put it on raw." They hung black lights everywhere there was an outlet.

"People kept asking, 'Is there LSD in the punch?' There wasn't. You didn't even need to have a *drink*, the atmosphere was so incredibly strong," Doris told me. The costumed hosts floated through the crowd in eerie phosphorescence. And of course they performed. Doris lip-synched "It's Impossible," the number Neely O'Hara sings at the telethon in *Valley of the Dolls*. Ginger lip-synched Judy Garland singing "Fly Me to the Moon" with the turntable speeded up from 33⅓ rpm to 45.

Maybe you didn't need a drink, but the crowd guzzled and smoked and snorted all the same. Inhibitions toppled as publicly as the elegant queen on top of the piano who mistook the sheet of chromed plastic behind which Doris had concealed a few items for a wall and leaned back into it. "I was sensible enough," Doris said, "to have my camera at the ready and ran in and took a couple of snaps." Men were having sex in

---

[*] Trivia note: The director Nicole Holofcener, who was in the San Francisco State film program at the same time, was another extra, in a different scene.

the hallway, to Ginger's consternation. ("How *can* you, with this green-faced drag queen standing right in front of you?") One of them lost his clothes and had to go home in a garbage bag. Doris's new boyfriend wound up in the arms of a stranger as Doris and Miss X sat chatting on the bed beside them. That relationship didn't last long.

When they all got up to face the wreckage the next afternoon, Doris beheld the vision they'd created and decided it was too glorious to just discard. So he phoned Phillip Ford: "Look, I've got the set. Let's make a movie." What he had in mind, he said later, was something knocked out John Waters–style—"Just turn the camera on one afternoon, make the movie, go home, that's it."

He didn't have a clue.

Phillip did. He knew how much work went into even a throwaway movie, and he was skeptical. Still, he agreed to meet with Doris and X at It's Tops, a pancake house on Market Street, and hear them out. What they had in mind was a twenty-minute-or-so goof on the outer-space movies of an earlier era, "when," as Doris explained, "rockets still had propellers and everyone could breathe and speak English through-out the universe." The plot would involve an expedition to an all-female planet, with Doris as the commander who has to undergo a sex change for the mission and the others playing extensions of their party charac-ters: Miss X as the Blue Queen, Tippi as the Pink Princess, and Ginger as the Green Empress. Most important, Doris had $5,000 to spend on the project; up till then, Phillip's parents had been bankrolling his movies. Intrigued, he told them to come back with a script. They did, and he was convinced. "I thought, *This is my big break. I have the one element that all film students are missing. I've got stars!*"

SOMETIME DURING THIS PERIOD MISS X RECEIVED A TELEPHONE call from one Randal West, the proprietor of a local greeting card company, who was looking for models. Randy West had launched West Graphics a year or so earlier with cards featuring black-and-white reproductions of his own homoerotic airbrush paintings. He recognized that expanding his business would mean going more mainstream, emphasizing humor, and switching to photography, since there was no way he could manage the growing company and keep creating the art. He began looking for models just as the Sluts were showing up all over town.

"At that point we had every sleazeball Tom, Dick, and Harry calling us," X remembers. So he hedged when Randy first phoned ("Mm, we'll have to talk about how much you're willing to pay and how much trouble it's gonna be") and palmed him off on Doris—who, being Doris, jumped at any opportunity to get his face in front of the public. Or, as it turned out, his faces.

Their first shoot, for which he was paid seventy-five dollars (later he earned more), took place in a beauty salon. Doris sits, legs folded, under a dryer, turquoise curlers in his yellow fright wig, wearing a fuchsia top, turquoise pedal pushers, white peep-toe pumps, and (too much) matching makeup, wide-eyed in what looks like despair. Randy had already written the cutline: "BOTH YOUR DOCTOR & HAIRDRESSER AGREE! THIS TIME IT'S GOING TO TAKE MORE THAN A COMB-OUT."

It wasn't brilliant, but it sold well, and it marked the beginning of a collaboration that would make Doris's face, if not his name, familiar nationwide into the '90s, through dozens and dozens of cards and as many personalities. The punch lines were often scabrous: "I LOVE YOU . . . BUT ONLY I COULD LOVE AN ASSHOLE." "I'VE TRIED TO FIND A GIFT TO MATCH YOUR PERSONALITY . . . CAN YOU USE A DOUCHE BAG?" An image of Doris in full makeup but wigless, with his own bright-yellow hair—"very Kurt Weill Germany," Randy called it—gagging himself with a finger: "THINKING OF YOU."

Most of them, though, were far less brutal. Artist, model, and photographer lavished great care on their work. Randy insisted on top-quality color separation even before the company could afford it. And Doris was peerless with a makeup brush; the cards, more than any of his other ventures, attest to his Lon Chaney level of skill. In addition to his own bevy of highly peculiar women, he created convincing versions—on himself and his fellow models, most of them friends and some of them actual women—of, among others, Katharine Hepburn, Lucille Ball, Tammy Faye Bakker, Leona Helmsley, Zsa Zsa Gabor, Nancy Reagan, and Barbara Bush.

The standing joke with Doris, Randy said, was that "she wants to do glamour, we want to do greeting cards." In reality, though, Doris had been willing to demean himself for a laugh ever since he'd performed with Sylvia and the Synthetics. It was harder for Tippi, who, along with X, was soon posing for the cards as well. Doris would patiently explain, "We're not real models—we're comedy models." Doris's bag-lady cards, some of them shot beside the garbage cans in the alley next to 422 Oak Street, propelled the Mildred look to a grubby extreme. They outsold the femmes fatales by ten to one.

What was probably the cruelest shoot took place in 1984. "It must have been February," X recalls. "She's wearing a strapless evening gown, and they've got two ladders set up out of camera range, and huge buckets of water which they keep dumping on her and dumping on her." The poor victim holds up a gloved arm in a futile attempt at self-protection, her wet hair plastered to her head, her mouth wide open in a sob. "INTO EVERY LIFE A LITTLE RAIN MUST FALL. (SORRY YOU GOT DUMPED ON.)"

The Sluts' presence—and their willingness to do whatever he asked of them—always lifted Randy. By 1986, when I interviewed him, he was a successful entrepreneur who kept a close eye on surveys and sales records. (He died in 1992, from AIDS.) Seventy percent of his clientele, he told me, was women in their thirties, another 15 percent was gay men, and what worked for one worked for the other. "We've tried to make almost every shot with Doris—with a few exceptions—vulnerable," he explained. "There's heart in that character. There is a sadness there, and people relate to that. It doesn't matter whether it's a real woman or somebody doing drag."

On that point I'm quite sure Randy was wrong. Once, West Graphics got a call from a group of Texas office workers who had a pool going as to whether this Doris Fish (model and photographer always received credit on the back of the card) was a woman or a man; there was cheering when they got the answer. Randy himself admitted that as he was driving to their first shoot, he wondered whether Doris was a drag queen "or just a very bizarre woman—that's how naive I was." Except when Doris was doing high glamour or a celebrity, though, he didn't disguise his gender. Both his politics and his aesthetics required him to look crook—if only slightly—and that dab of the off-kilter was what made the cards so potent. When West Graphics used female models, even goofy ones, they didn't have the same edge.

Greeting cards are such a low-art medium that few gay people viewed them with pride—or with shame or irritation, either. They were just funny, which was how the rest of the country saw them, too. Yet it's hard to envision their taking off the way they did a decade earlier. The very people who might once have been appalled to learn they had a queer family member were snapping up these artifacts of gay humor to mark birthdays and holidays in places far outside the Castro. Drag queens were tiptoeing in from the fringes; gay humor, like Jewish humor before it, was breaking out of its ghetto. Something had happened.

MEANWHILE, PERFORMANCES CONTINUED. IN OCTOBER 1982 DORIS appeared as a drag queen in a play called *Torn Tulle* at Theatre Rhinoceros. The small but prominent Theatre Rhino, which calls itself the world's oldest continuously producing queer theater, was founded in 1977 and is still around today. Doris's association with it would continue, as would his relationship with the play's director, Chuck Solomon. The role was small, and he agreed to do it, he told me, "for the credibility and the change of pace." He later learned that the audition had been solely pro forma: "They thought it was a plus to have someone who had some kind of a vague following." As it was—at one point or another everyone in the cast mentioned a friend or acquaintance who had said, "Oh, you're in that play that Doris Fish is doing."

But Doris was most excited about the movie. Once he convinced Phillip Ford to direct, Phillip began assembling a crew. A. P. Gonzalez, a grad student in film, had his own Éclair camera, which made him a natural choice for camera operator. Todd Ritchie, a burly, fun-loving straight guy, took charge of recording the sound. They both remained loyal, professional, and incredibly good-natured through the eighteen-month ordeal. Most important, Robin Clark, another student in the film program's Core group, agreed to serve as director of photography. Robin, who'd been taking still photographs since he was twelve, was the group's masterly technician, and his meticulousness provided the perfect complement for Phillip's much more hang-loose approach, just as his shy demeanor balanced Phillip's buoyancy.

The first production meeting is imprinted on Robin's memory. Ginger had an old restaurant booth that served as the kitchen table at 422 Oak Street. Robin was seated there with Doris and Phillip when X swooped in and barked, "There are no straight people allowed on the set!" Robin, who is straight, was mortified and—like everyone else who knew X only peripherally in those days—intimidated. He said nothing, and neither did Phillip.

The first segments were shot on video. Doris had been one of the early adopters of home-video technology; on yet another trip to New York, he made up Miss Abood as an alien and taped him. Back home, they taped Miss X as the Empress of Earth (the smaller of his two roles) instructing the astronauts on their mission.

At the beginning of March 1983, Doris wrote Ace that the script had just been typed up: "Hopefully the filming will be completed in two weeks." Preparations for the first shoot began on Friday, March 18. The scene was a small one in which Tippi's Princess Angel and Ginger's Empress Nueva Gabor are in the palace's communication room, tracking the arrival of the spaceship from Earth. Doris had built the set in the foyer from construction paper, with mirrored stalactites. But lighting the small space proved to be complicated; the high-powered lamps kept blowing the circuits. Robin finally figured out how to tie into the main power line in the basement ("I was terrified, because you can get killed in an instant"), but they weren't ready to start rolling until Monday. Tippi and Ginger spent hours sitting around in their heavy makeup and uncomfortable costumes. Phillip knew what Robin was doing, but nobody else did.

And then, after they were finished, the lab Phillip had taken the film to for processing called to inform him that, because of a power outage, the negative had been damaged as it went through the developing machine. It was too late to reshoot the scene; Doris had already struck the set and started on the next one. Phillip and Robin brought the marred film back to the house.

Parts of it had been severely overprocessed, producing changes in density and color that were bizarre. Nevertheless, they were stunned by what they saw. "It looked so phenomenal," X says, "that it was like a drug." They had all been seething at Robin's painstakingness. Now, suddenly, they gazed at him with admiration. "My whole relationship with everybody changed," he says. "X was nice to me, first of all. And Tippi put her arm through my arm and walked me to my car, and she said, 'Thank you for making us look so beautiful!' It broke my heart. So they had me. It just snowballed after that."

Next they filmed the opening scene, in which the four male astronauts swallow sex-change pills in order to land on the "all-female pleasure planet" where most of the action takes place. The four were Doris, Timmy Spence, and two women friends, the blonde Lori Naslund and the dark-haired Ramona Fischer.

That first scene is long. They were just getting started and didn't really know what they were doing. The actors, accustomed to the stage, land too hard on their forced lines. ("But that's a babes-only planet— no dudes allowed!") The paramount problem, though, is that—apart from Freda as Jane the Computer, a glamorous head in a glass box— the characters are men, and, aesthetically speaking, men bored Doris. He barely tried to make Lori and Ramona look masculine, beyond a ridiculous mustache he plastered on Lori; he didn't even play up his own handsomeness. After the sex change, the women have better hairdos, and Doris—formerly Captain Dan Tracey, now Captain Tracey Daniels—has acquired a lush chestnut wig (a tribute to Jane Fonda's Barbarella) and regained his flair.

No one had anticipated the excruciating pace of filmmaking. After several all-night sessions, Timmy, who had professional commitments as a musician, bailed: "Just get me out! I don't care how." They offed him during the sex change. His character, Lieutenant Dick Hunter, is so manly that he demands two pills instead of one, and the overdose atomizes him.

As they went on filming, pouring in more and more time and money, their aim tacitly shifted. "It wasn't like we made the decision," Phillip says. "It was just assumed: 'We've got enough ideas to flesh this out.'" They were no longer working on a short but on a feature that might actually be seen and—a notion that increasingly tantalized them—turn a profit. Little by little, their small folly turned into a big one.

For the penultimate sequence, during which the three astronauts, posing as showgirls from Earth, perform a "traditional twentieth-century lounge act" at the empress's soirée, they rented the 544 Natoma Performance Gallery, south of Market.* The number was a tacky pileup of snippets from '60s and '70s pop hits—"By the Time I Get to Phoenix," "Leaving on a Jet Plane," and so forth—that Doris and Jackie had concocted years earlier. The script called for more drag queens to play the empress's guests, but they knew surprisingly few. Doris recruited the three drags he'd acted with in *Torn Tulle*; Freda took a second role; and a filmmaker friend named John Canalli joined the cast as the yellow-hued Princess Jaundice, along with a couple of biological women. Everyone had to be costumed for this climactic scene, in which the crime the astronauts have been sent to investigate is solved. The principals' drag had to climax, too.

It did. Doris is caped in metallic red-orange fringe, with enormous gold Statue of Liberty spikes jutting out of a gargantuan red wig and a matching spiked necklace above his plastic "pleasure chest" with its glittering nipples. ("Don't they have mirrors on Earth?" one of the

---

* 544 Natoma had a brief but distinguished history. The brainchild of the composer and impresario Peter Hartman (1940–1988), it operated from 1981 to 1984 as a gallery and avant-garde performance space (and, on certain nights, a sex club). Ethyl Eichelberger and Whoopi Goldberg both appeared there, the latter as a member of the Blake Street Hawkeyes; so did Silvana, before I knew him, in arty performance pieces on which he and Peter Hartman collaborated.

guests is heard to inquire.) Miss X swaggers around in a blue-black velvet toga with a black cape, an indigo Louis XIV poodle wig festooned with pearls, and black gloves that shoot out Freddy Krueger nails.

"I couldn't believe how uncomfortable I was and how long I had to stay in those outfits," X told me. "We didn't design them with that in mind, because we didn't know! So then we were stuck with it, pinning *this* layer and then *this* layer, so it took a *long* time to get on, and then if you had to go to the bathroom . . . !"

"The more it hurts," Doris would remind them placidly, "the better it looks. If it doesn't hurt, it isn't glamorous."

He insisted on applying everyone's makeup himself. "It was her vision," X explains. "She wanted everyone to look a certain way—like her. Or versions of her, but with blue skin or red skin or pink skin." Miss X and Tippi designed their own makeup, and Tippi drew helpful color maps for Doris. Everybody else was Doris's creation. The actors would put on their foundation, usually a primary color, erasing their features, and then sit quietly as Doris transformed them. "Doris always had a cool head and a smile," Ramona says. "You never saw her lose patience. As she was putting on your mascara, she would say, 'You have such lovely long lashes!'"

Robin was impressed to find Doris as exacting as he was—which was probably why he was one of the few straight men that Doris admitted into his circle. They had a special relationship on the set, especially when no one else was around. "We were both very quiet," Robin remembers. "If I needed something and I was on the top of a ladder, I would turn around and there she'd be with it. It was symbiotic." Citing Doris's talent and his dedication, Robin—who since *Vegas in Space* has gone on to a career as a rigorous and serious painter—ranks him as a first-tier artist.

Amid the continuing all-nighters, the prophetic words of Coco Vega came back to haunt them: "The saddest thing is when your beard starts showing through your makeup!" They would have to break when that happened. Nobody slept; a line had to be added to the budget for beer and speed.

The speed came mostly from Carmel, who, since arriving in San Francisco, had descended into the drug world. She became Ambi Sextrous's dresser, but that gig hardly paid enough to support a $300-a-day heroin habit. So she turned to prostitution (she must have been one scary-looking hooker) and dealing, which got her by until she was arrested.

Much of the energy that fueled *Vegas in Space* came from the amphetamines she supplied. "With speed, most people get over it very quickly," Phillip told me. "They don't like it. And the small percentage of people that do like it become addicted. X," he added, "didn't touch it"—which may have accounted for his perpetual crabbiness. Phillip stayed cheerful and focused with the aid of crystal meth, to which Freda had introduced him. Doris managed on stamina, and perhaps a snort of speed now and then.

After finishing at 544 Natoma, they returned to 422 Oak Street to shoot the segments in the empress's pink plush throne room, including the arrival of the party guests. Since they didn't have enough fun fur to cover the whole living room, they stapled what they had on one side, shot what they needed, took it all down, stapled it up on the other side, and shot from that angle: a process that was, like everything else in the movie, makeshift and laborious. The extras were then dismissed, much to their relief.

In May, Phillip graduated from the San Francisco State film department's Core program at the top of his class.

By then, Doris's original $5,000 had been depleted. They needed more. "Many was the time," Phillip says, "we'd be having discussions about our script or planning our schedule, and the phone would ring." Anyone who spent time at 422 Oak Street during those years can do an impression of Doris dropping his voice: "Hullo, this is Phil . . . Got a hairy arse . . . Oh, I'm pretty versat'l." The john would arrive, "and twenty minutes later," Phillip recalls, "Doris would come out and give me a check for fifty or a hundred dollars."

Still, even with Doris turning tricks as fast as he could, you couldn't make a feature film, as he put it, on a prostitute's salary. They had to find other sources of funding. When Phillip's good-hearted parents won a prize in the Irish Sweepstakes, it went into the movie. Cheryl—Doris's erstwhile roommate Paul Tudman—was still making a bundle in cocaine, and he enthusiastically offered them $5,000. Phillip went over one afternoon to pick it up; Cheryl answered the door in a T-shirt and nothing else and invited him in to watch *I Love Lucy*. "I'm sitting there," Phillip recalled, "and thinking, *I'm certainly not gonna blow him for five thousand dollars.*" But he didn't have to. When *Lucy* was over, Phillip said, "Well, I must be going!" and Cheryl cheerfully handed over the check. I asked him if he had an explanation. "When you're on drugs," he said, "you just take your pants off. As soon as you get high, you just take your pants off and proceed with your business."

By August they'd scrounged enough to start shooting again. X loved film noir and had insisted from the beginning that the movie include a black-and-white sequence, which he contended would give the audience's eyes a rest from the oversaturated color of everything else. ("Well, if that's what outer space is like," Mildred said later, "we'll all have to wear sunglasses, won't we?") They headed up to Corona Heights Park, a rocky precipice between the Castro and the Haight, to film. August is chilly in San Francisco, and the wind was so high that Miss X's ponytail stood straight up. The next shoot, at Slut Central (where X, Tippi, and Freda were still living), went smoothly enough, but when the film came back from the lab it was blank. At the time the mishap seemed like a catastrophe, but they would reshoot the material the next year, incorporating two new actors, with more experience under their belt and more professional results.

As exhausting as filming was, it barely cut into the Sluts' schedule of public appearances. "Someone was always throwing an Easter party," X says, "or Thanksgiving—it was always something. We'd get all dressed up and go and look for what we could steal." Tippi, inspired, no doubt, by Jackie's stories of Sylvia and the Synthetics, liked to empty ashtrays under sofa cushions—"Oh, wait till they find this!" They were runway models in a gala show at the Fashion Institute of

Design and Merchandising; Doris wore a near-transparent pantsuit covered with appliquéd daisies, and at the end of the runway he performed a cartwheel, which would become one of his signatures. They were the Solid Plastic Dancers for the ZaSu Pitts Memorial Orchestra, a popular big band that covered '60s hits; Timmy, the group's organist, was their entrée. Although these appearances didn't bring in much more than cab fare, by another marker they were living their fantasy. They really had become hardworking showgirls in the gum-cracking, tough but lovable mold of Joan Blondell and Betty Grable in the backstage movies of the '30s and '40s. Even their hard-up circumstances fit.

In April Doris did a solo piece, *Ego as Art Form*, in a studio attached to Squid's, a then-hip restaurant riding the fried-calamari vogue. He incorporated slides and video, performed a headstand, and talked about Romantic Cruelism, cosmetics, and *Vegas in Space* ("due for release later this summer"). His work on the movie, he said, in a formulation that was, typically, both self-mocking and self-promoting, combined both sides of him: "the shy, curious artist" who does all the work, and the "public persona" who hogs the credit—"a true merger of the two parts of an artist coming together as ego as art form."

But the performance from the spring of 1983 that people remember most vividly took place at the South of Market nightclub the Oasis. The Sluts had recently been hired there for a socialite's private party (X remembers a wall covered with orchids), and they returned to do a show of their own. *Screamgirls*, a loose parody of *Dreamgirls*—the Broadway musical about a Supremes-like group, which ran from 1981 to 1985—was a compilation of their girl-group lip-synch routines. In the title number, they bunched together in long yellow gowns trimmed in green and silver zhuzh, then pulled apart to reveal that they were wearing one big garment—a joke they'd lifted from the Supremes parody in *Hair*. Doris did a quick costume change and went into *Dreamgirls'* showstopper, "And I Am Telling You I'm Not Going," while X and Tippi retired backstage.

The club had a dance floor at ground level and a staircase ascending to a balcony with a railing whose midsection had been removed so that it could serve as a stage. "And I Am Telling You I'm Not Going" is close to hysterical in its emotion, and Doris gave it the full drag queen treatment: he shimmied and he pumped, he quivered his lips (another signature move), he hung off the railing, and then, misjudging the space, he did a side roll that took him over the balcony and down into the screaming crowd below.

Luckily for Doris, if not for the guy who got a high heel in his head, the place was packed. He landed on a cushion of spectators without missing a note. "That was our thing," X says. "No matter how sick you were, how bad your head felt, how horribly the costume hurt—you went on!" Doris continued, giving the number his all, more than his all, wailing, flailing as he hoisted himself over the banister and vaulted back up the stairs.

X: "So we're sitting back down and having a cigarette, and we're thinking, *What the hell is she* doing? *What could be so fabulous?* Because it was like the 1906 earthquake was happening out there. They're *screaming* and *pounding*. We're looking at each other: 'Oh, that fucking bitch. And *we* have to go on after that.' So we get out there, and we're doing our choreography and—'Doris! Doris! What did you do out there?' And she can't even talk, she's in shock from it."

8
NAKED BRUNCH

NOT LONG AFTER THE BLACK-AND-WHITE SCENES FOR *VEGAS in Space* that had been shot at Slut Central came back from the lab blank, circa September 1983, X, Tippi, and Freda lost their bargain lease on the large apartment. Another mild crisis: it had been, up to this point, the central storage unit for all their drag. Doris transferred his to Oak Street. Tippi and Freda found seedy single rooms in the Tenderloin. Phillip recalls the gloomy day they rented a truck and carted Tippi and her stuff to her new place, leaving her all alone behind "a *mountain* of dolls and toys and crap." X procrastinated for so long that finally a room opened up in Oak Street. Tippi hated her Tenderloin rental so much that effectively she became another roommate.

Publicity still for *Naked Brunch*, episode 1, 1983. *Left to right*: The actor Joe Cappetta, Sandelle, Miss X, Silvana, Doris, and Ginger. Photo by Daniel Nicoletta.

So then there were four, plus a couple of cats, in the classic configuration that Esther Newton had described in *Mother Camp*: "By living together," one of her subjects told her, "you surround yourself with your own image by surrounding yourself with other images."

Thus began the constant repainting and room swapping. The thrift-store shopping grew even more obsessive. For a while many of the ceilings and walls were covered with pink fun fur. Then, sick of the odor of cigarette smoke that it harbored, they pulled it down, along with much of the paint. Which launched the marbleizing—of ceilings, walls, mantelpieces, dressers, the piano. The painting and furniture-restoration skills that Doris had picked up long ago in Sydney were paying off. One room had sky-blue walls with puffy white clouds; in another, the clouds were pink. For a while a room was painted with the eyes that Doris had been sketching on available surfaces since childhood. On the floor were his rugs; the walls were crammed with his paintings and West Graphics blowups. Among good pieces of '50s and '60s furniture, all purchased for a song, there were clusters of kitsch—Madonnas, Cleopatras, chandeliers, trophies, vases, Barbies—and ferns. Doris especially delighted in molded plastic, such as the framed frieze of a female nude in front of one fireplace, which he spray-painted black and gold in a period style he called "Hollywood rococo."

In the eighteen-by-twelve-foot designated drag room, five commercial racks hung from the ceiling and another three stood on the floor. There was a wall of shelves for cosmetics, with room for more in the bathroom. The stockpiles included fifty pairs of eyelashes, four hundred pairs of shoes, a hundred wigs (plus switches and hairpieces), bras and panties and pantyhose in every color, gloves, scarves, handbags, dozens of vats of color pigment for makeup, and—Doris once rattled off the categories as he was showing me through—"brown suits, gray suits, yellow, green, mumsy suits, fashionable suits, unfashionable suits, waitress outfits, nurse outfits, doctor outfits, inmate outfits, tuxedos and tails for when we need to look really elegant, blouses in every style, shape, and color, cloth coats, Barbie coats, vinyl coats, '60s plastic raincoats, evening gowns, showgirl costumes, feather boas, tinsel boas, wedding dresses, sequined slack suits, and I don't know how many hundred pairs of earrings, necklaces, and bracelets. I've bought things from ex-strippers, theaters that were going out of business—you just buy whatever you can, thinking you can use it somewhere down the line." Not all of it, he allowed, was in the best condition, but "makeup can hide a lot of crimes, I can tell you. They don't notice the safety pins holding everything up in the back."

It all functioned beautifully for a while, a hothouse of ideas and a cozy, daffy home, with Doris and X bonding ever more tightly. And then, as in the old movies playing on tape on the TVs they never turned off, a woman came between them.

New theatrical vistas opened when Doris connected with the director Marc Huestis.

Doris lifted weights not just because it made him more desirable and gave him, as he said, "cleavage for days" but also because he had aspired to some version of healthy living since his teenage discovery of yoga and fasting; he went to aerobics classes, too. Sometimes he put a weight-lifting routine, as well as headstands and cartwheels, into his shows. His gym was the International Center, a decrepit facility on Oak Street not far from the house. The gym was also, of course, a place to cruise. He wasn't a drag queen there, and so when Marc Huestis approached him and said, "You're Doris Fish, aren't you?" he reacted with alarm. "Shh! Shh! Don't say that here! You'll spring me!"

Marc had begun working out himself, he told me, because "AIDS was first starting—there was just an inkling something was going on—and I wanted to keep my body in fighting condition." He had spotted Doris on the gym floor some time before he introduced himself. They'd both been in San Francisco for a decade, in separate niches of the drag world, though Marc, rather remarkably, hadn't gone to any of Doris's shows. "I remember first hearing her name: 'Doris Fish—ick! How politically incorrect! What a horrible last name! She has no consciousness about feminism!'"

Marc most definitely did. He belonged to a group of gender radicals who, unlike many activists, regarded drag not as offensive but as a profoundly feminist statement. "We were oppressed as men as they were oppressed as women, and the way of getting rid of the oppression was to dress up and free parts of our psyche that couldn't be freed in the stiff, hard-core vision of what a man's supposed to be. We were dressing up as women not to mock them but to show them that we felt, almost, like we were sisters."

Marc was born in Bethpage, on Long Island, in 1954. He studied theater at the State University of New York's Binghamton campus but hated the rigidity and the irrelevance of the program so much that when he was twenty he decamped, a few credits short of graduation, for the lotus land of San Francisco. Through an acquaintance he was introduced to the Angels of Light, a faction of the Cockettes that had broken off over its principled commitment to keeping performances free. "Seeing people living collectively and eating together and taking care of children and everybody choreographing stuff together and learning how to tap dance—it was a beautiful way of being initiated into an aesthetic that I had no idea existed." The Angels introduced a number of new arrivals to their glittery notion of community theater, among them Silvana and Lulu and Tommy Pace, three drag queens about whom I'll have more to say shortly. They were all drawn to Marc, who was magnetically cute—compact and chestnut-curled and as hyper as a squirrel, with a rat-a-tat laugh you can still hear across a crowded room.

He did drag, too, until a notorious incident when, during a melodramatic monologue onstage as the character Ellen Organ—a name arguably not that much less objectionable than Doris Fish—he flung open his arms and the bottle he was holding torpedoed into someone's head. An ambulance had to be called, and Marc, humiliated, retired his high heels. ("Only years later," he wrote in his own memoir, "did I learn my victim was into S&M and he relished his battle scar.") He then turned to directing and producing, for which he had the classic volatility. His temperament was nothing like Doris's, but, like Doris, he knew how to make things happen. He was destined to have a profound impact on the tone of San Francisco's gay culture and, especially, on the way the community would respond to AIDS— which was just around the corner.

But Marc was making his presence felt long before that. In 1977 he was prominent among a group of filmmakers who launched what was then called, somewhat redundantly, the Gay Film Festival of Super 8 Films; it would develop into the largest festival of its kind in the world. Marc's Super 8 movies were generally more politically pointed than Phillip's, if no less zany. In 1982 he made his first feature, *Whatever Happened to Susan Jane?*, an excursion through San Francisco's underground gay culture starring his Arkansas-born friend Anne Block as a clueless but enthusiastic tourist. It included a scene at the Café Flore, then a prime hangout, with Lulu and Coco Vega dancing on the tables.

But he never lost his love for theater. The most ambitious of his early collaborations, staged in 1977 and 1978 at various venues, was *Strange Fruit*, a radical-camp mixture of songs, sketches, Marc's poetry, and Marc's movies that satirized the widening divide between macho men and sissies in a community that was growing increasingly hostile to effeminacy. Other shows were just silly fun, like *The Night of the Fallen Stars*, an "Italian extravaganza" Marc and his friends put together in June 1983 at Club 181, a decaying Tenderloin nightspot turned newly hip. Doris came backstage after that show, but not to greet Marc. The previous summer, Silvana had made Jackie's acquaintance in Paris, and then in the spring he'd gone backstage after the Oasis show (when Doris tumbled off the balcony) to introduce himself. Doris reciprocated at Club 181.

I ought say something more about Silvana, though the subject is uncomfortably close to home. It *is* home. He was born Robert Tumbelston in Hamilton, Ontario, in 1951; when he was twelve his family moved to St. Petersburg, Florida. He found the near-total absence of culture there stifling and got out as soon as he could. He arrived in San Francisco in 1975, met Marc and Tommy and Lulu, and named himself Silvana (after the Italian film star Silvana Mangano) Nova. We got to know each other working at *Mother Jones* magazine in 1983.

By then he'd become a wage-earning citizen because he liked buying clothes in places other than thrift stores. His drag look was severe—dark eyeliner, topknot, and a skirt hiked up as a blouse over one alarmingly skinny shoulder—though, like Doris's, it became softer over time. Doris, like Jackie, recognized a shared sensibility as soon as they met.

Thus, when Marc introduced himself at the International Center gym, Doris certainly knew who he was, and what Doris probably thought was what he'd thought about Phillip: *He makes movies.* Over time they started discussing the possibility of a joint project. Marc loved the idea of the live soap opera that he'd heard was being done in installments at the Pyramid Club in New York. He was thinking about something in the beatnik era. Late '50s and early '60s was the Sluts' home turf.

"Tonight we're trekking up to Silvana's for the first *Bongo Beat* meeting," Doris wrote Jackie on September 22. The two cliques mingled warily. Phillip wasn't happy—he wanted the focus to stay on *Vegas in Space.* X and Tippi didn't much like anybody except Silvana. Ginger was more gregarious, especially with a drink in his hand.

Marc had also invited a young woman who belonged to neither group. Sandelle Kincaid[*] had grown up in La Jolla, the quintessential Southern California surfer girl, as she later described herself to me. Her exuberance combined with her beauty could have made her the most popular girl in high school, but, she said, "I was always interested in the edges." She hung out with the punk rock crowd, dated a boy in a band, and on graduating in 1981, at seventeen, she followed him up to San Francisco. The romance ended with a fight on her eighteenth birthday. Though she'd trained as a dancer, one day she found herself at Theatre Rhinoceros auditioning for a Marilyn Monroe–type role in a C. D. Arnold play, *Delivery.* (She had dressed as Marilyn the previous Halloween—though under the wig she was a brunette—and had savored the attention she'd drawn in the Castro.) She got the

---

[*] That's the name she goes by now. In those days she was Sandal (like the shoe) Hebert. Doris called her Scandal Sherbert. After a few years in show business she became Sandahl, then Sandelle. She adopted "Kincaid" because "Hebert" (ay-BARE) was so often mispronounced.

part. *Delivery*, which opened in March 1982, was directed by the same Chuck Solomon who would direct Doris in *Torn Tulle* that fall. That summer she and Silvana acted together in Lea DeLaria's one-act play *Fantasy in Flesh: Pay a Dollar, Talk to a Nude Girl*, at the 544 Natoma Performance Gallery. Marc saw the shows, and he was impressed with her. They lived around the corner from each other in the Mission, and he struck up an acquaintance.

There are people whose beauty is so startling that the conversation gets a little quieter when they walk into a room. Sandelle was like that. The word *statuesque* comes to mind. Her face had nothing of Marilyn's infantile fleshiness; her features were closer to Jane Russell's, very slightly, enticingly hard. Robin Clark, *Vegas in Space*'s straight cinematographer, said, "She'd come for photo shoots, and I would just turn into a klutz. I would knock over light stands. I just couldn't think straight." She was hardly unaware of her beauty, but she wasn't impressed by it, and I don't think I ever knew anybody who didn't like her. She wasn't innocent, either, but she had no experience of drag queens. At the first *Bongo Beat* meeting, she told me, "I had a little contact list that I was making for myself, and I wrote down 'Mr. X,' and everyone laughed and I felt *so* embarrassed." But her confusion was deceptive. *I'll play that part if you want me to*, she was thinking. *I'll just be naive and learn from you.*

By the time the production opened, the title *Bongo Beat* had changed to *Naked Brunch: A Story of the Beat and the Beaten*. They mined old movies for lines, though the shadow of the TV drama *Dynasty* was heavy, too: gay men were, if possible, even more obsessed than the rest of the nation with the weekly machinations of Joan Collins's glamorous, poisonous Alexis Carrington Colby, and the troupe billed itself the Alexis Carrington Colby Players. "We'd go to Doris's house," Marc says, "with all those fake marble pillars and the crazy art direction, and we'd just sit and watch old movies together, over and over again. *Valley of the Dolls*, *Virginia Woolf*, *The Pajama Game*—we copied choreography directly from that—*Suddenly Last Summer*, *A Streetcar Named Desire*, all the faggy things. *Baby Jane*, *The Snake Pit*,

The Heiress. To this day I'll watch these movies and I'll remember, *There's that line from* Naked Brunch!"

The principal characters, at the outset, were young Betty Van De Kamp (Sandelle), in search of her long-lost mother; Madame LaRue (Miss X), sinister owner of a North Beach hangout who's smitten by the girl (since the cast was almost all drag queens and women, lesbian plot threads were a given); LaRue's sister, Zizi LaFrance, a French starlet and junkie (Silvana); Connie MacAllister, a *Life* magazine snoop (Doris) later revealed to be LaRue and Zizi's sister; Cricket Kowalczyk,* a showgirl (Tippi); Darlene, a waitress (Ginger); and Zizi's pusher and the character with the best name, Nurse Junie May August (Anne Block). Phillip had a bit part—Doris had insisted—as a Chez LaRue patron. Almost everybody got a song, even Doris; Tippi got a dance. Sandelle and Marc choreographed an ensemble number to "Cool," lifting it straight out of *West Side Story*.

Getting the Sluts to rehearse was a challenge, and that first episode, Marc concedes, was pretty rough. But the in-crowd audience was screaming as soon as Doris and Silvana walked on. Part of the fun was the venue. Club 181, at 181 Eddy Street in the Tenderloin, had a semicircular bar, gobs of red velvet, and a titillating aura of decayed glamour. Few in the audience would have known about its gay history or even that it had one. It was opened in 1954 by Norma Clayton and Angela De Spirito, who had previously operated a popular lesbian bar on Broadway, and Edwin T. Atkins, who, as Lynne Carter, was one of the high-profile female impersonators that Esther Newton would profile in *Mother Camp*. The club featured dancing, live entertainment, drag acts, and, in the early '70s, nude go-go boys. A decade later it found a new, hip clientele. The singer Arturo Galster and his band started performing there as Patsy Cline and the Memphis G-Spots, a straight-faced drag act that drew a crossover audience. Marc had staged *The Night of the Fallen Stars* there, and so it was a natural venue for *Naked Brunch*.

---

* Marilyn Monroe's character in *Some Like It Hot* is Sugar Kane Kowalczyk.

Since Marc was also a savvy publicist, the room was packed for the first episode, on two Wednesdays in November 1983. The second, on two Fridays the following January, was "so jammed that people actually fainted," an excited Sandelle told a reporter for the *Chronicle*'s Sunday Pink Section—the most widely read arts-and-entertainment organ in the Bay Area and thus the brightest spotlight a show could wish for.

"That fucking 181 Club," Marc says now. "During the day you'd practically have to kill somebody to get the lights turned on. And there were rats stirring! And the smell of the place! It really reeked. And then they found out a couple of years later that there were bodies buried in there!" The dressing room was, to put it mildly, inadequate. So the Sluts made up at Oak Street; to set the mood, Doris played music from the "Gillian Girl" commercial in *Valley of the Dolls* on a repeating loop. Silvana set up his makeup station in the kitchen and then drove them all over, his glasses perched on the end of his nose to clear the enormous eyelashes Doris had fitted him with. Since there was no stage entrance, the cast created a stir when it arrived—painted but not yet costumed, loaded down with wig boxes and hanging bags—and clomped on high heels through the waiting crowd.

Two new performers joined the show's second episode. Arturo Galster—the Patsy Cline impersonator—would become a regular in Doris's shows; his fine voice was a plus. Janice Sukaitis was a Queens girl who had arrived in town in 1972 at twenty-five, fallen in with the Angels of Light, and discovered her own mad flair for drama. Small and voluptuous, she was a riveting performer. Marc cast her as Luz, a Raid-wielding prison matron loosely based on the Hope Emerson character in *Caged*, though Janice was half Hope Emerson's size.

She had a different role in the third and most demented episode, which ran on successive weekends in late March and early April 1984. That one consisted *entirely* of lines adapted from old movies. By now *Naked Brunch*, thanks in part to the Pink Section endorsement, had become a phenomenon. The roaring audience of San Francisco scene-makers electrified the actors. Doris, who at other times could be accused of letting his drag do the acting, was sensational: now that his character had evolved into a villainess, he got to be the show's Joan Collins.

As silly as it all was, it was silly in a hipper, more pop culturally literate way than *Vegas in Space*. The episode climaxed with "The Queens' Court," a plunge into surrealism that was both a trial and a game show. Janice, at her most deranged, played the prosecuting attorney with a different personality—Charles Laughton, Katharine Hepburn, Charles Boyer, Groucho Marx—for each witness she grilled. The presiding jurist, Justice Wayne Hockner, was played by Phillip, making his first foray into the unctuous stage persona by which he would, for better or worse, come to be known: in this instance a corrupt and fulsome phony fielding calls from Vegas stars. The trial proceeded according to the rules of "strip justice," and by the end Doris, the plaintiff, was down to bra and panties. He never looked more alluring.

Success was exciting—Marc even managed to see that all the actors got paid something—but the ongoing show turned out to be more work than anyone had envisioned. By the final episode, in July, Phillip and Ginger had dropped out. In exchange they got the unruly and hilarious Tommy Pace. Tommy, a San Jose native and already a star of the gay theater scene, "had the attention span of a two-year-old," Marc recalls with some disgust, though they were close friends. "Wouldn't give an ounce in rehearsal. And then he'd steal the show." Tommy was on the round side, so he was cast as the mother of Doris and Miss X and Silvana; their father—the climactic reveal—was Joseph Kennedy. Politics was in the air, since the Democratic convention had just been held in town, so they set this final episode during the 1960 campaign. (The Sluts had danced with the ZaSu Pitts Memorial Orchestra at a convention-related concert, and ever after they billed themselves as the Official Go-Go Girls of the 1984 Democratic National Convention.)

Amid all this wackiness there was one notable absence: Lulu, who, after growing up in Chicago, had arrived in San Francisco in 1974, performed with the Angels of Light, and been a regular in Marc's shows and movies. Part of the reason was his complicated friendship with Marc; they'd traveled together recently, and it hadn't gone well.

Moreover, there was frost between Lulu and Doris. They had very different personalities. Doris out of drag tended toward the invisible; Lulu had a brassy, campy voice that, like Marc's laugh, you could hear across a room. One day early on he had accosted Doris at the Café Flore and told him that *he* was the big blonde in town. Doris wasn't threatened, but he was insulted. Still, Doris expected him to be in *Naked Brunch*, mocking him in a letter to Jackie as an earlier version of himself, "lots of enthusiasm but no 'class.'" Lulu decided instead to stay away and pursue his interests in belly dance and butoh.

Meanwhile, early in the run of *Naked Brunch* a scandal broke out. It began when, during the lead-up to the first episode, X went over to Sandelle's to rehearse a duet to "Wouldn't It Be Loverly." "We were choreographing it," X recalls, "and it was *close*, one right behind the other and stepping in time, and just the sheer physicality of being close and rubbing up against each other . . ." For a while they tried to keep their relationship secret; that didn't last long. The universal reaction was shock. Few of X's colleagues knew about his bisexual past, and even if they did, he didn't offer up the kind of package, physically, that would have led anyone to think of pairing him with Sandelle. It wasn't just a fling, either. They were in love.

This romance was bound to affect the dynamic at Oak Street, especially after Sandelle began spending most of her time there. Doris didn't acknowledge the extent to which seeing X in a relationship with a woman hurt him, but their friendship was never the same. Everyone behaved like an adult, though. It helped that they all liked Sandelle so much. "I felt at home," she says now. "Later in life I reflected on it, and I realized there are a lot of times as a woman that people want you to be less than who you are. But gay men want you to be *more* of what you are." Doris wasn't warm—Sandelle likened him to "the older sister who didn't want to be disturbed too much"—but he was unquestionably "a mentor, encouraging me and pushing me, *yes!* and *yes!* and *more!* and *more!* and *more!*"

She took the cue. "I remember the first photo shoot. Doris comes up and she looks at me and she says, 'Oh, you're doing the *natural* look.' And I realized that *natural* was not good." The Sluts' makeup technique was a revelation. They all spent hours in front of the mirror, experimenting with eyeliner and eyelashes, and in front of the TV, educating Sandelle in the touchstones of camp.

The upshot was that the Sluts a-Go-Go had a new member.

Naked Brunch had, finally, another, sadder significance: Marc calls it the "last party before AIDS." In 1984 the hedonism of the 1970s was still baked into urban gay culture. Sex was everywhere and easy. Gay men regarded it the way the National Rifle Association views guns: Even the slightest curb on unbridled license was seen as a threat to hard-won freedoms. Monogamy was out. It would take at least a couple of years more for the nightmarish dimensions of the plague to sink in, and then the conflict between civil liberties and public health would explode—as it would again, nearly four decades later, during the COVID pandemic. But at this point very few people could imagine what was coming—brooding Marc was the exception—even though friends and acquaintances were starting to get sick. One of them was Chuck Solomon, who had directed Sandelle in *Delivery* and Doris in *Torn Tulle* at Theatre Rhino. "They were in so much denial," Marc says. "None of them wanted to hear about any of that. Every time I would say, 'Something weird's going on and this is really scary,' they would change the subject very quickly."

IN LATE FEBRUARY 1984, BETWEEN THE SECOND AND THIRD EPISODES of *Naked Brunch*, the *Vegas in Space* cast and crew spent ten days on their most grueling shoot, set in Plasworld, a kind of airport shopping mall where the astronauts await their first audience with the empress. The sequence plays like the happy afterthought it was, full of short comic bits for the drag queens who had secondary roles. Doris and Phillip rented Project Artaud, a performance space in the Mission District, for $500 a day and used industrial-size rolls of white plastic to cover its cavernous interior. Too late they realized that the exterior glass wall on one side meant they could control the light—and thus film—only after sunset.

But even then they couldn't really control it. In the smaller spaces where they'd shot before, Robin could aim the spotlights precisely; here they had to resign themselves to glaring overhead stage lamps. There were all kinds of other problems, too, including actors who kept flubbing their lines, probably from lack of sleep. Phillip says he stayed awake on speed for the whole ten days. He let Doris put him in drag for the sequence—he has a blue face and big blue hair and carries a parasol—and directing in this getup made him look deranged, especially when he removed the wig.

But the makeup, the costumes, and the sets for the Plasworld segment are so hallucinatory that the inexpert lighting is easy to ignore. The sequence also profited from the infusion of new talent from *Naked Brunch*. Silvana was cast as Wynetta Whitehead, a shopgirl with country inflections and a bad attitude. They enlisted Arturo to play the visiting Empress Noodles Nebula and staged a fender bender with the reliably lunatic Janice as a pop-eyed "Martian lady driver" spouting alien gibberish. (For the accident, Phillip exploded a cherry bomb in the back of Janice's vehicle, and she can be heard in a behind-the-scenes video screaming, "Get me out of here! It's on fire!") Sandelle they gave the part of the young shoplifter Babs Velour. Her memories aren't happy: "The stage shows had been so much fun, and here it felt like they'd gotten into the Vietnam War. I remember just waiting and waiting and waiting and waiting and waiting. They shot at 4:00 a.m. I had one take, and then they *ran out of film!*"

"My life may be interesting, but it's killing me!" Doris wrote Mildred when it was over. There's a video of him on the set, out of drag, talking mock-confidentially to the camera: "*Why am I doing this?* I ask myself. I mean, wouldn't poison be easier?"

The final shoot took place in August at the Farm, a community center on the edge of the Mission District, where they were redoing the sequence that had come back from the lab mysteriously blank. Phillip remembers those five days as pure pleasure, and both he and Robin consider this final footage their best work. It's also funny, thanks to Tommy Pace, whom they brought in to play Sandelle's aproned and antennaed mother, zapped by transporter to the detention center to take charge of her delinquent daughter. Tommy brandishes an egg-beater as he hisses at Sandelle in Long Islandese, "How could you *embarrass* me like this in front of the puh-*lice?*"

And that was it for filming, except for the miniatures, which Doris created in September, setting perfume bottles and lipstick tubes and costume jewelry around a tiny river and trees to create a girly fantasy of a city, a twist on the miniature landscape he'd once made for his model trains. They turned out to be the movie's most charming detail. The light at the end of the tunnel seemed to be glimmering.

LET ME PAUSE HERE TO OFFER A FEW OBSERVATIONS ABOUT THE movie, even though it wouldn't reach the big screen for another seven years.

Since *Vegas in Space* is one hundred percent camp, a good place to start is Susan Sontag's acclaimed 1964 essay "Notes on 'Camp,'" which is still, after more than half a century, fundamental to any discussion of the subject. The essay sheds light not just on the film but, more generally, on Doris's sensibility. Sontag's observation that "Camp refuses . . . the risks of fully identifying with extreme states of feeling" offers a gloss on his comportment after Jasper's death; and her dictum "The hallmark of Camp is the spirit of extravagance" could serve not just as an epigraph for *Vegas in Space* but as Doris's epitaph.

Where "Notes on 'Camp'" is most helpful in thinking about the movie is in the distinction Sontag draws between "naive" or "pure" camp and its "deliberate" ("manufactured, calculated") variant. Examples of pure camp include films such as the 1944 *Cobra Woman* and the 1967 *Valley of the Dolls* and Busby Berkeley's musical numbers of the '30s and '40s. They fall into the category of overwrought works that were meant to be taken at face value but fail, by ordinary critical standards, when they are; yet their decor or dialogue or acting or style is so over the top that by the so-bad-it's-good standard of camp—usually applied by a later, more jaded and ironic audience—they're a hoot. Deliberate or manufactured camp, on the other hand, includes the more preposterous Bond movies and their winking imitators, thousands of drag shows, and *Vegas in Space*: productions whose makers meant for them to be laughed at for their intentional lunacy, which is an homage to the unintentional lunacy of earlier works.

The supreme example of deliberate camp is *The Importance of Being Earnest*, the 1895 comedy in which Oscar Wilde both imitates and mocks the "more than usually revolting sentimentality" (as his Lady Bracknell sniffs) of nineteenth-century potboilers. Although Sontag tries to champion pure over deliberate camp—"Intending to be campy is always harmful," she declares incautiously—she undermines her argument with her clear delight in Wilde, whose epigrams dot her essay. I doubt that any sane person would try to claim that *The Importance of Being Earnest* isn't as good as *Cobra Woman*. But replace the "always" in her pronouncement with "usually" and you're closer to the truth. It takes an acute artistic intelligence to do a creditable job of manufacturing camp.

Doris himself was highly perceptive about the workings of camp humor. He once explained to me what fascinated him about *Valley of the Dolls*: "The first time you see it, it's serious, and it's actually pretty dreadful. The second time it just becomes funnier. I suppose repetition makes it funny." He estimated he'd seen *Valley of the Dolls* between twenty and thirty times. "It starts to look like it's satirizing itself, and in a way it is. It's a very serious satire, silly as all get-out, and yet it's done deadpan. And it does have a good element of glamour."

That last, seemingly tossed-off remark gets to the heart of camp. We don't embrace its artifacts only because they're clumsy or preposterous. Despite our better judgment, we also adore the glamour and the inflated emotions. The mockery works as a distancing maneuver that, historically, allowed men—gay men in particular—to explore stuff that mattered to them but that society identified as feminine. By assuming a stance of superiority and invulnerability, they could revel in these forbidden states—as we still do. Some less-jaded part of us *wants* to believe in those big emotions, which is what Sontag was talking about when she said, "Camp taste is a kind of love."

That's why the intentionally ridiculous dialogue in *Vegas in Space* falls flat. When a straight-faced Captain Tracey Daniels tells her subalterns, "Whatever happens, don't stop dancing—that's how you can *best save the universe*," the line doesn't elicit anything like the full-throated delight with which modern audiences greet Marlene Dietrich's "It took more than one man to change my name to Shanghai Lily" or Maria Montez's "Gif me that cobra jewel!" Every time *Vegas in Space* signals us that it's smarter than those corny old pictures, the mockery becomes unmoored. Without the undergirding of sincerity, camp superiority has nothing inferior to look down on.

Sontag, in fact, regarded camp as an "aristocratic posture," intellectually speaking. That stance made sense back in 1964, when camp was still an esoteric sensibility. She had no way of knowing that it was about to explode into the popular culture. Deliberate, winking camp became one of the signature styles of the late '60s; TV shows like *Batman* and *The Man from U.N.C.L.E.* and movies like *Barbarella* marked the end of anything aristocratic in the posture. (Phillip Ford grew up on *Batman*—he has copies of all the episodes.) This new, popular brand of camp, though at the gay end of the spectrum, is what fuels *Vegas in Space*.

It's also a driving force in the early movies of John Waters, from which *Vegas in Space* took so much inspiration. But Waters is a mordant and hilarious writer, closer to Wilde than to Doris and X. His movies have suffered, in fact, because often the kooks he casts don't have the skill to deliver his lines with the flair they deserve. *Vegas in Space* has the kooks but not the lines. Of course, one reason Doris and X didn't labor unduly over their screenplay is that they thought they were just tossing off another drag show, full of the usual groaners. I cringe when the astronauts identify their destination as a resort complex on "the planet Clitoris, in the Beaver System." As Mario Puzo is said to have avowed about *The Godfather*, if they had known what the movie was going to turn into, they would have written it better.*

---

* That's why I think the proper work against which to measure *Vegas in Space* isn't early John Waters but rather the gay cult picture *Pink Narcissus*. Shot by the late James Bidgood between 1964 and 1970, mostly in his cramped Manhattan apartment, where he

But Doris's principal concern—practically his only concern—was the way things looked. The campy plot was just a rack to hang the drag on. Ginger has suggested, astutely, that the best way to watch the movie is with the sound turned down. When you're not distracted by the words, you start to notice how literally unearthly the whole thing is. Now that I've seen *Vegas in Space* more times, I'm sorry to say, than I've seen *Hamlet*, the bad acting and the stupid jokes have flaked off. What remains is the dreamlike strangeness of its demented imagery. Most if not all great art is the product of obsession. *Vegas in Space* isn't close to great, but owing to the obsessiveness of Doris's vision, when it isn't bad it's spellbinding.

"YES, I'M REALLY 32!" DORIS CHIRPED TO HIS FATHER IN SEPTEMBER 1984, in a letter written, like much of his correspondence by then, on a series of West Graphics cards. His work for the card company was not only persisting but paying more—to his surprise, since he had never expected much out of it. Early that year they'd all (Doris, Tippi, X, and now sometimes Sandelle) gotten a 50 percent raise, plus the promise of continuing work. In one packed weekend, Doris had taken in $700. He would remain West Graphics' star model for the rest of his working life. It was the best and, in a way, the most challenging job he ever had: from "just changing wigs, more or less," he explained to me, he discovered that he was carrying around "this bevy of different characters that I wasn't aware of"—and, moreover,

---

managed to simulate fantasies of entire city blocks, this deranged semimasterpiece is laden with dreamlike costumes and sets that were heavy on glitter, sequins, and feathers and were made, like those in *Vegas in Space*, on a shoestring and almost entirely by hand. (It isn't surprising to learn that Bidgood began his career as a drag queen.) Both the handcrafted aesthetic and the obsessively queer vision make it a first cousin of *Vegas in Space*— although where *Vegas in Space* is deliberate camp, *Pink Narcissus* is pure: It wasn't *meant* to be ridiculous. The other major difference is that where *Pink Narcissus* is a pornographic fantasy that slavers over young male flesh sheathed in flimsy, femmy fabrics, there's absolutely nothing erotic about *Vegas in Space*. The drabbest Hollywood romance is sexier. Doris and Phillip had zero interest in female sexuality.

that he was marketable. He started to think that he really could have a movie career.

He was especially flattered when, in May, the company sent him ("all expenses paid," he bragged to his sister Marianne) to New York for the National Stationery Show. They printed up DORIS FISH WORLD TOUR T-shirts to distribute to buyers. He made personal appearances at card shops and got "tons of credibility" out of it. "A lot of people who were running stores would come up to me and say, 'If it weren't for your cards I wouldn't have made my rent this month!'" he told me. In August they sent him on the road again, this time to Denver and Salt Lake City. "I signed hundreds of cards and posed for dozens of photos and impressed a handful of people who are both anxious for my return!" he wrote Ace. "Seriously, it was quite successful and I really enjoyed the limo, the penthouse reception and being treated like a fucking goddess which is just how I behaved."

That fall he got another shot of credibility: a guest role on a network TV series. *Partners in Crime* starred the blonde Loni Anderson and the brunette Lynda Carter in a comedy-mystery about glamour girls who run a San Francisco detective agency. In the seventh episode (it lasted just half a season before NBC canceled it), "Is She or Isn't He?," which aired on November 3, 1984, they somehow wind up backstage at an audition for a drag show, and Anderson sideswipes Doris, who whirls around and snaps at her in a nasty male voice:

DORIS: Watch it, twinkle toes!

ANDERSON (*having moved away, to Carter*): Did you hear what I just heard?

CARTER: Uh-huh. Either she has a very bad cold, or—

ANDERSON: These women are too beautiful, too perfect, too *too* to be anything but—

CARTER: Men!

Though Doris was happy to have this clip on his résumé, it makes my skin crawl. First, the mean expression on his face is totally unlike him. (That's acting, I suppose.) Second, though he's called "The Blond" in the cast list, he was saddled with an ugly brown wig. Third, the only time he ever pitched his voice that low was when he was answering his business line. (Marc contended that Doris probably did his best acting in the bedroom.) If this moronic segment is of any interest at all, it's as one more demonstration that sexual variance, even as it was being ridiculed, was working its way into the national conversation.

Doris estimated that postproduction for *Vegas in Space* was going to cost $15,000. The Sluts staged their first fundraiser, a mock beauty pageant, one October Thursday at the Trocadero Transfer, a South of Market disco. According to the press release, "Excitement rages through the City as glamorous aliens drop from the sky to compete for the title of MISS SOLAR SYSTEM 1984." The contestants were actors from the movie and West Graphics models done up in outer-space drag. As the pageant's hosts, Doris wore his costume from the movie's finale, with Bride of Frankenstein streaks in place of the gold spikes, and Phillip donned tails. The evening's apex was a screening of the trailer for *Vegas in Space*, "set for release in early 1985." It got a thunderous response.

There was also song and dance—Timmy led the band, the Showgirls from Earth—including the "Space Surfin'" number from the movie, with Tippi dancing the frenzied lead. It was, in fact, Tippi's evening. As the blonde starlet who assists the hosts (Vanna White and *Wheel of Fortune* were then current), she wore a sequined bodice and radiated a cracked energy, seeming to float on her spike heels up and down the club's long staircase as she escorted the many contestants to the stage. Only now do I understand that her fizz was drug induced.

A month later a bunch of cast members appeared in *Sex Wars*, an intergalactic porn film that was being shot in San Francisco. They kept their clothes on, though. The producers had gotten wind of *Vegas in Space* and recruited Doris to supply extras, made up and costumed, for a bar scene that nodded, with obscene additions, to the cantina sequence in *Star Wars*. Doris was in fact one of two makeup artists, and it's easy to distinguish his colleague's pedestrian aliens from the outrageous *Vegas in Space* crew, which included Tippi, Miss X, Phillip, Janice, Tommy, Ramona ("I looked like a broccoli"), and Jacqueline Hyde, who had finally traveled from Paris out to San Francisco. Doris gave himself the most resplendent drag: apricot hair, green skin, bare green breasts with long-lashed eyes on the nipples, and—though they're visible only briefly—the giant padded ass and thighs he had lately taken up.

A few months later, a friend called Janice to ask her, "Do you know you're in a porno film on Market Street?"

IF SANDELLE'S ADVENT INTRODUCED STRAINS, IT ALSO BROUGHT A new energy to the Sluts. She and Tippi grew close; they would often dance as a pair in future shows, and when both those wildcats were letting loose, you didn't know which way to look. Moreover, they all recognized the theatrical value of the role disruption that she, like Jane Dornacker before her, added to the troupe: Playing with gender confines and extremes was more tantalizing when you had a woman playing, too. Eventually she started troweling on so much makeup that (though I find it incredible) some audience members truly were confused, like the young man who approached Sandelle after a show and, introducing himself as a student, asked, "I hope you don't mind this question—are you a man or a woman?" She replied, "I guess you'll have to do a little more studying, won't you?"

Sandelle's mother, who by then had also made her way to San Francisco, had found a spacious flat at the corner of 18th and Linda Streets, in the Mission District. Sandelle moved in with her but discovered they didn't make good roommates, which was one reason she became such a fixture at Oak Street. Had she been a little older, she might have been more sensitive to the growing exasperation there that she wasn't contributing anything toward food or rent.

Phillip, meanwhile, had lost the lease on his own small place. So when Sandelle's mother decided to move out of their shared flat, Sandelle invited Phillip to move in. Then Doris called a meeting. He said,

"You know, you're a big person, X. Living with you is like living with two people. And Sandelle is a big person. Having her around is like having another two people around. And Tippi—how many people is that? Really, it's too many. So why don't you think about moving in with Sandelle?" Tippi could then officially leave the Tenderloin for Oak Street.

"This was very Doris," Phillip explained to me. "She made this strategic plan and moved everyone around. It made sense—people just needed to be told."

X and Phillip wound up living in the flat on 18th Street for many years. After them came a younger generation of drag queens (though they're not so young now, either), who have always called it, with some pride, the House of Fish. Initially they must have thought that Doris had lived there, since so many of his things had wound up there.

The housing issue settled, Doris left to spend Christmas in Sydney. He hadn't seen his native city since the South Pacific Nightclub Tour, five years earlier. His star had not faded.

9

POLITICAL THEATER

D<small>URING</small> 1985 D<small>ORIS</small>'<small>S WORK GREW INCREASINGLY POLITICAL</small>,
in the broader sense. The outspokenness with which he pro-
claimed his identity as a drag queen was a political statement in itself.
It can be difficult to remember how scarce images of queer people used
to be. You hardly ever saw gay characters in movies or on TV, and
same-sex attraction was all but unheard-of in popular music and theater. As a consequence, it could be easy to believe, if you wanted to, that
gay sexuality was so rare as to be a statistically insignificant aberration.

On the battlefront against this invisibility, drag queens were in the
avant-garde. By the mid-1980s, Doris had come to understand what

Doris in *The All-New Happy Hour Xmas Special*, 1985. Photo by Robin Clark.

Esther Newton had argued in *Mother Camp*: That in the popular imagination, drags were symbols of homosexuality. Within the gay community itself, he was a standard-bearer for the notion that nothing in the fight for equal rights required gay men and lesbians to make a show of acting straight.

The need to see ourselves in the mirror of art is basic to human nature. But until late in the twentieth century, if gay men and lesbians wanted to see their reflection, they pretty much had to provide it themselves. Theatre Rhinoceros was one local institution that addressed this community need. Another was the San Francisco International Lesbian and Gay Film Festival, which in the eight years between 1977 and 1985 had grown from an evening of Super 8 shorts projected on Marc Huestis's bedsheet into a nine-day municipal extravaganza. There were also annual gay pride marches around the world, the most spectacular of which, by 1985, was the fancy-dress parade that crowned the Sydney Gay Mardi Gras.

The nutty drag shows and the noisy marches, the new gay-themed books, movies, and journalism—none of them, individually, looked hugely significant at the time. But now we can see that, taken together, they were. The Sluts, in other words, were more than showgirls. They were cultural workers, and their productions, combined with parallel projects, both lowbrow and high-minded, going on across the globe, were changing the drift of history.

BETWEEN *VEGAS IN SPACE*, CARDS FOR WEST GRAPHICS, THE MISS Solar System pageant, the *Sex Wars* shoot, and a spot on a prime-time TV show, 1984 had been a frenetic year for Doris. When he returned to Australia in December, he was looking forward to some downtime—unwinding with his family, getting to know his young nieces and nephews, seeing old friends. He stayed with Mildred in Manly Vale until Christmas Eve. Then the two of them joined the rest of the family (including, as always, Ace) at Marianne and Tony's large Balinese-inspired home down the coast in Wolumla, a few kilometers outside the pleasant beach town of Merimbula. It was the first of many Christmases Doris would spend there; Michael and his family had already moved down to Merimbula, and soon Andrew would, too. Liz has long been the only sibling left in Sydney.

Living halfway across the globe hadn't diminished their closeness, as Doris's many letters to them attest. He kept them abreast of his increasing celebrity (often using his cards as stationery), and they clearly enjoyed it. Once he even did a drag spot at a monthly folk cabaret Marianne and Tony sponsored in a small town outside Wolumla, doubtless a first for the rural populace. Mostly, though, his time with his family was an opportunity to shed his Doris mask and relax. No public appearances were planned for this vacation.

But then he received a call from his old friend Peter Tully imploring him to participate in what was then called the Sydney Gay Mardi Gras ("and Lesbian" was added in 1988). "We're building a float for you!" Tully promised. That was all the encouragement Doris needed.

THE YEAR 1985 MARKED THE EIGHTH EDITION OF THE MARDI GRAS. The first one, in 1978, had been a transformative event for the Australian gay movement. Activists had organized it for late June to mark the ninth anniversary of Stonewall. They'd planned a Saturday morning march, an afternoon meeting, and a more festive Mardi Gras parade in the evening, with costumes encouraged. (The term "Mardi Gras" was used from the outset; the event never had anything to do with the day before the start of Lent, though it now generally falls around that time.) Tension arose between those who saw the occasion as a political protest and those who saw it as a celebration of gay culture—a dispute that would play out again and again in the coming years, and not only in Sydney.

The morning march was a success. "We'd never been in a demonstration of five hundred lesbian and gay people," Ken Davis, one of the organizers, told me. A startlingly wide cross-section of queer marchers turned out—leather queens and sissies, butch and lipstick lesbians,

Catholic and Protestant and Jewish groups, and all manner of leftist organizations. The gay community is as diverse (or as splintered) as any other. "Everyone hated everybody" is how Ken puts it. But they united for the march.

The evening parade started even more promisingly, with a thousand revelers, some of them in fancy dress, gathering at Taylor Square. They drew several hundred more as they streamed along the gay Golden Mile of Oxford Street, shouting, "Out of the bars and into the streets!" and toward Hyde Park, where a small celebration had been planned. But when the crowd reached the park, the police, who hadn't issued a permit for the festival—from the start they'd gone out of their way to be uncooperative—ordered it away. A large faction, indignant but also exhilarated from the show of solidarity, headed for Kings Cross, that louche quarter of bars and streetwalkers where the cops were roundly hated.

"Then it became a march," Ken recalls, "because people were really angry." Once they reached the Cross they did start to disperse, but at that point the police blocked both ends of Darlinghurst Road and began beating marchers and dragging them to waiting paddy wagons. To the cops' utter surprise, the lesbians started punching. Many of the eyewitness reports recount the women's fierceness. "And then eventually the gay men start fighting back," Ken continued. "And then the sex workers and the junkies and the Indigenous people and everybody else: once they're seeing people fighting with the cops—*party!* So then it's a full-scale riot."

It's possible to comprehend the mindset of the thuggish cops who raided the Stonewall Inn early on the morning of June 28, 1969, never suspecting that a clientele ground down by years of harassment might resist—but not the monumental stupidity of the Sydney police on this parallel occasion. The gay-rights movement had been very visibly growing and strengthening for nearly a decade. Only a thoroughly myopic force could have expected a group of young, middle-class, politically fired-up men and women to cringe before such asinine brutality. And on that evening the police violence gave the Australian movement an enormous gift: its very own Stonewall moment.

Outrage broke out across the country, with the marches, rallies, and dismissals of charges—fifty-three people had been arrested that night—continuing for months. The result was the revocation, in May of the following year, 1979, of the Summary Offences Act, which until then had given the police carte blanche to deny permits to whatever assemblies rubbed them the wrong way. (They had wielded it avidly during the Vietnam War era.) That victory sealed the eminence of the Sydney Gay Mardi Gras.

Every year after 1978, it swelled: the first year's crowd of fifteen hundred had ballooned to forty thousand by 1984. Another change was a large-scale withdrawal of lesbians (over familiar objections that the Mardi Gras organization was dominated by men), who didn't return fully until the late '80s. Their absence probably encouraged the efflorescence of drag, always a contentious issue with some women who saw it as demeaning. Yet another was the shift of date, in 1981, from June to February*—that is, from winter to summer, when the warm weather encouraged bigger crowds and skimpier outfits. But probably the most far-reaching of these early changes came in late 1982, when the Mardi Gras committee decided, after receiving a grant of $6,000 from the Community Arts Board of the Australia Council, to hire an artistic director. The post went to Doris's friend the thirty-four-year-old Peter Tully, and there couldn't have been a more auspicious confluence of vision, talent, and locale.

Tully had originally set out to make jewelry. In his early twenties he'd spent several formative months in Papua New Guinea and had then traveled through much of Asia and Africa, captivated by tribal art and adornment. He met the artist and gay-rights activist David McDiarmid in Melbourne in 1973, and they soon became lovers. By the time they moved to Sydney, in 1975, their love affair was over, but their collaboration was just beginning. They easily found their place in the creative/bohemian society to which Doris and Jackie also belonged. Both of them

---

* That year rain delayed the parade to March 21. Recent ones have generally been held in early March.

were there for the first Mardi Gras, Tully decked out in one of his own assemblages, and for the free-for-all that followed. The following year, McDiarmid became Doris's rival for Bernard Fitzgerald's affection—though it's doubtful he saw it that way, and Doris doesn't seem to have held a grudge.

That same year, 1979, Tully wangled a travel-study grant from the Australia Council, and he and McDiarmid headed to New York. They arrived just in time for the annual Gay Pride march and found it far more exuberant than Sydney's as-yet stolid procession. New York's, which took place in the same city as the Stonewall uprising it commemorated, had attracted thousands of participants from its start in 1970, and in it liberation held hands with hedonism. But what really opened their eyes was the Paradise Garage, a popular drug-fueled gay disco downtown on King Street. Tully later said, "They played the best music I'd ever heard, and the people dressed." It wasn't about labels: "They could wear a paper bag and look like a million dollars." What he saw on the dance floor there fused with the ethnographic imprint of his earlier travels to create his mature vision: "I was looking at urban groups, the punks, blacks, Puerto Ricans, WASPS, gays, and they were all little components of New York society and I more or less saw them as little tribes. And so I started making things for my tribe." The name he came up with for his creations was Urban Tribalwear.

Tully's aesthetic beautifully suited both the operations and the budget of the Mardi Gras workshop. He was a genius at applying a glue gun to bits of cast-off junk and glitter. He was also, according to Ron Smith, his right hand at the workshop, "very aware, from demo experience, of the failings of the saggy banner and the anonymity of the T-shirt and jeans." Instead he wanted costume and ornament and music, in excess. He wanted spectacle. McDiarmid once called Mardi Gras the marriage of art and politics. It was this artistic element, enhanced by the nighttime setting, that Tully brought forward—and that by 1985, the year Doris was back home visiting his family, had already set Sydney's Mardi Gras resplendently apart from other gay-pride celebrations.

But 1985 was an unnerving year. Homophobia was deeply entrenched in the Australian press, which in the early years had dealt with Mardi Gras mainly by ignoring it, even as the crowds mounted into the tens of thousands. When the first Australian case of AIDS was diagnosed, in April 1983, gay-plague stories started appearing sporadically in the national papers. Then, in November 1984, three Queensland babies died after being infected via blood transfusions, and at that point hysteria broke out. The headlines tell the story: "GAYS ACCUSED OF BEING DONORS 'OUT OF SPITE.'" "'EXTERMINATE GAYS'— DOCTOR." "'DIE, YOU DEVIATE.'"

The parade had long had an indefatigable enemy in the Reverend Fred Nile, an Australian combination of Jerry Falwell and Anita Bryant. Nile was given to making thunderous pronouncements on the order of "If Jesus wept over Jerusalem, he must be heartbroken over Sydney." Every year he used to lead the members of his church in praying for rain to thwart the parade, and since February and March are wet months on Australia's east coast, sometimes their prayers were answered.

Nile, who is now in his late eighties and still ranting, can seem from afar like a comical figure. But in 1985 there was nothing funny about the controversy surrounding the parade and the Sleaze Ball, the dance party that followed it. Nile had already called for their cancellation. Then, at the end of January, Professor David Penington, the head of the commonwealth government's AIDS Task Force and a generally level-headed figure, worried publicly that the "Bacchanalian orgy" that followed the parade every year could become "the pathway to self-destruction." Though he was mainly talking about the importance of safe-sex practices—and he wasn't wrong about the hedonism—his remarks fed the fire.

"The Sydney daily papers are very sensationalistic," Doris told me, "so every day in the headlines there were more calls from the fundamentalists to halt the parade. And there were certain people in the gay community saying, 'Yes, we don't want to be presenting this kind of bad image.' And there were threats of violence." The arguments got so vitriolic that even some members of the parade's organizing committee suggested calling off the event. They were overruled. Thus the atmosphere was tense when Peter Tully and Ron Smith lured Doris down to the Mardi Gras workshop in early 1985 with the promise of his own float. The three of them had known one another for years, and Doris's showmanship held the promise of a splashy addition to the parade. What they may not have counted on was his optimism.

Ron is a friendly and loquacious artist, subversively clever. What he and Doris had, he told me, "was primarily a working relationship. That is, we were fabulous friends, but we worked as fabulous friends on *stuff*, because we both shared a passion for what Doris called 'turning shit into a birthday cake.'" With several thousand participants in the parade and tens of thousands more in the crowd, a typical workshop budget in those days might be $5,000. "So we *had* to turn shit into a birthday cake. We used industrial waste and masses of gold cigarette foil and gold cigarette card, waste from printing mills and waste fabrics. We used to go to couturiers and get very glamorous bits of off-cut brocades and stitch it all together."

The workshop was on Forbes Street, in the tough inner-city suburb of Woolloomooloo, in a derelict building that Ron describes as a rat's nest—"literally." Every bit of glass had been smashed out of the windows; there were one telephone, one toilet, and no garbage collection. "The committee never knew what we were doing. We kept everything secret from them, and they never came to the workshop. So we had an amazing amount of freedom." It came with responsibilities. "We used to produce the lead vehicle, several music trucks, a featured piece, which in different years usually featured Doris—funny how that happens— and then we would develop key pieces with community groups to teach the people skills."

For Tully, this participation was all-important. "There was a basic philosophy in the workshop, which was about identity and bonding," Ron says. "You wanted people to be able to talk. You wanted music. The process of making the stuff was as important as the finished product." He sees this notion of art by the people, for the people, which in his case went back to his days as a member of the Roxy Collective, as the same ethic out of which Doris had emerged. The acidly cynical Jackie and Miss Abood, he concedes, would despise the Synthetics' ever being associated with "community art," but the shared skills they brought to the enterprise—like Jackie's with gilding and Doris's with dime-store jewelry and a glue gun—had made it exactly that. The Doris he recalls is much the same quietly intent artist that Robin Clark remembers from the set of *Vegas in Space* the year before. "No one would recognize him out of drag," Ron says—"just some queen fiddling around."

Put him in makeup and it was a different story. Invited to launch the first Mardi Gras Film Festival that year—one of the numerous events leading up to the parade—Doris made a grand entrance in a silvery-gold gown and blonde curls, squired by his old flame Bernard Fitzgerald and Bernard's new beau. "We left from the house," Bernard recalls. "We had one of the first stretch limos in Sydney." Pink triangles embellished the mud guards; the Dykes on Bikes provided a motorcycle escort. "And she was half an hour late—they had to hold up the whole festival opening for her."

Doris's float in the Mardi Gras parade was the Fishmobile, a glittering sea creature with bulging eyes, puckered lips, and golden scales spotted blue and sea green, towed by strongmen in aquatic costumes; Thierry (back in Sydney with Jackie for the occasion) was one of them. Between the creature's head and its body was an open platform from which Doris waved to the crowd. He wore his big red wig, a tight red top with a long red boa, rainbow eye shadow, and, most remarkably, a stuffed sausage casing of gold lamé that tripled his girth from the backside down, like the one he wore in *Sex Wars*. (He was going through a phase of fascination with bottom-heavy divas.) It wasn't glamorous, but it was stunning. On one side he was flanked by a lavender-peruked Jackie in sequined culottes, and on the other by his mother, Mildred—crowned, radiant, and glorying in her return to the center of the scene. Eight thousand revelers attended the postparade party in the cavernous Royal Hall of Industries at the Sydney Showground, and "the only person you could see," according to Ron, "was Doris, because she was just so *unbelievably* fabulous."

After the months of warnings, recriminations, and fear, everything had gone off smoothly. Doris's sunniness played a part in the success. "A lot of people said to me personally that I did help to keep people's morale up," he told me, his pride showing. "It was really a boost to the community."

He got back to San Francisco at the end of February 1985, a lot less rested than he had anticipated. Oak Street, after two years of on-and-off filming, was a wreck. With nothing much on the schedule beyond a few go-go-dancing gigs with the ZaSu Pitts Memorial Orchestra, he put his energy into decorating.

Phillip, meanwhile, had rented a flatbed editing table and moved it into his bedroom in the apartment on 18th Street that he now shared with Sandelle and X. He literally slept in the editing room. In March he got his first nine-to-five job, at Monaco Film Labs. He stayed there for five years, learning the postproduction skills he needed on the job. Evenings and weekends he continued editing *Vegas in Space*. "The speed was cheap—it was the '80s." Within a couple of months he had enough footage assembled to present it at one of the works-in-progress screenings hosted by the Film Arts Foundation, an organization that provided grants and services to independent Bay Area filmmakers.

Bob Hawk, who was then its exhibitions coordinator, recalls how sparsely attended those evenings typically were. But Doris and crew put flyers in the bars and enticing notices in the gay papers and in *Release Print*, the Film Arts Foundation's newsletter, calling it "the talk of the San Francisco film/art/party/nightclub scene." The first screening took place on Thursday, May 23, at the small Adolph Gasser screening room on Second Street. "I won't ever forget the scene that night," Bob says. The crowd pressed up against the door and spilled out onto Second Street and down the sidewalk to Natoma Street. The buzz had started.

Once the movie began, the audience hooted gamely, even though the rough cut was clunky and barely coherent. "I knew we had something," Phillip says, "but I didn't know where to go with it."

Once again the group was kissed by fortune, this time in the form of Bob Hawk, whose career as a consultant to independent filmmakers has been so productive that in 2016 a documentary was made about *him*.* "I saw the potential," he says now. "There was an awful lot of lame footage," but it was "very much plugged into what camp and drag and parody and satire were all about." He also saw the potential—"unchanneled, unfocused imagination and talent"—in Phillip.

Doris, meanwhile, had been lying uncharacteristically low. The hiatus ended that fall. In October and December 1985 the Sluts and various friends staged the first two of what would be four *Happy Hour* shows at Club 181. *The Happy Hour Show* and *The All-New Happy Hour Xmas Special* were structured—though that's hardly the word—around a conceit that had originated with the Miss Solar System pageant: Doris and Phillip as TV cohosts. Then as now, talk shows were ground zero for junk celebrity prattle and thus gold mines of camp. It was Phillip rather than Doris who took charge onstage. Despite his initial reluctance—"My whole thing through the '80s was, 'We can do that *after* we finish the movie'"—in the *Happy Hour*s he became an equal collaborator on the script. Sandelle did much of the writing, too. Taking off from his earlier characters and inspired, no doubt, by the comedy of smarm that Bill Murray had introduced to *Saturday Night Live* in the late '70s, Phillip made himself into a glad-handing, bejeweled swinger who was transparently insincere—although unlike Murray's lounge lizard, who thinks he's a charmer, Phillip's character is fully aware of his obnoxiousness.

"But I didn't write that character," he clarified. "Sandelle, and then Doris—they all wrote it as a group." Still, he got so deeply into it that audiences confused the actor and the role. "I knew that. I said, 'It doesn't bother me at all. They'll find out what a nice person I really am.

---

* *Film Hawk*, directed by JJ Garvine and Tai Parquet.

Or they won't.'" As he was pondering, rather wistfully, the public's lack of perception, I was mortified, because I had been one of those people. I found him so grating onstage that I avoided him offstage. I didn't start getting to know him until long after Doris's death.

Sandelle and Tippi were the Happy Hour Dancers. (Originally so was Freda, but she had so much trouble remembering the steps that in the second show Doris announced, "The third dancer broke her heel and had to be shot.") The dancing, unlike the rest of the shows, was fresh, funny, and well rehearsed. Sandelle demonstrated how far she had advanced in the study of camp by choreographing with the movement vocabulary of a full-on drag queen. She made the numbers glamorous and Tippi made them hilarious, but it was the combination of the two that made them delicious. To see them side by side on all fours, slapping the floor with long ponytails they whipped in circles, was camp heaven.

The talk show format allowed whoever they could get to do whatever they wanted; Jennifer Blowdryer, for example, could come on to plug a recently published book without seeming more incongruous than any typical talk show guest. But it had a deeper resonance, even if nobody thought about it at the time. In the '80s, as I said earlier, openly gay people were still so uncommon on TV that when the rare program like *Dynasty* featured a gay character it was big news. So when Doris and Phillip referred to the club as "Channel 181" and to the crowd as the "studio audience," they were doing more than playing let's pretend. They were constructing a fantasy version of pop culture that included gay people. And they weren't doing it for the gay audience alone. Club 181 was no longer a gay bar; it was a mixed club, and the *Happy Hours* brought a queer sensibility to the mainstream in a way that was then starting to happen in many other cities as well and that, we can now see, played a big part in changing popular perceptions.

Soon they got a shot at real TV. Their filmmaker friend John Canalli, who had worked with them on *Vegas in Space*, obtained the San Francisco franchise for a public-access cable show called the Gay

Cable Network, or GCN. Public access had been an increasingly familiar part of the cable TV landscape since 1972, when the Federal Communications Commission mandated that large cable systems set aside a fixed number of noncommercial channels where groups and individuals could broadcast without corporate backing. GCN was the brainchild of Lou Maletta, a New York activist; he launched it in 1982 and was soon distributing his magazine-style programming in twenty metropolitan markets.

Some of them provided content in return. A teacher in Cincinnati, for example, contributed a regular feature called "This Week in Gay History." In the version of GCN that aired in the Bay Area, Tuesdays at 9 p.m., the first half hour, *Pride and Progress*, covered the news; the second, *The Right Stuff*, was devoted to entertainment, with Doris as host. The programming, in other words, comprised the same uneasy mixture of hard politics and sequined fluff that had originally raised furious debates around the Sydney Gay Mardi Gras—was it a demonstration or was it a celebration?—and continued to rankle the movement. For this reason alone, the Sluts' participation was destined to generate controversy. So was their relish for insult humor and treading the edge. Gags that broke up a hip and lubricated nightclub audience were bound to get a stiffer reception from TV watchers who didn't go to drag shows.

Every other week they would get into costume and trek to John Canalli's house, where, using a single video camera, he would shoot two weeks' worth of material. The brevity of the GCN segments imposed discipline and, thus, professionalism on the group. (The *Happy Hours* went on forever.) And it helped that they were used to working on a shoestring. When you look at the tapes now, what's fascinating is how polished their spots seem in contrast to everyone else's. The various newscasters, reporters, and interviewers on *Pride and Progress* try desperately to emulate their counterparts on network TV, and of course they can't; a deflating sense of playacting clings to them, and the seriousness of the topics they're covering—discrimination and AIDS—only points up the paltriness of their means. But when Doris made his first appearance in front of the camera, in late December 1985, he looked like what everyone else clearly wasn't: a professional.

His experience as a host for *Click TV* is evident. His timing is astute, and, unlike the newscasters, he's utterly at ease as a glammed-up anchorwoman, in scarlet lipstick, a long blonde wig, a tux top with a scarlet bow tie, and rhinestone earrings—Doris's version of understated and elegant. His first words herald the wicked tone he's going to take: "Good evening and welcome. I'm Doris Fish, and this is the very first San Francisco edition of *The Right Stuff*. Tonight we'll meet world-famous Sister Boom Boom* and a couple of his weirdo friends. I meant that kindly. Also, we'll put our finger up—I mean *on*—what really happened in 1985." After Boom Boom's segment he comments drily, "Well, I'm not getting *paid* to laugh at anybody else's jokes," as though he were getting paid at all. Then he introduces Phillip's calendar feature, "That's San Francisco."

Phillip's first words, too, give a taste of what's to come—manic phoniness: "I've got your whole week planned out for ya, so grab your pad and pencil!" He was followed by Tippi, in a striped sweater and a blonde flip, with the weather report: "[*Giggle*] Well, it's still winter, and it will probably be fairly cold, specially at night! [*Giggle*] So wear your fun fur!"

Doris quickly got more outrageous. Aware of the anger that drag provoked among some lesbians, he took a special pleasure in needling them: "Tune in next week, when we'll be laughing at women!" He was alluding to a guest spot by two lesbian comics, whom he introduced the following week by saying, "Now, while their humor has a definite

---

* Sister Boom Boom—Jack Fertig—was then the best-known member of the Sisters of Perpetual Indulgence, the drag nun troupe. He'd gained further notoriety when he ran for the San Francisco Board of Supervisors, in 1982; an impish campaign poster, based on the famous scene in *The Wizard of Oz*, had him on a witch's broom over City Hall, skywriting a warning to the mayor: SURRENDER DIANNE. In the late '70s he'd been the first Dunya Kalmeabich (the part Jane Dornacker took over and ran with) in *Blonde Sin*. Randy West had used the Sisters on some early West Graphics cards, and it was Sister Boom Boom, too busy with his supervisorial campaign to pose for Randy, who'd referred him to Miss X, who'd referred him to Doris.

lesbian flavor"—he touched his finger to his tongue—"mmm . . . it is still universally funny."

Phillip's calendar feature grew more outrageous, too. So did his out-fits: garish dinner jackets, open ruffled shirts with chains, rings on ev-ery finger, dangly earrings. His inspirations were Tom Jones, Elvis, and Liberace. His bleached-blond pompadour mounted into ever-higher and stranger styles, and every week he seemed to get more handsome.

"TV is very powerful," he observed of their new celebrity. "All of a sudden everyone knew who I was." He grew accustomed to being rec-ognized in stores, but that didn't mean he was loved. I don't think I've ever seen anything quite like what he did on those calendar spots, jab-bering so fast as he tweaked on speed that he had to gasp for breath as he ascended, week by week, into a kind of ecstasy of unction: "Really, there's no need to thank me. I do it because I *care*. I mean, we all are in this together, aren't we? All right, ya knuckleheads—go fetch your datebooks!"

Miss X and Sandelle played advice-columnist sisters. They dressed conservatively in Lilli Ann suits; X had found a job at the San Fran-cisco fashion house, which specialized in outfits for the business-woman. Dianne Feinstein was among its clients. Their routine involved milking bromides ("When all else fails, talk it over with your mother—she's your best friend!"), but the real frisson they offered—though you had to be an insider to appreciate it—was the knowledge that these two dowdy sisters were lovers.

The glut of projects on Doris's calendar late that year, following several fallow months, may have had something to do with his growing suspicion that he was ill and time was precious. That ap-prehension didn't put a brake on his hooking, though the movie contin-ued draining most of those profits. But then, Doris was always relaxed about money. He placed his confidence in what he called the Bank of the Universe: "The theory is, you have a bank account somewhere in the universe that has an unlimited supply of money," he explained to me. "And you just have to believe that you can take money out when you need it—which seems to have happened to me easily enough." What he was referring to specifically was the 1986 Mardi Gras.

Since he was more than usually strapped that year, he hadn't planned on attending. And then, he told me, "I got a call out of the blue: 'Come! We need you! We'll pay your way, give you a job! We're building a fabulous float for you!'"

The anxious mood of the previous year had shifted. "I had the most fantastic time," Doris told me, "working twelve hours a day, seven days a week, looking for the hammer, looking for the scissors, where's the silver glitter?" Once the season began—the Sydney Mardi Gras festival lasts a month and in 1986 comprised thirty-three separate events—he did manage to get out of the workshop to make personal appearances. That year the honor of opening the film festival went to the American film critic and activist Vito Russo, and Doris was there, in a white Cleopatra wig and a slinky white dress, to interview him for GCN.

A more meaningful evening for Doris was the opening of the art, photography, and crafts exhibition. It wasn't the solo show he'd dreamed of—he was one artist among more than fifty—but he was the star. His self-portraits, framed by his brother Andrew, drew a gratifying amount of attention, and the hall itself was dominated by a full-length oil portrait of him by Ron Smith, four feet by six feet, after a West Graphics shot of Doris kneeling in a leopard-spotted pantsuit of black-and-white fun fur with a black bra. Doris greeted the crowd in the very same drag, a GCN camera close by. A local pastry virtuoso had produced the gala's centerpiece, a multihued cake delicately sculpted in the shape of an Indian deity. Mildred, hurrying across the room, dragged her handbag right through it. The artist was apoplectic. Mildred was annoyed to discover icing on her purse, but she shrugged off the destruction: "It won't make the cake taste any different."

For the parade, Doris's float, conceived with Ron, was a fantasy of Halley's Comet (just then making its once-every-seventy-five-years appearance), with Doris waterskiing on top of the spherical body. Mounted on a flatbed truck, it looked like a giant chrysanthemum with disco lights whirling inside. The enormous tail was made of long strips of tulle that had been dip-dyed (by Doris, in Ron's bathtub) in a riot of colors and filamented with strings of Christmas lights plugged into a generator on the truck. A half-dozen drag queens, costumed as the planets, held the twinkling strands aloft on long poles. Doris's old Sylvia cohort Denis Norton was one of them; another was Miss Abood.

Doris wore a solid-gold jumpsuit with gold boots and a gold hood. His skis were mounted on scaffolding, and he had pipe handles to hang onto—"But of course he wasn't hanging on," Ron says; "he was waving the whole time." Fabulousness trumped safety. Ron walked alongside, anxious. As the truck rounded a corner, the scaffolding came loose and started to tip over. Ron jumped onto the flatbed and managed to push Doris back up; but then, as he was retightening the bolts, he smelled something burning. The generator, which they had wrapped in black plastic, had caught fire—"And he's dressed from head to toe in synthetics!" Somehow Ron managed to jettison the flaming mass.

February showers, as I mentioned, often threaten the parade, urged on by the prayers of Fred Nile and his followers. That year the downpour came. Miss Abood, one of the planetary tail-bearers—he was Venus, with three sets of breasts and a unicorn horn—was still fuming decades later. "No one had worked out the logistics of it! It rained, and it was really windy, and that post was so fucking *heavy*. We had on heels, and we had to walk about two miles. By the time we got there, I had one tit left. I was so angry—I was looking for Doris with a *brick*. If I had found her within the first ten minutes, she would have died a lot sooner."

From Doris's perspective—above it all, waving to the crowd—the 1986 Mardi Gras parade was one more triumph. He never minded punishment in the service of glamour.

10
NIGHTCLUB OF THE LIVING DEAD

T HE EVIDENCE THAT DORIS WAS AWARE OF HIS HIV STATUS by 1986 is in a letter he wrote Ace several years later, in April 1989, announcing his diagnosis of "full-blown" AIDS: "I have known or rather suspected for five years so I'm fairly unruffled by it." He couldn't have really known as far back as 1984 since a test wasn't widely available until the following year; it's unlikely that he was even symptomatic then, since 1984 was such a busy, productive year. But he was obviously a prime candidate for a sexually transmitted disease.

Doris's approach to health and nutrition always had a New Age bent. He once tested positive for syphilis (or possibly gonorrhea; memories differ) and, skeptical of antibiotics, decided to cure himself with diet.

Publicity still for *Nightclub of the Living Dead*, 1986. *Left to right*:
Miss X, Doris, Sandelle, Phillip, and Tippi. Photo by Greg Foss.

But the health department monitored cases of venereal disease, and the letters he received demanding that he submit to treatment eventually turned into letters threatening his arrest. His friends were frustrated. "You can't cure syphilis with avocadoes!" Janice Sukaitis shouted at him. "Just get the shot, Doris," Ginger kept urging. Finally he did.

Sandelle described his constant cheerleading for natural foods, and X chimed in with an imitation: "There's no sugar in these cookies—they're sweetened entirely with juice!" When I went to interview Doris, I spotted the *International Journal of Holistic Health and Medicine* and the magazine *Australian WellBeing* on his coffee table. He sang the praises of wheatgrass juice and told me he ate no meat but lots of fruit—"If I'm going to overeat, I might as well overeat foods that are digestible."

This New Age gastronomy harmonized with the strain of hippie spiritualism that still ran strong in San Francisco. So did the Buddhist ideas that had attracted him since his adolescence. He came to see his obsession with drag in terms of reincarnation. "Every man was once a woman and every woman was once a man," he told an interviewer in 1985. "I think my personality is a mix of both sexes, and I'm happy with that." Phillip Ford rolled his eyes at much of what Doris told him but still listened. "She had very hard and sharp feelings about heaven. And that we choose this life, and everything that happens to you is because you've chosen it."

Doris's major sounding board on these matters was, perhaps not surprisingly, Mildred. Though he mocked her piety, he was also affected by her strong faith. He certainly took her views seriously enough to argue with them. "You don't have to worry about me!" he snapped in November 1983, in response to some unasked-for spiritual counsel. "My relationship with God is coming along nicely! You really must see that the theory of reincarnation is so much more sane and realistic than the Catholic religion, but at the same time it does not negate or deny any religion." Like his siblings, he could find Mildred exasperating, and he wasn't above dealing tough love. To a letter she sent in one of her depressed phases, he answered sternly, "I'm in no mood to commiserate with you—I just hope you've been able to get your friend God to help you! Don't be afraid to ask for his help." But more often he was warm and chatty, as in the letters filling her in on the New Age literature he was reading. After finishing Bruce Goldberg's *Past Lives, Future Lives* he was itching to find out about his own via hypnosis: "I'm too talented not to have been famous or highly creative in a past life."

But if it's unlikely that in 1984 Doris knew for certain he was infected, by 1986 it appears he had little doubt. The epidemic had been growing rapidly: the number of AIDS deaths in San Francisco had increased from 8 in 1981 to 534 in 1985 (nationally, from 130 in 1981 to 6,996 in 1985). "People were getting sick," Janice remembers, "and there was no name for the sickness, so we made believe that people weren't getting sick. But all of a sudden we knew something horrible was going to happen. I had a dream during that time. There was a big war, a world war, and I was left. The dream said, 'You're there to clean up'—I saw myself cleaning all this gray stuff. And I thought, *This is more than a dream. This is a prophecy.*"

One reason denial was easy, at least for some time, was that it was the federal government's position. President Ronald Reagan didn't say the word *AIDS* in public until September 1985, and then only in response to a reporter's question. The administration's foot-dragging—its lackadaisical approach to research and its reluctance to even acknowledge that a crisis was in the making—has been extensively and damningly documented. To cite a single revealing statistic: in the years 1985 and 1986 the City of San Francisco's AIDS budget exceeded the federal government's.

San Francisco distinguished itself not just from the feds but also from other cities—notably New York, where the indifference of the closeted Mayor Ed Koch and his administration gave rise to the theatrical protests of ACT UP. In San Francisco ACT UP never gained the same kind of traction, probably because there was less to protest. From the onset of the crisis, the city's politicians and health officials treated AIDS like the emergency it was. In 1982, when Harvey Milk's successor on the board of supervisors, Harry Britt, brought Mayor Feinstein his first AIDS funding proposal, she told him, "Fund everything." Paul Volberding, the physician who headed the AIDS team at San Francisco General Hospital, has recalled, "My staff and budget at the AIDS clinic doubled every year, and Feinstein didn't blink an eye."

During the 1980s, the city of San Francisco came together in a remarkable way—the whole city, not just public officials and the gay community (which isn't to say that there weren't angry arguments over some significant controversies, like the decision to close the bathhouses). Gay men and lesbians buried the hatchet over many of the issues that had been dividing them. It was an era of drawing up schedules for getting sick acquaintances to medical appointments, of dog walking and grocery shopping for the housebound, of answering phones at the new organizations that were emerging to serve the afflicted, and the volunteers were men and women, gay and straight.

Being gay in San Francisco was probably unlike being gay anywhere else during the crisis. "I still think that that was the golden period," Marc Huestis says. "The best of times, the worst of times. We came together as a community and created this whole system. We created institutions: the Shanti Project, Open Hand, the AIDS Emergency Fund. Part of our nature as gay people, I think, is nurturing." David Weissman, who codirected *The Cockettes*, made another very fine documentary in 2011, called *We Were Here*, about the city during this awful period, and the reaction he's received from many of the young gay men who have seen it has been surprising, or maybe not so surprising: "I wish I could have lived there then."

"A whole different kind of depth and compassion and wisdom started to come out of Doris in the context of the epidemic," David observes. "The first time I remember seeing it was the night of the Chuck Solomon party. Doris was hosting that, and was catty and tacky and bitchy, but in a way that was so indisputably inseparable from the fact that Chuck was dying."

As one of the principal creative forces behind Theatre Rhinoceros in the early '80s, Chuck Solomon had directed Sandelle in *Delivery* and Doris in *Torn Tulle*. He began getting sick, or sicker, during the run of *Naked Brunch*, and unlike many of those infected (including, initially, Doris), he was public about it. As Chuck's fortieth birthday approached, Marc had an idea: Why not combine the inevitable memorial with a birthday party, so that Chuck could enjoy it? "So many people thought it was morbid," David recalls. But gradually they embraced the idea, and so did Chuck.

It grew into an event for 350 of Chuck's colleagues, friends, and family members, with performances by, among others, the San Francisco Mime Troupe (to which he'd once belonged) and cast members of *The AIDS Show*, a collaboration of some twenty Theatre Rhino artists spearheaded by Leland Moss (who would later direct Doris onstage). The community was just starting to confront AIDS artistically. And so the party was a natural for Marc to film. *Chuck Solomon: Coming of Age* pays tribute to its subject's determination to find something of value in his diagnosis, to connect with family and friends, and to squeeze as much juice as he could out of every moment left to him.

Doris emceed the party on March 10, 1986, only four days after stepping off his flight back from Sydney, in a new look: Marie Antoinette, with a white panniered wedding-cake gown and a two-foot-tall hot pink wig. He was charming and drily funny as he addressed Chuck: "I would like to just say that, you know, it's very inspiring to us all, your commitment to living and chain-smoking." Sandelle came out in gold-sequined Marilyn drag and shimmied her way through a breathy "Happy Birthday, Mr. Director." Marc got it all on camera, zipping around to interview various guests.

Chuck Solomon's party became a turning point in the culture of the epidemic in San Francisco. "Marc crossed a boundary and really altered the way our community responded to death and dying," David maintains. The evening formed the template for the ever more elaborate predeath memorials and fundraisers that would culminate in Doris's own. At the close Chuck mounted the stage, moved and thrilled, to thank the crowd for one of the great nights of his life and to say, "You're all invited to my fiftieth birthday party!" drawing shouts and applause. He was dead before the end of the year.

CHUCK'S PARTY WASN'T THE ONLY REASON DORIS HAD NO TIME TO rest upon his return. "I was not prepared to find myself the subject of some controversy on my homecoming," he wrote in a letter that appeared in the *Bay Area Reporter*, San Francisco's most widely read gay newspaper, three days after the event. The *BAR's* letters column was and still is a combative community forum, and in Doris's absence the old anxiousness about drag queens had once again surfaced, this time in the context of the Gay Cable Network. One writer demanded, "Doesn't anybody have any pride [in] how the gay image is projected on television[?]" Another maintained that having Doris and Tippi report the news was "akin to having Aunt Jemima anchor the news of the black community! This type of programming undermines all of our efforts and merely strengthens every negative image held against us by the straight community."

Doris noted in his reply that he did not, in fact, read the news on GCN, and then he drew himself up:

> I am not interested in acceptance from . . . the "straight community" if it means I have to pretend to be something I am not. What is the point of our years of struggle if people who present a "negative image" are to be hidden and excluded from our community media and from their full rights as citizens of this planet? Freedom and equality are not just for those who present a positive image. They are for all.

He said much the same thing when a very hyper Phillip interviewed him (as a blonde with mint-green doughnut earrings and deep-tan back-from-the-beach foundation) on his return to the Gay Cable Network. Referring to the recent censures, Phillip asked, "Do you feel that you have a social responsibility towards the gay community?" Doris answered evenly,

> Yes, I think so. But "to thine own self be true" is the first thing, and once you get that taken care of, social responsibility just comes from that. Now, the gay community is not made up of any one particular

type of person, and I can't represent everybody. But I think everybody must realize that we are a very, very diverse mix of people, and you can't just have acceptance for one type of person within that gay community. There has to be acceptance for all of us, even the misfits.

If his argument seems obvious today, it was radical then. The Castro was starting to emerge from the conformity of jeans and flannel shirts that marked its clone period, and Doris, who'd never thought of himself as political, had been cast as a spokesperson for diversity.

He and Phillip discussed the difference between the "political roots" of the New York and San Francisco pride parades and the "party roots" of the Sydney one, though they agreed that holding a parade was a political act in itself. In later shows, Tippi joined Doris as cohostess. But their enthusiasm for GCN had begun to wane, and soon their routines were pushing the bottom edge of irreverence:

DORIS: I don't think there's anybody really watching out there, you know.

TIPPI: They are too watching! Why, the producer says we get hate mail every single week!

DORIS: Oh yes, that's right. And who do they hate most?

TIPPI: And now presenting Phillip R. Ford with "That's San Francisco"!

Harking back to Doris and Jackie's snarky introductions at Cabaret Conspiracy, they heaped derision on the people they were bracketing: "Well, this next segment's probably going to be pretty boring for you all." "Thank you for your movie review. Oh, how we appreciate having you on the show blah blah blah." "If you're still tuned in and you didn't throw up during that interview . . ."

What finally did them in was one of Doris's lesbian jokes. Doris had been needling his detractors with politically incorrect effrontery since his days with Sylvia and the Synthetics. In the autumn, after ten months on the show, he finally went too far. There's no knowing whether he intentionally got himself fired—as I suspect—but it happened on camera, and John Canalli, who wasn't without his own sense of theatricality, retained the segment and edited it for maximum drama (or comedy). Doris and Tippi are seated in their cohosts' chairs, Doris in a grasshopper-green knit top pulled over giant torpedo breasts. ("The director said he thought I was a little flat last time.") At some point he begins fondling them obscenely and licking his lips: "This is for the lesbians!"

> JOHN'S VOICE: Cut! Forget it! Forget it. I can't. No. Uh-uh.
> DORIS (*to Tippi*): I thought it was really funny.
> JOHN'S VOICE: It's not. It didn't work.

Cut to the very same chairs, now filled by two hunky guys who announce, "Doris and Tippi couldn't be with us tonight." They were the show's new cohosts. Doris and Tippi had walked off the set and off the program.

DORIS MUST HAVE FELT TIME BREATHING DOWN HIS NECK. "SHE really accelerated," Phillip says, "when she realized the clock was ticking." Shortly after the party for Chuck Solomon, Doris and Phillip hosted an Oscars benefit for Frameline, the organization that runs what was then called the San Francisco International Lesbian and Gay Film Festival. He and Tippi did *Nudies Go Berserk*, a two-woman show in July and August; one of the routines was a five-minute *Valley of the Dolls* with Tippi as Neely O'Hara and Doris as everybody else. On August 6 they joined Tommy and Lulu (as Lucy) for a show in honor of Lucille Ball's seventy-fifth birthday. Doris did Lulu's makeup—it must have been easy, since he'd done Lucy himself on a 1984 card. Their animosity had waned.

It was a busy year for everyone. In March, Silvana, X, and Tippi performed Tennessee Williams's one-act *Hello from Bertha* at Theatre Rhino. In the fall, Tippi entered the *Chronicle*'s Barbie look-alike contest, choosing the circa 1960 "Solo in the Spotlight" Barbie, in a tight black sheath with a tulle zhuzh from the knees down. The *Chronicle* wasn't about to award first prize to a drag queen, but it did give her more attention than anybody else. "I'm la la years old," she told the reporter. "My hair is an unnatural color." She said that she had close to fifty Barbies and a subscription to *Barbie* magazine, that she admired Barbie's "stacked figure" ("I'm built more like a stringbean"), and that sometimes she went downtown to look at Barbie in shop windows.

On June 5 they all participated in a mock runway show, *Dragon Ladies and Their Fashions*. Doris emceed as Marie Antoinette, and the usual crew played such notables as Evita Peron (Tippi in the gold sheath), Jacqueline Kennedy (Sandelle in a pink suit), Safia, wife of the Libyan dictator Muammar al-Qaddafi (Janice, trailing bloody baby dolls and jabbering a gibberish Arabic that got her booed), and Raisa Gorbacheva (Silvana, who yanked off his wig to reveal a bald post-Chernobyl scalp). But the show belonged to Tommy Pace as Imelda Marcos. After Ferdinand Marcos had been deposed in February and the couple had fled the Philippines by helicopter, en route to Hawaii, an angry mob had breached Malacañang Palace and discovered the thousands of pairs of shoes she had left behind. At once she became a world symbol of vile excess and a hero to drag queens everywhere. Tommy's Imelda had a black beehive, a flowing multicolored caftan, and a heavy Filipino lilt that today would probably be considered beyond the pale:

DORIS: Imelda, honey, there's been a lot in the media about—

IMELDA: *Don't ask me about the pucking shoes!* All I can find in Hawaii are *platporm plipplops!*

DORIS: It must have been quite frightening leaving your country.

IMELDA: I thought we were going shopping! If I'd known, I would hab jumped out of dat whirlybird!

DORIS: I know that not only are you a famous beauty, but you're also a talented singer.

IMELDA: I'll sing you some!

He launched into a medley of "My Punny Balentine," "Peber," and "Like a Birgin." Mere description can't capture what may have been the funniest five minutes I've ever spent in a theater. The audience was beside itself. Alas, there's no tape—John Canalli, who was in charge of the video camera, forgot to press the Record button. (The dialogue quoted above comes from the script.) Poor John: Those queens never much liked him, and when they found out about his goof they were livid. I have to admit that I've always held it against him myself, though he's been dead since 1992, yet another casualty of AIDS.

The show was a fundraiser for Marc's movie. When *Chuck Solomon: Coming of Age* came out a few months later, Doris's role turned out to be more potent than anyone who'd seen him wisecracking from the dais at the party could have predicted. Marc had taken the camera into the dressing room, shooting into the mirror as a wigless, shirtless Doris painted his lips. At first he jokes—"The thing I liked about Chuck was that he agreed with everything I suggested"—but gradually he turns thoughtful:

Well, most people think the AIDS diagnosis is "That's it" and they say goodbye, but it's not really. It can be really quite a fantastic thing, and I think in Chuck's case it certainly is. And I think, however long he lives—and he seems to think he's not going to live forever (I suppose none of us will)—but he looks like he's making incredible things out of these last times, and we're all getting to share it. So that's something fantastic, isn't it? I mean, any of us can be knocked over in a car tomorrow, and I wouldn't have said goodbye to anybody. So I think that's actually, we can look at it from the positive side from that point of view. And life goes on. Even if you're dead you still exist, so it's not as if he's not going to exist anymore. And everybody will meet again somewhere, sometime in the universe. So I mean, it's just really a passage from one existence to another. It's a sad goodbye, but it's not forever.

The poet Aaron Shurin, who was also onstage that night, discerned "a certain gravitas" from Doris at the event, but it wasn't until he saw

Marc's movie that he fully perceived the extent to which Doris was "so deep and so rich and so grounded." Doris may not have fully perceived it himself. There are people who are flattened by catastrophe, and others who, when the historical moment arrives, rise to meet it. Aaron compared Doris to Harvey Milk, who hadn't really impressed him—"until the last time I saw him give a speech at Civic Center, when he was mesmerizing and courageous and *huge*. I thought, *He's changed. History has fed him and lifted him up and altered him.* I felt that about Doris, too—that she had changed, and San Francisco had changed her and deepened her."

The summer's big event, on two weekends in late June, was *The Happy Hour Celebrity Backyard Barbecue and Pool Party* at Club 181. The show was as sloppy as its predecessors, but this time the writing showed a real advance in terms of character. The Happy Hour Dancers were now also the beleaguered flunkies of the imperious Ms. Fish and of the alcoholic Mr. Ford, who had acquired a new vice: womanizing. Tippi and Sandelle had to fight him off. The show may be best remembered for Doris's first rendition—that I know of, anyhow—of Shirley Bassey's histrionic "This Is My Life." Honing what was by then an established drag queen routine, he whirled in a white caftan and then braked with his arms spread, turning into a screen for slide-projected images of his many looks as Bassey wailed, "This is my life, and I don't give a damn!" Even at that point the number meant more than it could have in prior years—by then probably everyone in the audience knew someone who was sick. It was a show-stopper every time he did it.

That summer, Phillip also completed a video teaser for *Vegas in Space*. It begins with Doris in a red Lilli Ann suit and Phillip in a green blazer and lavender ascot speaking to the camera at their most mock-sincere. After commending the movie as "easy-to-understand, no-hidden-meaning entertainment," they make their pitch: "Although very near completion, we are circulating this sneak preview to encourage persons like yourself to consider this fantastic and unique investment opportunity." Seven well-chosen minutes from the movie follow.

Earlier in 1986 I had proposed my profile of Doris to *Image*, the Sunday magazine of the *Examiner*. He was a timely subject, since his celebrity was growing but many people who now recognized his name weren't quite sure what he did. Somewhat hesitantly, the editors agreed. Although the *Examiner* was a gay-friendly paper, drag was still a touchy subject even in the gay community, and elsewhere it produced mainly bewilderment. Though attitudes toward gay people were changing, it seemed possible they were changing for the worse. Only that June the Supreme Court had handed down its ruling in *Bowers v. Hardwick*, upholding the right of the states to criminalize gay sex. With AIDS climbing to epidemic proportions, much of the public now saw homosexuals as disease vectors. But all the AIDS news was also having another, more positive effect, and not just because it was bringing gay life into public consciousness. The stories were often moving accounts of people dying tragically young. It was hard to read them without a lump in your throat (even in the stuffy *New York Times*, which in 1986 was still refusing to let its writers use the word *gay*). The ranting of the bigots, and the shouting of the antibigots in response, were drowning out a quieter advance. All of which is to say that the *Examiner*'s willingness to run a long story, with photographs, in its Sunday magazine about a personality as off the wall as Doris was more than an editorial blip.

I interviewed Doris, Tippi, X, and Sandelle, plus Marc Huestis and Randy West. I didn't talk to or even mention Phillip, I assume because, after seeing him onstage, I wanted nothing to do with him. It all went smoothly until the day the *Examiner* had arranged a photo shoot at Oak Street. A distressed Doris phoned me to ask if there was anything I could do about the photographer, who had set up her equipment to create the kind of high-contrast glare that exaggerates every line and shadow. Tippi, who knew lighting, had locked herself in her room and wouldn't come out. It was clear that the paper had decided to make them look like freaks. If it was taking a risk by running a story about drag queens, it was also shielding itself by looking at them askance.

The article came out on Sunday, August 17, and the opening portrait of Doris, in a flowing gold gown, gold opera-length gloves, and a blonde bouffant, is one of my least favorite pictures of him. It doesn't make him look like a man—his makeup is too canny for that—but it does make him look like a woman on the other side of fifty. (He had just turned thirty-four.) And that wasn't all. At the last minute my nervous editors chopped out my few references to prostitution without telling me.

Whatever its flaws, though, Doris was pleased. He sent a copy to Ace, bragging that the Sunday paper was "probably read by about 1 million people!* I'm now quite famous—the next step is to get rich." To one of his nieces he reported, "The reaction has been quite good. I've raised my fee for performing from $100 to $300!" A month later another profile appeared in the *BAR*, adding heat to this burst of fame. It was gratifying and potentially lucrative, but—what to do with it?

"The problem," Phillip later told me, "was that Doris didn't have an act. People started calling for her to do things, but they didn't know what she did." Doris hardly knew himself. He fully believed he was at the head of a march into the future, but that future hadn't arrived, and so the opportunities he might have taken advantage of today weren't available. "We all thought that Doris should have her own—blank," Phillip continued. "Now we could say her own Comedy Central program or her own Fox show that will last for six months. Back then we didn't know what." Simply put, Doris was ahead of his time. No one could foresee the extent of the shift that was coming. In 1986, the admiration of drag that would begin, in only a few years, with RuPaul's rise to national fame seemed as inconceivable as the legalization of same-sex marriage.

THE HIGH POINT OF 1986 CAME ON TWO WEEKENDS IN OCTOBER, when the troupe mounted the finest of all their shows. The venue was

---

* He wasn't exaggerating: the morning *Chronicle* and the afternoon *Examiner*, though separately owned, published a joint Sunday edition that went to subscribers of either paper throughout the Bay Area.

once again Club 181. At the end of that summer's *Happy Hour*, Phillip had ad-libbed, "Come back for *Nightclub of the Living Dead* around Halloween time!" The title, he claims, just popped into his head. Like *Vegas in Space*, it proved to be a fertile one. They all wrote the show together, but Doris's fingerprints are the ones most evident.

In the baroque plot, the famous Doris Fish has had a nervous breakdown after getting fired from the nationally broadcast *Happy Hour Show*. Phillip, Tippi, and Sandelle, jubilant to be free of her, are boozing it up on their way to Las Vegas when Tippi crashes their car. Lights up on a strange club where the dazed crash victims wander in, to weird theremin-like music, followed by the imposing Big Brenda:

PHILLIP, SANDELLE, TIPPI: Doris!

PHILLIP: What are you doing here? We thought you were in the nuthouse!

BRENDA: Oh no, my dears. I'm not Doris. Why, people often mistake me for someone they left behind.

SANDELLE: But you look so much like Doris Fish.

BRENDA: That's a funny kind of a name for a woman.

PHILLIP: She was a funny kind of woman!

BRENDA: Well, she must have been extremely beautiful!

PHILLIP, SANDELLE, TIPPI: Wellll . . .

BRENDA: You know, Florence Ballard still thinks I'm Diana Ross!

Then begins the evening's entertainment: a revue featuring long-dead camp icons—Silvana as Tallulah Bankhead, Miss X as Joan Crawford, and Tommy as Billie Holiday, phenomenal once again. His junked-out Billie wanders past the mike, nods out, scratches, nearly falls over, and slurs out an introduction to "Town Without Pity": "This song was written aftuh Ah died. But Ah like it anyway. And uh. Hit it, mothuhfuckuh." Even more than with his Imelda, he was pushing the bounds of racial humor in a way that I doubt would be allowed today, though, with his superb voice and his gift for mimicry, he sounded hauntingly like the real thing. After the song, Billie crosses the stage to Doris's Brenda and gripes, in the plaintive nasality of an '80s Valley Girl, about the clueless new people perceiving her as Black: "Don't they know that, like, you know, Black and white are just, like, relative concepts that have nothing to do with life on this plane?"

Though *Nightclub of the Living Dead* had the contours of the usual clownish drag show, it was more than that, as Tommy's weird pivot hints. And you could feel it. Phillip pointed out to me that the story Doris came up with was very much a manifestation of his spiritual beliefs—about heaven and the afterlife, filtered through his Catholic upbringing (it's set in Limbo); about reincarnation (Brenda's subjects are there to prepare for their next roles on earth); and about seeing the reality you want to see (hence Brenda's crack about Florence Ballard and Diana Ross, and Billie Holiday's line about "relative concepts"). Phillip continued, "Life is eternal and we don't die; we just change form." He noted the emphasis on the concept of karma, "whereby we're not punished for our sins: our sins, in and of themselves, *are* our punishment. Our sins are our shortcomings—greed, self-centeredness." Doris had taken the cartoon personalities they'd been developing in their shows and turned them into components of, as Phillip called it, a morality play.

Nightclub of the Living Dead was a pinnacle. Unlike most of the group's other shows, it was tight and well rehearsed. The actors were generally in very pale makeup, befitting the dead, and their costumes were splendid: Silvana wore a black-and-white evening gown that evoked Charles James, Miss X wore a caped satin ivory sheath that had started life as a sheet set but looked magnificent under the lights, and Janice (as Doris's servant) wore an astonishing black-and-pink petticoated outfit that fully exposed her pastied breasts. Doris's set, on which, for example, the Wheel of Misfortune revolves to reveal, on its reverse, a golden toilet containing a telephone that Brenda uses to talk to Satan, was perhaps his cleverest. The metaphysical underpinnings gave the show a coherence—more important, a *feeling* of coherence—that was new.

It seems obvious now, though it wasn't at the time, that *Nightclub of the Living Dead* was also an acknowledgment of what was on everybody's mind even if not everybody was talking about it. Janice re-members a bit of stage business that she and Tommy shared: "I had to take off his glove or something. I pulled the sleeve of his dress up too high and I saw those KS lesions on his arm, and he quickly pulled it down and looked at me like, *Don't you dare ask me.* But we knew." Everybody knew, on some level. The season of death was underway.

11

COUPLES

A S THE CAST OF *NIGHTCLUB OF THE LIVING DEAD* WERE polishing their macabre roles, they received a macabre piece of news: Jane Dornacker was dead.

Doris had first met Jane at the Tubes' Talent Hunt, when she was already an adjunct member of the band. She and the Sluts had stayed in touch since she had joined them in *Blonde Sin* at the start of the decade. They went to one another's shows, and she sometimes got them gigs, though since she was a single mother with her own career they seldom spent much time together. She was popular around town and had found an offbeat job as a helicopter "trafficologist," adding some wit to radio reports of freeway backups. Late in 1985 she moved to New

Bob and Tippi, Valentine's Day 1989. Photo by Greg Foss.
Courtesy of the Louise Lawrence Transgender Archive.

York to do the same thing for a radio station there. In April 1986 the helicopter she was reporting from crashed into the Hackensack River, but she managed to swim to safety. It took some time for her to work up the nerve to get back in the air. On October 22, in the middle of a broadcast, her copter crashed again, this time into the Hudson River, and she drowned. (Horribly, you can hear her last, frantic words—"Hit the water! Hit the water! Hit the water!"—on YouTube.)

The sold-out memorial in late November, a benefit for her teenage daughter, featured seventy-nine performers at the cavernous War-field Theatre on Market Street.* In introducing Jerry Garcia and other members of the Grateful Dead (Deadheads filled the balcony with pot smoke), Bill Graham, the rock impresario, called it, accurately, an only-in-San Francisco event. There were performances by members of the erstwhile Jefferson Airplane, Todd Rundgren, Boz Scaggs, Paula Poundstone, and the locally famous stripper Carol Doda. The Tubes played house band, and Jane's Leila and the Snakes partner, Pearl E. Gates—now Pearl Harbour—flew in from London to perform one of their old numbers, a Hula-Hoop spinning around her bare midriff.

It was a career high for the Sluts, who had never shared the stage with such an illustrious crew. They arrived in drag and struck poses for the news cameras out front. When a reporter asked, "Isn't this an exciting night for you?" Doris responded, "Well, I can only say what Jane always said to the audience: 'You think I'm up here for you. That's not the case at all. *You're* actually there for *me*.'" They had the luxury of their own dressing room, which they needed for several costume changes.

They did Jane's "Drag Queen," of course, and joined in several numbers, taking center stage on her mildly obscene "Señor Jalapeño." ("First you hear them moan / Then you hear them shout / It's too hot! Take it out!") The nearly four-hour show "ran like clockwork," the *Chronicle* reported, "building splendidly to a finale where the entire cast assembled

---

* A second show on the following evening included Robin Williams and Whoopi Goldberg.

to sing the Leila and the Snakes anthem 'Rock and Roll Weirdos'"—
the number that Jane had written a decade earlier on the night before
Doris and Pearl won the Tubes' Talent Hunt.

A FEW DAYS LATER, DORIS LEFT FOR AUSTRALIA. THIS TIME, ON
what would be his longest trip back between his departure and his
death, he stayed until spring 1987. My guess is that, with thoughts of
mortality swirling, he wanted time to spend with friends and especially
family. "You may see more than an hour of me!" he promised Ace. Once
again the Mills clan spent Christmas down the coast at Marianne and
Tony's house near Merimbula, Doris happily surrounded by nieces and
nephews.

Ron Smith, who had succeeded Peter Tully as artistic director of
the Mardi Gras workshop, had spent much of the previous year cleaning up after the deluge of 1986, which had dissolved everything. His
ambition was to produce a waterproof parade; his solution was molded
plastic. The theater production facility at the Australian Broadcasting
Corporation had giant vacuum molds: "I modeled some giant gems,
some smaller gems—and then the shoes, of course, the shoes!"

The shoes were the fruit of a clever observation of Jackie's that the
waterlogged Divine—a fifteen-foot-tall puppet of John Waters's obese
drag star, with a carved sponge head, tulle wig, and crimson gown—
looked like Imelda Marcos. Ron loved the idea. Hence the high heels,
dozens of them, each one more than a meter long, devised for myriad
groups and individuals to customize with their own wild designs—
exactly the kind of community endeavor that Tully had envisioned
and Ron lived to foster. Doris was captivated. He took charge of transforming the sodden Divine into Imelda, cloaking her in an enormous
hibiscus-print muumuu with puffed pink sleeves and gold gloves.

For his own part he decided to forgo a float that year and, true to
his "bigger is better" aesthetic, see just how big he could take the Marie
Antoinette drag he had debuted at Chuck Solomon's party. He would
walk on stilts encased in fiberglass molds of black-and-white-stockinged

legs atop ruby pumps. His pink-satin-and-white-crinoline skirt, orna-mented with jumbo jewels in molded plastic, took six people to lift onto him; his hot-pink wig, anchored on a motorcycle helmet, was a meter high and topped with more jewels plus a glittering miniature of the Fishmobile.

Both Imelda and Marie Antoinette were sensations. One of Imelda's gloved hands, held up on a pole by a puppeteer, dabbed at a tear as she reached with the other for the dozens of fantastical heels—they, too, held aloft by marchers—floating just beyond her grasp. Doris's colossal Marie Antoinette, nearly as tall as Imelda, waved regally from among a forest of meter-wide gems raised, like Imelda's shoes, on long poles. Both of the tableaux have attained the status of Mardi Gras legend.

But Marie Antoinette was another almost-disaster. The puppet maker who crafted Doris's fiberglass legs, Ron says, "had *no* idea about costume. Each of them was as heavy as a *heavy* suitcase." And once Doris was perched on top of them, he couldn't see his stilts under the enormous dress or where they were going—and this back in the era when the parade was still largely unmarshaled, much of the crowd milling in the street. Ron ran ahead, kicking beer cans and bottles out of the way. The route, from the Art Gallery of New South Wales to the Sydney Showground, covered some three miles, much of it uphill. Doris made it all the way without toppling. When it was over he had to change outfits quickly for the postparade party, where he was to compere the costume contest; a crew helped him out of the huge frock. "When the legs came off," Ron says, "the fiberglass was awash with blood. They had sawed into his legs, and the whole way a frozen smile, waving to the crowd. He just pulled black tights on over the blood, went straight into the party, and was onstage for an hour and a half."

Doris stayed in Sydney for another month in order to host the Gemmys, the awards for Mardi Gras excellence. The ceremony took place on the last Friday in March at Kinsela's, a gay bar near the site of the old Roxy on Taylor Square. He shared the stage with the Showbags, a much-loved trio consisting of Miss 3D, Twistie, and Cindy Pastel,* and wrote the bitchy script. ("Showbags? Scumbags! Douchebags!") And he reprised "This Is My Life," with the slide show of his multifarious looks projected onto his white caftan. Miss 3D pronounced it "a very moving and enlightening audiovisual presentation of her favorite subject."

NEITHER DORIS NOR TIPPI HAD HAD A SERIOUS ROMANTIC relationship in the years since Bernard Fitzgerald and Tom Faulkenbery. To some extent they fulfilled the mutual need that, in a conventional couple, lovers might have—although since both of them were so guarded, it's hard to know exactly what their intimacy was like. Doris had played a big role in encouraging Tippi to blossom from an effeminate boy into the quintessence of femininity she had become. Anyone who knew her could see the fragility, and Doris watched her with a maternal eye, but that didn't mean he kept her on a short leash. Tippi had always had boyfriends, though she tended to be tight-lipped about them. There was Mr. Natural, the big bearded guy she sold roach clips with in Berkeley, and Tom, and, in Sydney, the unseen Mr. Whippy. X recalls that during the Oak Street era she had regular beaux, one in particular: "She'd go out walking after a show, in drag, and he'd find her and pull over in his little sports car. They never even knew each other's names. He was 'James Bond' and she was 'Marilyn Monroe.' That went on for years. Needless to say, none of us ever met him."

They did meet Stanley, or at least they knew who he was, since he co-owned a chain of video stores and put Tippi to work in one of them, although she claimed to be incompetent. During the filming of *Vegas in Space* Doris noted wryly that after shooting till dawn three nights

---

* *Showbag* is an Australian term for the swag bags handed out at fairs. In the 1994 movie *The Adventures of Priscilla, Queen of the Desert*, the Hugo Weaving character—the drag queen with a young son—was modeled on Cindy Pastel.

in a row they were shutting down "because Tippi has to go to her four-dollar-an-hour job." Later on Tippi regarded Stanley with bitterness, evidently because she thought he had given her HIV.

Shortly after Doris's departure for Sydney, probably in December or January, Miss X and Tippi, still in costume from a West Graphics shoot, attended a party at Project Artaud, the roomy Mission District performance space where the Plasworld sequence of *Vegas in Space* had been filmed. Bob Davis, a lanky, bespectacled composer who taught music at City College of San Francisco, was there, too, because he had written the music for a play that was being performed at Project Artaud. Bob was also a straight or straight-identified cross-dresser, fascinated by all things feminine, including Tippi. "I knew who she was," he told me. He had seen her in the *Happy Hour* shows. "I went over and I said, 'Could I get you a drink?' trying to be a gentleman. She said, 'No.' And that was it.

"And then I could not get Tippi out of my mind. For weeks. I phoned my friend Magenta Mason, a seamstress who had made costumes for the Sluts, and said, 'Magenta, what do I do?' Magenta phoned Tippi with this 'I know a boy who likes you'—it was just like high school—and then finally, after a conversation or two, I was given Tippi's number and I phoned her."

Despite her ingrained wariness, she must have been flattered, since she invited Bob to a casino-themed party that Phillip, X, and Sandelle were throwing at their flat on 18th Street. The date was February 28, 1987. (I was there, too, and noted it in my diary.) Bob was glad, if uncomfortable, since the only person he knew was Silvana, but he lingered hopefully. As the hour drew late, two women discovered that their fur coats had disappeared. Someone quickly fingered the probable culprits. Bob joined the posse. As they waited—and waited—in the car outside the thieves' home, everyone else nodded off. Finally Bob saw the two guys come bouncing up the street, happy in their new coats. He got out and confronted them, and as the others emerged from the car, he warned them, "They're *really angry.*" They handed over the coats meekly, and he returned to the party a hero.

He stayed on. At one point he overheard Ginger asking, "Who *is* this guy?" At the end of the evening Tippi allowed him to take her home to Oak Street and, much to Ginger's surprise, up to her bedroom. The sun was coming up when he left.

Tippi later told Bob that had Doris been in town it probably wouldn't have happened. What she meant, I think, was that she herself wouldn't have allowed it to happen. And although Bob was quickly absorbed into their circle (he eventually did the sound design for *Vegas in Space* and worked on several stage shows), he, like Tom, always perceived Doris as a rival, and rightly: he knew where Tippi's loyalty lay.

Still, he and Doris remained cordial. The three of them watched a lot of TV together. Bob remembers one evening when Tippi had left the room for something—"We heard Tippi's heels go click click clicking down the hall"—and as she was returning Doris threw his arms around him and said, 'Bob wants to be with me now, because you're too much of a sissy!'" They all laughed. "But," Bob says, "what fascinated me about Tippi *was* that she was such a sissy. That *is* what I was attracted to."

Tippi understood, all too well. Probably because of bad experiences with previous lovers who'd wanted nothing to do with her maleness, she would never let him see her undressed (though she loved for him to be), which didn't prevent them from making love constantly. It was like having sex, he says, "with a sylph or a fairy or an angel." So much of her, he says now, "was wrapped up in the idea of who she wanted people to *see* she was, feeling a horrible disconnect with who she physically was." That was one reason she loved performing: when she was onstage, the roles were defined.

Tippi had a touchy relationship with her audience. She loved the applause, in the theater. But once she was on the street, she wanted nothing to do with her fans. It was hard enough just to let in a few friends. ("I can't stand living with me," she said when I interviewed her for my Doris story, "so for other people it must be even more difficult.") She had been terrified of people since childhood, and with good reason: no man as girlish as Tippi is safe from violence. I imagine she would have jumped at surgery had she been able to afford it, but it was less common then, and she was happy enough to call herself a drag queen in solidarity with Doris and Miss X, even though she was a very different creature. Unlike them, she didn't like to be seen when she was out of costume because she didn't accept her body.

For quite a while she was like that with Bob, too. It was hard for him to make her trust the durability of his affection. "You don't shave the day before a big performance," he told me, "and I can still remember her saying, 'Don't kiss me!' It took me a long time to convince Tippi that our relationship was past that." Only toward the end did he succeed. Among her effects is an off-the-cuff note in her childlike handwriting that hints at the snugness she found with him:

Bob,

Hi Honey! Thank you for Letting me come over today. I had a really lovely time. I watched "Key Largo" in the Big sunny room.

Mmm, the cranberry bread was lovely.

I took the Liberty of watering some of your plants. I hope you don't mind.

Lunch was swell, thanks Honey.

I love you
Tippi

Meanwhile, as Bob and Tippi were finding each other, X and Sandelle's romance was drawing to a close. Sandelle wanted to go to Los Angeles and find out if she could scorch the screen the way she burned up a stage. X had lived in LA and hated it. Their rapport deteriorated. He moved out of the bedroom and into what had been the drag room. "It was OK," he says—"but no, it was awful." Tippi told Bob that she would have X crying on her left shoulder and, an hour later, Sandelle crying on her right. Finally Sandelle left the 18th Street flat, though she wouldn't move to LA for several years yet.

DORIS'S NOTORIETY WAS WELL ENOUGH ESTABLISHED BY 1987 THAT in June TV stations in Pittsburgh and Baltimore flew him out to appear on their daytime talk shows—more evidence that the culture was advancing. Now drag was worth the attention of Middle America. The stations wanted good, which is to say scandalous, TV, and they had no reason to regret their invitations. Doris handled both appearances nimbly, winning over studio audiences who had probably never before seen a drag queen in the flesh.

The host of *Pittsburgh 2Day*, Jon Burnett, was flummoxed at first. Who wouldn't have been? Doris walked onto the set clad in the metallic red-fringed halter top from the movie's finale, a tight fringed purple skirt, cobalt-blue opera-length gloves, gold platforms, and grapefruit-size gold-and-amethyst earrings under a teased blonde wig. But he put everyone at ease with his calm intelligence, his wit (Burnett: "Have you ever had anybody who's just wanted to flat haul back and cold-cock you?" Doris: "Well, not *cold*-cock . . ."), and above all his obvious happiness with the outrageous identity he'd created. Though he was jokey at first, he showed his reflective side, too—"People think that there are two sexes, male and female, and that's just a little too hard and sharp." And he talked about the thrill of becoming a famous movie star: "You can have anything you want in life!" Burnett, who by this point had begun to enjoy the sparring, noted that this claim "might be just a bit of an exaggeration, much like your makeup" as he introduced a clip from *Vegas in Space*. But it was evident that Doris had charmed them all.

In Baltimore, on *People Are Talking*, he appeared alongside three local drag entertainers who, with their seemly outfits and their "it's just a job" arguments, were on a mission to convince viewers that what they did was perfectly normal. Doris, who was dressed like a streetwalker, was the sole clown. When the host inquired, "On the street will you be men or women?," he jumped in with "We'll be men or women, yes!" As the celebrity queen from San Francisco he had something of an air of visiting royalty, and his humor gave the show's dull plea for tolerance what buoyancy it had. The other queens were friendly, though, and, in the case of Miss Gay America (who sang "The Impossible Dream" with no hint of irony), talented. The audience, which looked like it had been bused in from nearby farming communities, was again enthusiastic.

Later that June the Sluts, minus Sandelle, put on a Sunday night show, *Box Office Poison*, at Lipps Underground, a basement club (Doris called it a root cellar) across the street from the film lab where Phillip worked—he'd struck up a friendship with the owner during his lunch breaks. The first part was a sketch that Phillip and Janice had written for themselves when Doris was in Sydney, about the disgraced televangelists Jim and Tammy Faye Bakker, the former a philandering con man and the latter a makeup addict as shameless as Doris; in fact, Doris had turned Janice into Tammy Faye for a West Graphics card. But Janice wound up backing out of the show, and Doris stepped in for her, lip-synching pop tunes about the Lord. In the second segment, Miss X, with help from Tippi, offered a motley set of songs, from Tammy Wynette to "My Way." Phillip closed with an Elvis impersonation that had started life in *Nightclub of the Living Dead*, when his character was doomed to "the lowest form of entertainment known to mankind."

Since Doris hadn't participated in either the preparation or the publicity, Phillip gave him a little less when he divvied up the minimal takings—"It was like twenty dollars versus thirty dollars"—and Doris quickly set him straight. "She said to me, 'They're not coming to this show because your name is on the postah. They're coming to this show because *my name is on the postah*. I am not a twenty-dollar act.' It was all quite nice, but educational. I said, 'Of course. I was wrong.'"

The reason Janice had defected was that she'd decided she needed to put her energy into caring for Tommy Pace. His illness was nearing a crisis stage, even though he was still refusing to acknowledge it. Marc Huestis recalls a day when Tommy dropped by the video store where Marc had a day job. "He was sweating like a pig. I looked him in the eye and said, 'Are you OK?' and he was like, 'Yeahyeahyeah, I'm fine, I'm fine.'" He told another friend that his lesions were flea bites from his cat. Janice says, "He was getting weird. I was interrogating him. He didn't want that. Finally Lulu and I confronted him: 'Please, we love you, we want to know what's wrong.' He goes, 'Mind your own business!'" But they wouldn't, and ultimately Tommy could no longer deny the obvious. Janice was disturbed by his resistance to even considering the protocols that various doctors were trying out on an experimental basis and that everyone else with AIDS, lacking any other hope for a cure, was desperate to get in on (even though some of them were producing effects that were arguably worse than the disease). "He decided that he was going to be holistic," Janice says. "He found this doctor in New York that would give you vitamin C shots."

In July Doris made a long-planned, long-delayed trip to Paris. Jackie and Thierry, he reported to Mildred, were "terribly sweet and kind" to him. In the evening he and Jackie went out in drag; during the daytime he would put on shorts and a T-shirt to cruise in the Parc des Buttes-Chaumont—"hot mountain butt," as Jackie likes to translate it. He took her along once, and she still shudders at the memory of "do-gooders handing out condoms from a basket like cigarette girls." Doris told her that he liked to find a group of men loitering in the bushes and start things off with the ugliest one; then everyone would join in and he could choose the plum. There was touring and culture, too, including a trip to Versailles, which became a new decorating inspiration.

In August the Sluts were back at Lipps for several more Sundays of a revamped show they now called *Who's Afraid of Box Office Poison?* Doris came up with some funny stand-up, including a routine about yearning for sainthood—"St. Doris Fish, I think it has a good ring to it!" The other addition, a bravura one, was a deranged reenactment of Richard Burton and Elizabeth Taylor in the opening of *Who's Afraid of Virginia Woolf?* Phillip played Burton's George, and Miss X and Tippi did Liz together in one giant dress—two heads, two arms, and four spidery (as Doris noted) legs—trading off lines, chomping on chicken parts, and swilling back drinks as the Incredible Two-Headed Martha.

THE YEAR'S MOST AMBITIOUS PROJECT WAS A PLUNGE INTO legitimate theater: the horror melodrama *The Bad Seed*, though it was really the 1956 movie version they loved. "We watched it so much," X recalls, "that we used to walk up and down the halls spouting off dialogue. Then we started to think, *This was* made *for us.*" As Phillip remembers it, "I said, 'Let's do this sometime.' And Doris said, 'No, we're going to do it *now.*'"

The source material, a 1954 novel by the Alabama-born writer William March, recounts the career of the eight-year-old serial killer Rhoda Penmark, mostly from the point of view of her wan, conventional mother, Christine. It isn't funny (not even unintentionally), but it does rest on a prankish foundation: the idea of turning the saccharine postwar view of children, and of American society in general, on its head. The iciness with which adorable little Rhoda dispatches her victims is salutary for anybody who grew up on *Father Knows Best*.

The popular playwright Maxwell Anderson turned March's eerie novel into a stagy melodrama, compressing the action onto an unlikely single set, and it was a success on Broadway. The 1956 Mervyn LeRoy film ignored March's much superior book and stuck to Anderson's turgid play, retaining the principal Broadway actors. Nancy Kelly had won a Tony as Christine Penmark, but onscreen she suffers nobly in the Joan Crawford mode, which is partly why the movie lives on as camp. Eileen Heckart is accomplished as the drunken, blowsy mother of a murdered boy. But the element that makes the picture hard to shake off is an indelibly evil performance by Patty McCormack, who was eight when she started playing Rhoda onstage and ten when the movie was made.

Tippi was thirty-five when she played Rhoda, but her age hardly worked against her. Mounting the play with drag queens brought the malevolent joke underlying March's vision into full view. And Tippi was mesmerizing. Her demeanor was already juvenile (Doris used to introduce her as "the oldest living child star in captivity"), and her impishness could shade into meanness, a side she'd drawn on to play Princess Angel in *Vegas in Space*. Plus she was tiny. "People like small people," Timmy Spence reflected when he was trying to put his finger on her popularity. "They're drawn to them. They want to help them"— which allowed the audience to savor Rhoda's fiendishness all the more.

The Mills siblings, 1984: Michael, Andrew, Liz, Doris, and Marianne. Courtesy of Andrew Mills.

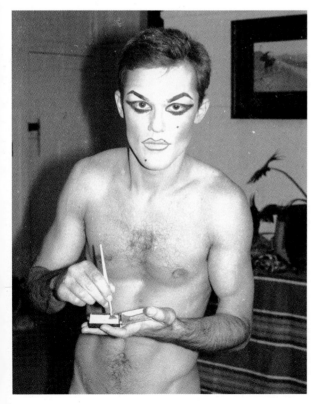

Doris preparing for a Cabaret Conspiracy show at Garibaldi's, Sydney, 1979. Photo by Eddy Hackenberg. Courtesy of the Australian Queer Archives.

Doris on the Fishmobile, with Mildred (crowned) and Jackie; Thierry Voeltzel, standing, in aquatic drag. Mardi Gras 1985. Photo by William Yang.

Doris, on stilts, as Marie Antoinette. Mardi Gras 1987. Courtesy of Ron Smith.

Doris donning Marie Antoinette's pumps, Mardi Gras 1987. Photo by Ron Smith.

The head of Fred Nile on a charger, Mardi Gras 1989. Photo by William Yang.

Impress Me! West Graphics, 1983.

You Know, If It's Not One Thing, It's Another. West Graphics, 1983.

CHRISTMAS? It's Just Another Excuse Not to Work! Doris, Tippi, Randy West, and Miss X. West Graphics, 1984.

Nine Planets in Seven Days, Never Again! Doris and Miss X. West Graphics, 1984.

Get Shit-Faced! West Graphics, 1983.

Free Leona and Zsa Zsa! Doris and Janice Sukaitis. West Graphics, 1989.

Self-portrait as a hippie chick, 1982.
Courtesy of Andrew Mills.

Mildred and Doris, with Doris's
paintings, at the opening of the art,
photography, and crafts exhibition,
Mardi Gras 1986.

Self-portrait at CBGB, 1979.
Courtesy of Johnny Allen.

Self-portrait with (left to right) Doris, Bob, Miss X, and Tippi, 1990. Photo by Glenn Bachmann.
Courtesy of the Louise Lawrence Transgender Archive.

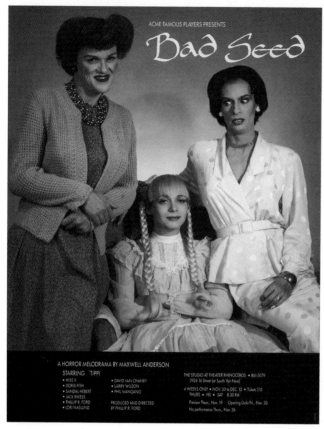

Poster for *The Bad Seed*, 1987.
Doris, Tippi, and Miss X. Photo
by Rico Schwartzberg. Courtesy
of Phillip R. Ford.

Poster for Doris's benefit, 1990. Photo by Steve Savage.

The poster was an instant classic: Miss X, genteel and alarmed, in the maternal role; Doris, dowdy and absurd, as the elderly neighbor; and the pigtailed, pinafored Tippi blandly radiating sweetness and malice. Once you'd seen it, you almost didn't need to see the show. But in fact it was the most successful one they ever put on in terms of attendance. Phillip had booked the forty-nine-seat basement space at Theatre Rhinoceros for four weeks in November and December; they wound up extending the run all the way into February—which is one reason Doris didn't return to Sydney for Mardi Gras in 1988.

Like *Nightclub of the Living Dead*, *The Bad Seed* looked unrelated, on the surface, to the epidemic. But its ghoulish fun had an edge that reflected the general anxiety. March's novel had come out at the height of the McCarthy era, and his implied critique of American sanctimony felt no less caustic in the Reagan era to an audience that saw itself as all but abandoned by its government and its fellow citizens. Maybe that's why the troupe, with Phillip directing, decided that the wisest approach was to play it straight—a first for them—and let the anarchy of drag speak for itself. Miss X toned down Nancy Kelly's histrionics; there were no laughs, either, in Sandelle's skillful rendition of the soused grieving mother.

Doris more than made up for their earnestness. As Monica Breedlove, the corpulent busybody who provides the one comic note in both the novel and the play, he was extraordinary. Years of transforming himself into frumps and scatterbrains for West Graphics had made him an expert at antiglamour. Mildred, now in her sixties, provided a helpful model, and he studied the older actresses on the then-popular sitcom *The Golden Girls* to master their stiffness. Obsessive, as always, about his makeup, he used light and dark shading to render the musculature of a sagging neck and painted liver spots on his hands and arms, all so convincingly that when A. P. Gonzalez, the cameraman from *Vegas in Space*, came backstage after the show, he gasped. He thought Doris was sick.

Doris *was* sick. His friends now think the liver spots, like the long gloves Tommy wore in *Nightclub of the Living Dead*, were there to mask the small lesions that had appeared on his body. He was also having throat problems, possibly caused by thrush, a yeast infection common in cases of immunosuppression, or by the onset of the esophageal ulceration that would later put him in agony. But since Monica rattled in the cracked tones of an old bag, if his voice was affected it wasn't apparent. And anyway, denial is a powerful force. Doris wasn't yet talking about his illness, and no one in his immediate circle wanted to even consider the possibility.

THERE MAY HAVE BEEN ONE EXCEPTION. THAT YEAR, 1987, AT THE Muscle System, a Castro gym familiarly known as the Muscle Sisters, Doris had met a man I'll call Maurice. He was of Mexican descent, with curly black hair, blue eyes, and caramel-colored skin, and had grown up Catholic, like Doris, in a small town in the far north of California. Soon they were an item. Words that tend to come up when people talk about Maurice are "gentle," "kind," and "quiet"; also "private." Among Doris's friends and family, he was liked more than he was known. Everyone was beyond pleased to see Doris in love.

The reason I'm using a pseudonym is that he adamantly didn't want to talk to me. He wouldn't respond to my letters and emails and phone messages, and when I finally did manage to get him on the phone, he snapped "That's too private" and hung up. Thus anything I say about Doris's relationship with him, it should be understood, comes from others, except for a few instances when Doris wrote about it himself. The side of Doris that Maurice and no one else saw will always remain veiled.

And so I don't know when Doris told him that he was seropositive, but it can't have been long after they started going out. For one thing, Doris was already feeling pangs over clients he had almost certainly infected; Maurice admonished him that he had to stop hooking. For another, by that point Doris appears to have been symptomatic. Among gay men the question of HIV status was then a basic one when you started a new relationship. A lot of men understandably didn't want to fall in love with someone who was about to get sick and die. For others, like Maurice, love was the only question, and either they didn't ask or they went in with their eyes open, not only to the inevitability (as we then thought) of death but also to the ghastliness of the decline that was going to precede it. In Maurice's few words on the phone I heard the remnant of wounds that, after decades, hadn't healed.

But for Doris and Tippi, Maurice and Bob came onto the scene like angels draped in clouds. They both had devoted friends who would soon enough have a chance to show their devotion; with or without lovers, neither of them would have died a lonely death. But love brought a special grace to the end of their lives.

Once Maurice got involved with Doris, he was unavoidably drawn into the glare of the spotlight. Even as Doris weakened, the pathological need for attention he joked about didn't. Maurice remained good-natured about it, but for him, especially when they were alone together, his lover's name was Philip, as it had been for Bernard. It was different for Tippi, who didn't have a male side; to Bob, and everyone else, she was always Tippi.

At first Maurice knew nothing about Philip's other identity. Then, after several dates, Doris invited him to Oak Street. The stairway that rose from the front door to the parlor floor was dominated by the fluorescent six-foot-by-six-foot self-portrait that Doris had painted as a billboard to promote *Fish for Christmas* in 1981. Maurice looked from the fantastic image to the man he was falling in love with, and he said, "That's *you*."

12

STILL ALIVE!

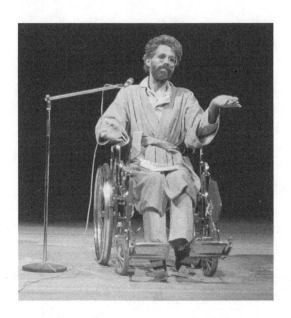

I T WAS DURING THE LATE '80S THAT THE HOSTILITY DIRECTED
against drag queens began softening into affection. Back in 1972,
Esther Newton had identified their potency, and thus their threat, in
the open celebration of homosexuality they represented. Since those
days the gay community had advanced light-years in terms of self-
confidence; now that it was being assaulted from one side by disease
and from the other by disease-fueled bigotry, it needed that spirit of af-
firmation. AIDS transformed the standing of drag queens in the community and, eventually, in the world. They went from being, depending
on your perspective, weirdos, public embarrassments, or misogynists

Rodney Price at *Gimme da Damn Money*, 1988. Photo by Daniel Nicoletta.

to keepers of the flame of gay culture, embraced for the courage it took them to be themselves. The erstwhile pariahs became heroes.

APART FROM A FEW ONE-NIGHTERS AT BARS AND AIDS BENEFITS, the first half of 1988, following the long run of *The Bad Seed*, was mostly quiet. Phillip, the movie still gnawing at him, retreated into the editing room. Tippi had Bob; X had his job at Lilli Ann. Doris, who was getting sicker, tended his spiritual garden, spent more and more time with Maurice, and grew closer to Tommy Pace.

KS lesions had bloomed across Tommy's body and over his face.* His nose was an eggplant, his ears two purple cauliflowers. He frightened strangers. "And Tommy was impeccable," Janice says. "He always dressed well. He always had a haircut. He was manicured." Disfigurement changed his personality. Lulu remembers the way Tommy reacted to the stares he got as they were leaving a movie: "Don't look at me! Don't look at me!"

Marc Huestis says, "People either go up or down when they die. And you never know what's going to happen. My mother, who was the biggest bitch in the world, mean and bitter and angry—she was really nice! I was like, *What happened?* And Chuck, of course. And then there were people like Tommy, who were horrors, absolute horrors."

Perhaps Tommy's explosiveness was the flip side of his genius for making people laugh. But no matter how vile he got, Janice and Lulu refused to let him push them away. He was more equable with Doris, who must have found comfort in talking to him frankly about his own symptoms. (Some friends, like X and Phillip, Doris never opened up to.) They were both into New Age spiritualism; they meditated together at the Zen Center and attended macrobiotic dinners there. Sometimes Doris would invite Janice, too—"I think because Tommy was being so mean to me"—and she would dutifully tag along despite

---

* Kaposi's sarcoma—KS—is a skin cancer, characterized by purple lesions, that had been largely unfamiliar before it became a common affliction of AIDS patients.

the boring programs and "these *awful* meals. Doris would act like she loved them. I would go, 'You want mine?'"

The inevitable benefit for Tommy took place on Saturday, July 2, at Project Artaud. Unlike Chuck's, it was open to the public; admission was free, but the flyer said, "Bring a checkbook." Tommy himself, in a flash of spleen, had come up with the title: *Gimme da Damn Money.* There was a lot of talent on that stage. Doris came on to deliver a bitchy-funny tribute before calling on "the ever so slightly youthful" Miss X and "the almost totally illiterate but still adorable" Tippi to join him in a fun fur–clad version of "Take Back Your Mink."

The showstopper, though, was Rodney Price, a founding member of the Angels of Light. Not everyone knew that Rodney had been diagnosed with AIDS the previous October, and when he rolled onstage in a wheelchair, dressed in pajamas and a bathrobe, bearded and shockingly thin, there was an audible gasp. He sang the new, darkly funny lyrics that Janice had written to Kurt Weill's "One Life to Live":

> You say I'm thinner
> Take me to dinner
> 'Cause I've got less time than you!

When he broke into a seated tap dance, using the footrests of the wheelchair, a roar went up. David Weissman, who had conceived the number with Rodney and Janice (and who captured it a couple of weeks later in a short film, *Song from an Angel*), remembers that people were "screaming and screaming. It was beautiful and moving and tragic."

David now looks back on the benefits of those years as an extension of the free drag shows and Angels of Light shows of an earlier era, when being in the audience made you feel like an insider and everybody was dressed to the nines: "That same spirit extended to these events so clouded by the tragedy underlying them: 'Everybody cool is here tonight!' You could feel the whole culture of free theatrical shows slowly dying, and on some level what was keeping it alive was the dying—this tradition was being revived to honor the dying."

There were video clips and a slideshow assembled by Daniel Nicoletta, the photo-historian of gay San Francisco, of Tommy mugging at home and in his many roles, including Billie Holiday and, of course, Imelda. At the end, Anne Block emerged, as she had before the intermission, to dun the audience for contributions. Her Arkansas accent has a fresh charm that made her a natural for this kind of appeal. Then the full cast assembled to lead the audience in "Red River Valley," a song Tommy had requested. As hundreds of voices joined in the corny old cowboy song, the lyrics took on a fresh poignance: "We will miss your bright eyes and sweet smile, / For they say you are taking the sunshine / That has brightened our pathways a while."

Tommy never appeared. Most of the audience assumed that illness was keeping him at home, but he was far up in the theater, watching alone, too mortified by his lesions to show his face.

The fundraiser took in more than $4,000, surpassing the organizers' hopes. The next day, David—who had done video tech for the show and then, uncharacteristically, donned a wig and a frock to join the cast onstage at the end—saw Tommy at a friend's house, and Tommy told him, "You know, I was looking down from the rafters and I thought, *Who is that ugly ugly ugly drag queen?* And then I realized it was you!"

He died a month later, on August 1. Rodney Price died on August 15.

THAT FALL, DORIS GOT HIS FIRST (AND LAST) DAY JOB IN YEARS working behind the counter at the vegetarian Green Gulch Grocery, an offshoot of the Zen Center close to the house on Oak Street. Between that gig and his continuing West Graphics work ("It's one job where older and uglier is a plus," he wrote Ace), he could put away enough to return to Sydney for Mardi Gras in the new year, and he was planning to bring Maurice.

And then, boom, a bolt of bad news: the owner of 422 Oak Street—a gay man who knew the state of Doris's health—announced that he was evicting them because he'd decided to sell the building. Ginger found a small apartment nearby, where he still lives. But the timing was hard on Doris, since it meant that he was simultaneously planning his trip and managing his illness and organizing rehearsals for their upcoming fundraiser and looking for a new home for himself and Tippi and their two cats and, not least, their mountains of drag. They wound up cramming everything they could, including Tippi, into the front room of Phillip and X's flat on 18th Street. Doris moved temporarily into Maurice's house on Walter Street, in the Duboce Triangle, the neighborhood across Market Street from the Castro.

Meanwhile, they were still scrabbling for postproduction money—by Phillip's estimate they needed $50,000. The success of Tommy's benefit gave him an idea. Doris, Tippi, and Miss X had first performed *Sluts a-Go-Go* in October 1979; the tenth-anniversary year was approaching. They could hold a benefit for the movie. The director Leland Moss had approached Doris about starring in *The Balcony* in the spring, but with little else in the works, everyone was game. And so on January 14, 1989, a Saturday evening, at the Victoria Theatre, a 480-seat venue on 16th Street that dated back to the era of vaudeville, they greeted the crowd in *Sluts a-Go-Go: Still Alive!—The Last Chance 'Vegas in Space' All-Star Greatest Hits Gala Benefit Revue.*

Despite the obvious AIDS joke, the title wasn't quite as morbid as it sounds now. Doris was always lamenting his advancing age (in August he had turned thirty-six), and when, in introducing himself to the audience ("I'm Doris Fish—if there's anyone who didn't know that, they should leave"), he added, "And I'm still alive!" it mainly meant, "The old bat is still here!" Miss X even sang "I'm Still Here," the old-bat number from *Follies*. Doris performed "This Is My Life," with the caftan and the slides; Tippi, Miss X, and Phillip reprised "The Incredible Two-Headed Martha." The most spectacular number was the second-act opener, "These Boots Are Made for Walkin'," with a red-wigged Doris in oversize boots (he was on stilts inside them) surrounded by a dozen supine dancers invisible except for black-light-lit boots and gloves moving in synchrony. The show went on for nearly four hours, but it was more professional than anything they'd done before, and the audience ate it up. They took home $6,000.

STILL ALIVE! FEATURED TWO NEW PERFORMERS WHO WERE ALSO growing closer to Doris offstage, as part of his care group. With the advent of AIDS, women had stepped into their traditional role as care-givers. The period saw a general rapprochement between gay men and many of the feminists, gay and straight, who had blasted them as heirs of male privilege. Anybody who accused Doris of misogyny, though, didn't know him. There had always been women in his inner circle, and in his last years they drew ever closer.

Carmela Carlyle had a solid day job directing the counseling pro-gram for university staff members at UC Berkeley. By night she was a party girl. Doris and Tippi and X found her so much fun to dance with that one evening they pulled her into the kitchen of the flat on 18th Street and invited her to join them onstage; Sandelle was drifting away and would soon leave for LA. It wasn't by chance that Carmela was an excellent dancer: she'd had years of ballet training and had done a stint in a modern-dance company. Nearly six feet tall and small breasted, she was nothing like Sandelle physically, and, unlike her male counter-parts, she had no interest in enhancing her bosom—which only added to the gender confusion onstage.

By the time she met Doris and Tippi, she was already working as a volunteer with AIDS patients, and she recognized that they were ill. Not that it was slowing them down. She remembers how fatiguing re-hearsals could be: "I would look at them and think, *No, we shouldn't do this again.* And then Doris would go, 'One more time!'" The years of letting his drag do the work were behind him. Doris would get to know Carmela's black Volvo well. He had never learned to drive, and now his doctor's appointments were mushrooming.

One of the highlights of *Still Alive!* was a sensational rendition of "(Theme from) *Valley of the Dolls*" by the rising chanteuse Connie Champagne. A decade earlier Connie had arrived at Mills College in Oakland as Kelly Brock from Roseville, northeast of Sacramento, a theater arts major and a spiky-haired punk—although vocally, as she says, she had more in common with Rosemary Clooney than with Patti Smith. (She once auditioned for Jennifer Blowdryer's punk band and was rejected by Jennifer as "too musical.") The Connie Champagne persona was a kind of female drag queen who, as originally conceived, would croon rock numbers torch-style. With a show approaching, she went looking for a drag queen to help her with her makeup and was directed to Doris. A friendship was born. More than a friendship: Doris, Connie says, was like "a strange and magical mother." The amphetamine-like high that came with the cosmetics Doris showed her how to apply changed the way she perceived herself onstage, just as it had for Pearl a dozen years earlier: "It gave me permission to do anything I wanted." She performed with the Sluts in several shows and benefits, aided Phillip in the late overdubbing of *Vegas in Space*, and became a central member of Doris's care group.

Pearl, meanwhile, was back in town. Her marriage to the Clash's Paul Simonon at an end, she had come home from England broken-hearted to find a San Francisco chillingly transformed: "AIDS was in full swing, and I was so sad I didn't know what to do. I had lost myself." Caring for the sick and dying brought her back, she says, "out of all my bullshit heartbreak" and made her feel like she was doing something good. She had always loved Doris; now she could help him.

Gwyn and Jennifer Waters had arrived in the Bay Area in 1976—the year of the Tubes' Talent Hunt—and had found it far less welcoming than Doris had. Only two years earlier the Symbionese Liberation Army had kidnapped Patricia Hearst, and the city, Gwyn remembers, was swarming with cults—Jim Jones's Peoples Temple, the Rajneeshpuram, Hare Krishnas, Moonies. Polk Street was a drug zone, and in the Castro, she says, "Bars would come up with rules like 'no open-toed shoes' to keep out women, and walking down the street we were met with hostile glares." She and Jennifer found community in the city's budding punk scene, which, especially in San Francisco, interlocked with its drag scene—"We were *all* yelled at when we walked down the street." The Sluts performed at the city's premier punk club, the Mabuhay Gardens; Jennifer became Jennifer Blowdryer and started her eponymous punk band, with Timmy Spence on keyboards. Gwyn first met Doris when she went to Slut Central to photograph him for

Jennifer's "Transvestite of the Month" column in the punk zine *Ego*. After that she was almost always in the Sluts' audience and at their postshow parties. Like Carmela, she had a car, and Doris needed drivers. As he got sicker, their friendship deepened.

SOON AFTER THE BENEFIT, DORIS AND MAURICE LEFT FOR Australia, making the usual holiday trip (even though Christmas had passed) down the coast to Merimbula and Wolumla, with Mildred and Ace in tow. The family took to Maurice at once. It would have gladdened them under any circumstances to see Doris in love, but now it reassured them to know that he had a partner to care for him, since he was growing unmistakably gaunt. His face was more worn than a thirty-six-year-old's. His toenails were misshapen, and something was terribly wrong with his digestion.

Mildred noticed nothing. In fact, she was as thrilled as ever to have Philip back home, which, once they were back in Sydney, meant a new round of Mardi Gras socializing. After years of accompanying him to parties and events, she was almost as familiar to the gay community as he was. Mildred didn't just love a crowd; she couldn't bear solitude, which was one of the reasons for her reliable presence at Mass every morning, as well as for her chirrupy spirit of Catholic volunteerism. She regularly pitched in at a center for the homeless, and in recent years she'd thrown her energy into AIDS care. The family loved telling the story of her first AIDS patient, who had gotten a morphine injection from her and promptly died.

For the 1989 parade, Doris painted himself blue and flourished a dark-red metallic miniskirt with matching cone bra, à la Madonna, and gold Statue of Liberty spikes over a red ponytail. He danced with the Showbags on a bright flatbed float designed by David McDiarmid, who had succeeded Ron Smith as workshop director. But it paled next to another tableau Doris had a hand in, one that retains a place of honor in Mardi Gras memory right beside Imelda and her shoes.

The idea originated with Ron, who the year before had started working on an effigy of that "horrible obsessed homophobe lunatic" Fred Nile as a Godzilla-style monster. He'd gotten only as far as a maquette when a visiting friend gave him another idea: forget the body—just set the head on a serving dish. When Doris arrived, the giant papier-mâché head was waiting for his expertise. He created thick hair and bushy eyebrows by folding over hundreds of strips of paper and gluing them down. Beads of hot-glue sweat dribbled down the pore-pocked flesh, and saliva bubbled from the lips. The severed head was mounted on a silver charger, surrounded by papier-mâché fruit, and borne along the parade route by the Sydney branch of the Sisters of Perpetual Indulgence. Nile was so incensed that he tried to have the Sisters arrested. He had to content himself with fuming to the press.

It was Doris's last Mardi Gras. A few weeks after he and Maurice departed for San Francisco, Ace got a letter with a clipping of one of the enthusiastic reviews Doris was receiving for his part in *The Balcony* at Theatre Rhinoceros:

> It's very hard work for me as I'm constantly fighting the urge to make jokes out of all the dreadfully serious things we have to do! I am good in it but it's not the sort of show that leaves one feeling especially happy at the end. And there is the problem of my now delicate health.

He then confirmed what the family had feared:

> I've been for all the tests and they've done biopsies and the results are as I expected; full-blown AIDS with a viral infection of the gastro-intestinal tract which is so painful that I can't eat more than one small meal of vegetables each day or else I can't sleep because of the pain! So doing the show is an ordeal but at least it keeps me away from the fridge.

His tone was frank but not bleak. "I hope that I haven't disturbed you too much with my news, I have known or rather suspected for five years so I'm fairly unruffled by it." He hadn't yet written Mildred, he added, but he would soon.

Not long afterward, Michael's wife, Anne, in Merimbula, got a call from her mother-in-law, in Sydney. "Did you know that Philip's got AIDS?" Mildred asked, bewildered. Anne replied, "Didn't you know that he wasn't well?" Mildred said she'd had no idea. The shock plunged her back into the depression that had intermittently threatened to overwhelm her since Gina's death and the divorce. This time she went in so deep that she wound up being admitted to Manly Hospital for electroshock treatment. It must have worked, since she rallied.

IT WAS LELAND MOSS WHO'D HAD THE IDEA OF STAGING A production of Jean Genet's *The Balcony* around Doris. Leland had helped develop *The AIDS Show* at Theatre Rhinoceros—he had the virus, too—and had written his own AIDS drama, *Quisbies*, and his theatrical universe was pretty much the opposite of the Sluts'. Their ethos was camp and pop; Leland's bona fides included a degree in drama from Harvard and directorial stints in New York. But he was also a warm and funny gay man who got a huge kick out of Doris. In "Some Notes from the Director" in the printed program, he explained, "By casting a man as Irma, I hope to shed light on Genet's obsession with gender, appearance and reality." Did he ever.

Genet wrote his first version of *The Balcony* in 1955 and seems never to have stopped working on it. He had reason to be dissatisfied. The opening tableaux, set in a brothel, with clients and whores dressing up to act out various fantasies, are gloriously theatrical and, as Leland directed them, funny; the moral and political philosophizing that follows is a hard sell, since it's very difficult to figure out what, exactly, Genet is selling. *The Balcony* isn't an easy play to make entertaining, and the reviews make it clear that Leland didn't fully succeed. But they were nearly unanimous in their praise for Doris, and the show was another hit.

The brothel's business is selling illusions, and since artifice, transformation, and role-playing are all major themes, casting a drag queen in the central role of Irma, the madam who assumes the robes of the Queen when the real Queen is assassinated, was such a fitting stroke that from a distance of three decades it borders on the obvious. Leland magnified this emphasis by giving Doris onstage wig and drag changes (at one point Doris even refurbished his makeup and painted his teeth—without a mirror) and by filling the other roles with a gender hodgepodge, including Tippi, Sandelle, X (in two parts, respectively credited "Miss X" and "D. B. Chandler"), and the trans performer and activist Kate Bornstein. But it was Doris who carried the show, as Leland knew he would.

Irma is a cold, smart businesswoman—a stock madam; her authority is what makes her such a suitable Queen. Doris was used to being in charge offstage, and his somewhat frosty inflections, which had a way of saving even his filthiest jokes from vulgarity, were ideal for Irma. The critic Misha Berson, describing his performance in the *San Francisco Bay Guardian*, wrote, "She (if that's the right pronoun) exudes nothing *but* authority." Doris, she continued, "never camps it up, never flashes some exaggerated notion of femininity at you," and she captured the essence of his drag aesthetic when she noted that "Fish seems neither male nor female, but some elegant, unidentified third gender designed to keep you guessing." She added that Doris was "stone gorgeous—or handsome, or whatever you want to call a square-jawed person who looks flawless in a cascading blonde wig, a slinky purple evening gown and a rhinestone tiara."

It was true—Doris had never looked more stunning. But there was a deflating irony behind this fashion-model glamour: it was an effect of his accelerating thinness. He was sick and in pain. "She would *scream* at rehearsals and backstage," Kate Bornstein remembers. "She never did in performance." His esophagus had ulcerated; hence the misery that eating caused him. On top of that, he wouldn't take painkillers. Why? Kate wanted to know.

"This is my *kaama*"—Kate does a good impression of his Australian vowels. "And I don't want to have to do it again next time if I don't do it this time."

Kate was then still near the beginning of her career as a performer, author, transgender lesbian, and gender theorist. The former Albert Bornstein was only three years into her life as a woman and was still exploring, not always confidently, what the transition from male to female meant.* "Doris Fish became my first drag mom," she wrote in her 2012 memoir *A Queer and Pleasant Danger*. To me she said, "I watched the bravery of being both man and woman, and that was one *hell* of an example for me."

In addition to encouragement, Doris offered practical advice. "I came in one day. She said, 'Ohhh, particularly high rouge today, *aa we?*'" Despite the Carmel-inspired extremes to which he took his own makeup, he understood that Kate wanted to pass, "but that I didn't want to be schlumphy about it. Jeans and a flannel shirt—I never got into that phase of my dykehood. But I did get into jumpsuits. She said, '*Daaling*, show off your legs!'"

Thrilled with the success of *The Balcony*, Leland wanted to do a season of Tennessee Williams's women with the Sluts. But he was too ill, and he died the following January. Doris did write his father about the idea, though, and Ace wrote back, "I agree with your Director. You would be outstanding in *Desire* as either woman—they are both parts which require much study and concentration. I would of course prefer you as Blanche."

By this point, Ace knew what the future held. Cases were skyrocketing—that year the number reported in the United States reached one hundred thousand—and mortality rates were grim. But Doris wouldn't countenance gloom, as he admonished the family via a letter to his father:

I was taken aback by everyone's assumption that it's the end of the show for me. It definitely is a serious situation but not at all as bad as the

---

* Early in her 1994 *Gender Outlaw* she observes, "I know I'm not a man—about that much I'm very clear, and I've come to the conclusion that I'm probably not a woman either, at least not according to a lot of people's rules on this sort of thing," making her a pioneer of nonbinary thinking. The volume's subtitle is *On Men, Women, and the Rest of Us*.

media has led you all to believe. I personally know of a few people who have lived 6 to 8 years since their diagnoses. It's lots of work and much self discipline but I firmly believe in my own ability to survive. I want to impress upon you how important it is for others to have positive thoughts too. . . . So please let them all know that all is well under the circumstances. And don't bury me until I rot!

Ace replied that he'd conveyed the contents of Doris's "cheery letter" to the family: "They were all very pleased to learn your spirits are so high & they agree totally that you must retain that outlook. . . . I have checked with clinical AIDS staff here & find that some 'full blown' AIDS patients have been going 7 & 8 years since diagnosis. They don't have any set period for the disease." In reality he was far less sanguine. "Dad was pretty practical," Liz says. "He knew he was dying even if Doris didn't. Dad was just like that—he accepted it." He advised the family that if they wanted to see Philip again they should get plane tickets.

Meanwhile, with Tippi and half their stuff still in the front room on 18th Street and the rest in storage, Doris was hunting for a new place. "Living with Maurice has been surprisingly pleasant," he told his father, "but I'm dying to redecorate! There's too much brown wood in this apartment and I need a little hot pink and gold!" They wound up in a third-floor walk-up with stairs on the outside, at 1275 South Van Ness Avenue in the Mission District. "And the rent is only $625!" Doris told Ace—a bargain, given what was already happening in the city's real estate market. "At least Tippi and I will have some food money left. Although it's a dump I have a good feeling about it." It *was* a dump compared to Oak Street, and I always dated Doris's and Tippi's real declines from that move. But Doris's energy seemed to leap back as soon as he began redecorating, with Versailles as his new model.

Heeding Ace's counsel, Mildred, Liz, Andrew, and Andrew's wife, Sally, arrived on July 21 for a two-week trip. Doris met them in Los Angeles, and they toured Disneyland and Universal Studios before heading up to San Francisco, where the visitors slept on air mattresses in the new flat. Doris was in good spirits and, judging by their itinerary, good condition. "We just didn't stop," Liz says. They drove north to Muir Woods to see the redwoods and to the Napa Valley wine country, and south to Santa Cruz and Big Sur and William Randolph Hearst's eccentric castle at San Simeon; they toured the Berkeley campus and wandered through the arboretum in Golden Gate Park.

Only once did Doris bow out of an excursion—when they were headed for Alcatraz. "I can't bear all the sadness over there," he said. Liz decided he was right and stayed home with him. "He was very kind in every way," she recalls. His openhandedness with the homeless, when they were all on tight budgets, so rankled Mildred that he took to slipping them bills when her back was turned. Often Maurice and Tippi joined their outings. Janice had them over for lunch, and Doris gave a party so the family could meet more of his friends. "Nothing was going to stop Mildred from having a good time," Liz says—not even her oldest son's approaching death. "She just put that out of her mind and didn't dwell on it, till the end." The sadness went unmentioned.

13

WHO DOES THAT BITCH THINK SHE IS?

I N THE AUTUMN OF 1989, DORIS BROUGHT A LISTING FOR A
show to the offices of the *San Francisco Sentinel*, a gay weekly, and fell
into conversation with the paper's arts editor, Kathleen Baca. She had
seen *Who's Afraid of Box Office Poison?* and thought it was a hoot. Kathleen felt strongly that one of the paper's duties was to represent every
segment of the community, but she realized as they were talking that it
lacked the voice of a drag queen. "Hey, would you want to write?" she
asked, and Doris said yes, not least because any income was welcome.

By then his name was familiar to San Franciscans, but only a small
portion of them went to his shows or to the AIDS benefits where he'd

Doris's final performance, 1990. Photo by Marc Geller.

become a regular presence. The weekly column he wrote over the next year changed his stature in the city. He had an unforced voice on the page that went from funny to catty to bleak to wise with conversational ease, and almost immediately the column became a must-read for gay San Francisco.

Although Doris had always been a good writer, early on he'd conceived his scripts primarily as vehicles for his astounding looks—and maybe one reason his shows were so enjoyable was the airiness with which he tossed them off. Over the years the words had taken on greater import. Now that he was performing in a different medium, he extended his range in a different direction. But Doris in print was considerably less cartoonish than the *monstre sacré* who'd been on gaudy display in the city for the past thirteen years.

In those days, the gay press held a central place in the queer life of San Francisco. Everybody in the community followed it, and when I say "everybody" I mean that just about literally—certainly every gay man and lesbian I knew, young or old, comfortable or scraping by, read the gay papers, both for cultural reporting and for news. The *Bay Area Reporter*, or the *BAR*, had the largest readership; the *Sentinel* had the same kind of scrappy, second-place rivalry with it that the afternoon *Examiner* had with the morning *Chronicle.* By 1989 the *Sentinel* belonged to Ray Chalker, a bar owner whose main interest in the paper was the clout it brought him—politicians were eager for the gay papers' endorsement. He certainly had reason to be happy with his new columnist; Doris wrote Ace in January, "I've managed to gather a good following, which eventually the publisher of the paper found out about

---

* Both the *BAR* and the *Sentinel* were vital sources of information and sounding boards during the AIDS crisis, but only after initial reluctance. As Rodger Streitmatter details in *Unspeakable: The Rise of the Gay and Lesbian Press in America*, at first the *BAR* "downplayed the spread of the epidemic in the bathhouses, partly because it saw any attempt to ban sexual activity as a setback for gay liberation and partly because it did not want to lose the revenue it received from bathhouse ads. . . . The *San Francisco Sentinel* also rates harsh judgment. Also because of the double fear of losing ground in the gay rights battle and losing revenue from advertising, the newspaper appears to have deliberately misled its readers."

(people were raving to him about my work!) so now all the staff smile and gush at me when I drop my little tomes off."

Kathleen assumed that Doris would cover the drag scene, but she gave him free rein, and one of the pleasures of his column was that you never knew what his next topic would be. There was indeed a lot about drag—contest reports, makeup tips, and gossip, as well as reflection. In his debut, which came right after the October 1989 Loma Prieta earthquake and before "that other earth-shaking event—All Hallows' Eve," he offered a how-to for anyone planning to go out as Zsa Zsa Gabor. The septuagenarian actress was in the headlines after slapping a cop who had pulled her over for a traffic violation; at trial she'd been sentenced to a few days in jail, making her a bonanza for comedians. West Graphics was on top of it, with Doris transforming Janice into a terrifically convincing Zsa Zsa. (The paper ran one of the shots with the column: Janice as Zsa Zsa behind bars next to Doris as Leona Helmsley, the famously mean hotel magnate, who had also just been sentenced to jail time.) Not long afterward there was a moment of terror at West Graphics when a call came in from the actress herself. She demanded, "Who is that old, fat cow? She doesn't look like me!" and then placed an order for three dozen cards.

Doris gazed with dubious fascination on the new generation of drag performers, like the "talented and volatile" Popstitutes, a troupe of musician anarchists that he found "just awful" and at the same time "just about the nicest folks who ever shaved their heads in weird patterns." One Miss Romé, whom he encountered at a drag competition, left him even more ambivalent. He recoiled at her garish and crudely applied makeup and her scuzzy drag even as he was aware that older queens had once reacted to Sylvia and the Synthetics with equal perplexity; now he found himself on the other side of the "gay generation gap." In any event, Miss Romé's coarseness disturbed him less than the "arch-conservatism" of the competition judges who denounced it: "If they weren't gay," he wondered, "would these people still be pro-gay?"

The Popstitutes and Miss Romé were in fact exponents of the tattered genderfuck aesthetic once claimed by the Cockettes and the

Synthetics, filtered through punk and updated to the late '80s. Other performers heralded more lasting change. Doris was impressed by the young Justin Vivian Bond's performance as a hermaphrodite in Kate Bornstein's *Hidden: A Gender* at Theatre Rhinoceros, though it barely hinted at the cyclone that was brewing. Vivian and her performing partner, Kenny Mellman, would eventually take their invented duo, Kiki and Herb, all the way to Carnegie Hall and Broadway. But she arrived in San Francisco too late to do much more than look up to Doris and Tippi—"I felt like they were the guardians of the keys to the kingdom—queendom—in which I was moving," she says—though in time she and X did become good friends.

But if anyone Doris wrote about demonstrated that drag was becoming less niche, it was John Epperson's celebrated alter ego Lypsinka, already a hit with New York audiences. Lypsinka's evening-length show, an entirely lip-synched mash-up of song and movie snippets that collaged the suffering and the madly bubbling divas of the past, both ridiculed the pop-culture construct of glamour and, in so doing, offered a startlingly feminist critique. Doris was out of town when she made her San Francisco debut: "Lypsinka, Lypsinka, Lypsinka! It's all I've heard for the last two weeks," he mock-griped. "My answering machine is full of the bitch." They did meet later at a party, where a melancholy Doris passed the torch: "Now it's your turn."

Tippi and Miss X were in the column constantly, with Miss X in particular a running joke. It was as though Doris's honor as a drag queen required him to sprinkle venom somewhere. "Miss X is like an old wine—kind of bitter and vinegary." Talking to X on the phone: "I could hear her face cracking as a smile spread across the old prune." After months of similar barbs, Doris wrote,

Many readers have expressed concern about our friendship. "Can she read? You couldn't possibly still be friends after all the terrible things you've written about her." The truth is Miss X loves to see her name in print almost as much as I do. And with her reputation what's a few more bad words matter. Without me she'd be just another aging, bitter and twisted, frustrated chanteuse giving her roommates hell. I'm doing her a favor telling the world what a witch she is.

A West Graphics photo of Miss X as a witch, for a Halloween card, accompanied the column.

On one level, this relentless dishing was a way of keeping the Sluts front and center. But the edge was real. The rift Sandelle had opened between Doris and X had never fully healed, and now Doris had entered a brooding stage. One evening, as Doris and X and Tippi and Phillip were driving somewhere and listening to a female vocalist on the radio (X thinks it was Joan Baez), Doris said, "If I could sing, I'd be a solo act—I wouldn't need you bitches!" The line lived on as a bon mot, but was it? Talking about X to Timmy Spence, Doris said bleakly, "You know, we worked all this time—ten years—and now I've come to the conclusion that we just have very little in common." But his real feelings were less resolved. Doris and X went on performing together, and they never stopped seeing each other, even when Doris was close to death.

Sometimes he wrote about parties he'd been to. Gwyn Waters threw one in December 1989; he praised the dips and described his own "traffic-stoppingly beautiful" Christmas outfit and the other guests' bad behavior. After a cocktail party that Silvana and I gave, he tried to decide who the worst person had been; Marc Huestis won for saying, "There's too much about Miss X in your column! Write about me!"

In a column called "A Quiet, Dressy Evening," he recounted a more elaborate soirée. "The host Mr. Bob Davis, a big handsome straight musician, greeted his guests in a purple gown and matching turban—not that that was too disturbing, but he was braless!" Bob had planned the party partly to offer (as the invitation stated) "An Opportunity to Peruse Mr. Davis' Library of Female Impersonation & Related Arts"* and partly to unveil a painting he'd commissioned from Doris depicting Doris, Bob, Tippi, and Miss X as their most glamorous female selves;

---

* The collection has grown into the Louise Lawrence Transgender Archive, housed in Vallejo, California.

Miss X's Kabuki pallor and narrowed eyes add a disquieting note. Knowing Doris needed the money, Bob had kindly offered him $800 for the portrait.

Ambi Sextrous was there, and Doris praised his "very successful transition from serious substance abuser to sober socialite," as well as his appearance, "despite the glittered beard, though even that was not unattractive." Another longtime friend came, too. "While we're on the subject of self-decor, the winners would have to be that lovely couple Carmel Sanger and her husband, Robert. Only a few areas of their bodies remain tattooless." Carmel Sanger was the married name of Carmel Strelein, his old Synthetics cohort and makeup inspiration, who, like Ambi, had put substance abuse behind her. She'd met Robert Sanger in in the drug-treatment program she'd agreed to enter in order to stay out of prison after a bust. A few weeks later Doris got a card from her, thanking him for "the nice words you wrote in your gay rag column," enclosing a check ("I've only owed you this money for the past 8 yrs. but it always comes when you need it the most"), and adding—obviously concerned about his health—"Well lovie I just wanted you to know that I love and care about you and thank you for your friendship your the grooveiest person I know if it wasnt for you Id still be liveing and posibley married to something in Australia wishing Id come to the USA."[*]

In March 1990 Doris left for a month in Australia; the swishy comic Tom Ammiano (later he would be elected to the San Francisco Board of Supervisors and then the California State Assembly) took over the column for him. Doris felt well enough to keep up his visits to the gym and spend time at the beach, "going topless, and sometimes totally nude," he wrote on his return. "I didn't even wear lipstick!"

Naturally there were columns about the Sluts' still-frequent appearances. West Graphics threw itself a tenth-birthday party at DV8, a

---

[*] Carmel's spelling and punctuation are so hair-raising that I've left them uncorrected, but it should be noted that not only had she turned her life around while remaining an edgy style-setter, but she was also running her own very successful salon, Pink Tarantula Hair.

South of Market nightclub, and Doris performed "This Is My Life," with the caftan and the slides, "my really truly best number." At another South of Market club, DNA, they mounted yet another revue, *Sluts a-Go-Go All-Star Celebrity Gang Bang*, which Doris devoted a whole column to plugging.

Sometimes he just reminisced in his columns—about Sylvia and the Synthetics, about whoring, about Cheryl, about Coco Vega, about old shows. He devoted a February column to Sydney's Mardi Gras and a Mother's Day piece to Mildred's high jinks. He wrote about what he was thinking about. When the subject was Christianity (it came up a few times), his sense of humor paled—"Most people who call themselves 'Christians' today are not fit to be fed to any poor lions." A lighthearted column about his Catholic childhood curdled at the end: "No matter how old I get, there's still a little child in me who's still hearing the nuns, still fearing their Hell, and most of all now hating them with a rage that seems not to diminish but to grow."

One summer week when he couldn't think of anything else to write about, he just copied out a letter from Jackie. On the phone Jackie asked, "Are you still a Romantic Cruelist, Doris?" and Doris replied, "Darling, I'm a *victim* of it." An ambiguous response—was he referring to the many AIDS jokes that were circulating, or to the Romantic Cruelist joke the cosmos was playing on him? He never did open up to Jackie about his illness, even when she and Thierry came for another visit and Doris looked so ghastly that Jackie said, "Can you *please* get into drag for us to go out?"

Doris didn't talk about his illness with Miss Abood, either, until he came through San Francisco on one of his occasional trips from New York to Australia. Since his move to New York, Miss Abood had been through a novel's worth of ups and downs. For a while he had lived a fast and very lucrative life: "I was spending nights in the Waldorf and getting flown all over the country. I was making so much money out of being a boy whore that I didn't have *time* to do drag." He must have found time somewhere, because a 1983 *Village Voice* story about him, "Dressed to Overkill," by the scene-maker Michael Musto, provides an account of his getting dolled up for a night on the town (his very Doris motto: "When in doubt, add more") and, once the drinking started, his descent from charming to disorderly to semiconscious at a disco where he was finally shown the door.

Beyond booze, Abood had returned to his old heroin habit. The glamour faded further when people started getting sick. Then *he* started getting sick, first with an infection of the spleen, then with HIV. The money dwindled. Ultimately he was reduced to living on the streets. He found a place in a rough (now gentrified) section of Brooklyn. "One morning I woke up—I'd started getting into doing coke, heaps of coke—and I thought, *If I don't get out of here, I'm dead.*" Boring Australia and its efficient health-care system beckoned. It was on a stopover during one of his trips back, before this final return, that Miss Abood made Maurice's acquaintance and was shocked to learn that Doris had AIDS.

Doris had another Australian visitor. "Who is that funny old man?" a friend inquired at a party (he reported). "I think he fancies me." Doris reassured her: "He's 65, slightly drunk, and definitely a bit of an old perve. But he's recently had by-pass surgery so he's probably impotent. . . . Oh, and he's my father." Ace had arrived for a three-week stay in California in mid-July 1990, his timing good since Doris had just emerged from a stretch of physical agony. Ace was so amused by the decor of the apartment that after returning to Australia he began a letter, "Hi, Louis Philippe of France!"

Doris's frank and affectionate correspondence with his father provides a record of his vacillating health during this period and gives some idea of how baffled doctors treating HIV were before the advent of protease inhibitors in the mid-1990s. When Doris was first officially diagnosed, in April 1989, he was put on AZT, a controversial drug because of its known toxicity; it "makes me a bit queazy [*sic*]," he told Ace, "but it is supposed to for a while then one is expected to get 'better.'" In January 1990 he reported "the most shocking sore throat I've ever experienced! . . . I couldn't even sip water for a few days, and any time I had to swallow it was just excruciatingly painful. And to add to that, as if I needed more, was a mouthful of ulcers. . . . I couldn't chew, I couldn't swallow and I couldn't digest anything." He talked, hopefully, of "a new Chinese abortion medicine, a cucumber root extract"—Compound Q, which an unsanctioned research group was testing without authorization from the Food and Drug Administration; it appeared to kill HIV in the test tube, "but it will not be available for a year or two as the pharmaceutical companies have to patent it and make a million bucks. And of course the FDA will do lots to stall it."[*]

By then the FDA's foot-dragging regulatory protocols and its apparent unconcern about the mounting death toll had made it the target of furious protests, though Doris didn't join them—in his column he called himself a "political couch potato. (Though it has been said that my very existence is a radical act!)" He was skeptical about Western medicine in general and his own physician in particular: "He's an absolutely lovely fellow but I don't think he knows anything about alternatives to the drugs he's giving me, or anything about diet, or even vitamin and mineral supplements." In fact, after the AZT began causing him liver and muscle damage, his doctor wanted "to double the dose so he can document the bad effect to prove that I'm having trouble with the medicine so then THEY will send us some ddI, the half-brother of AZT, with different toxic side fx. Naturally I'm considering not following this particular plan as it breaks the first rule of medicine, 'Do no harm.'"

He did manage to get onto the ddI he mentioned in that letter; the drug gave him "a few bouts of diarrhea, but I'm still managing to put on a little weight and feel fine most of the time. I'm going to the gym regularly and I'm getting back into shape." He also tried an alternative regimen, ozone therapy: "It's a very 'gay' process as we have to ingest the gas up our butts for twenty minutes and try not to fart!" The sad fact, though, is that nothing much worked well, or for long. Doris being Doris, he seldom lost hope, but the first effective anti-AIDS medications weren't developed until several years after his death.

---

[*] Compound Q did not live up to its promise.

A topic that showed up as much as AIDS, drag, and parties in Doris's column was animal rights, which toward the end of his life became a political fixation. It began with his and Tippi's cats—now there were four—who, Doris wrote, "quite correctly think I'm God." In a later column extolling fake fur he argued, "If we demand our civil rights, then it follows we should extend rights to those who've served us faithfully for so many thousands of years." It wasn't an easy subject from which to mine humor, and in "Fish on a Soapbox" he made fun of himself by listing various ideas he had rejected as unfunny before landing on his theme again, asking his readers to "imagine an even superior species to us" that "ate your mother then cured her skin to make pants and vests to wear to their bars. (No one could possibly make a nice ensemble from my mother, but you see what I mean.)" In June he and Maurice flew to Washington, DC, to join the March for the Animals, resulting in "Our Little Brothers and Sisters," in which he described the horrors of factory farms and advocated a vegetarian diet.

But he probably went too far when, after almost a year as a columnist, he attacked leather queens—"The Dead Animal Crowd"—and sadomasochistic sex: "I just don't get it. Why does adorning oneself with the skin of a dead animal make one more attractive?" The whole phenomenon, he said, made him "a little scared. I think dead animal people must be into kinky sex. I get nervous and even turned off if someone slaps me. The thought of having to endure lots of discomfort and hard work to have an orgasm leaves me cold."

No one could have been less entitled than Doris to judge other people's sex lives, and to top it off he mocked the all-too-often-unsightly bodies that peopled this milieu, citing as an example "one older gentleman wearing nothing but a leather G-string, a pot-belly and a really saggy old butt" at the Folsom Street Fair, the annual leather street party. Outrage followed. For several weeks the *Sentinel*'s letters column carried heated responses, many of them as angry about Doris's "looksist" body-shaming as about his denunciation of leather.

Finally, Doris responded. In a column titled "Did I Say Something Wrong?" he admitted, "I stuck my neck out so I have only myself to blame!" And though he joked, "It's hard not to be judgmental when you're right about everything!," he was contrite: "Dear critics, you were not as harsh as you could have been." While holding steady in his defense of animal rights, he composed his own version of the letter he felt his detractors could have written: "How dare you criticize something you know nothing about. Not only is it in questionable taste to condemn the private consensual sex habits of others, it is also bigoted. Keep your prejudices and ignorance to yourself." He added, with un-Doris-like humility, that "no one questioned the condition of my own butt—it's definitely not fit for public scrutiny!"

But he was getting tired. "It's dreary to have AIDS as a hobby, a career or a life," he'd written that summer. "I hate that 'gay' equals 'disease' in most people's minds." Karmic aspirations had receded in the face of constant pain: "Remember when Percodan was a recreational drug? Now I take them like vitamin C." In September, at the beginning of a serious decline that would be punctuated by hospital stays, he wrote, "I was so sick last week I thought I was going to die!" and then he launched into a breezy column about his obituary. "Would my demise make it into the *Chronicle?* Maybe the *Examiner.* . . . Do you think Queens sit around in Heaven comparing the length of their obituaries?"

By now he'd become one of the city's best-known AIDS cases, and his cheerfulness, his wit, and his public-spiritedness had won him admiration beyond the gay community. But it was time to bow out as a writer. October 1990 marked the one-year anniversary of his column. "Unfortunately," he told his readers, "that challenge has begun to overwhelm me. It's no secret that my health has deteriorated." After the years of reticence, he was all the way out of the AIDS closet:

I know you're all dying to have every detail of my condition exposed and you might as well have it from the horse's mouth. I have a few "popular" problems like KS and T-cells of 75 (on a good day) but I also have "non-specific" ulceration of the esophagus which seems to defy all treatment so far, hence the pain-killers. My doctor assures me I'm not dying (yet) so I shall continue to seek relief. I often envy the ones who died quickly.

He made a last appeal for animal rights, "my number one concern," and then asked readers for help placing his cats in new homes.

He ended with a mock apology to Miss X, whose cocktail-party boozing had been the source of regular digs:

> She doesn't actually drink but loves to pretend she's had a few too many then behaves badly and starts to sing! But she's been such a saint lately that I can't bring myself to dish the bitch.
>
> In fact she's helped to organize a wonderful send-off/tribute for little me with a cast of all my fellow performers from many great shows. I hope you can all come, Saturday, November 3 at 8 p.m. at the Victoria Theatre on 16th Street.
>
> So this is goodbye and it's hard to say it because you've all been so sweet to me. I'll miss you.

THE BENEFIT WAS TITLED *WHO DOES THAT BITCH THINK SHE IS?* and was held at the same Mission District theater that *Sluts a-Go-Go: Still Alive!* had filled nearly two years earlier. Marc, Silvana, Phillip, and X organized it; Sandelle came up from LA to choreograph; Bob took charge of the complicated technical and sound aspects. The three dozen performers had almost all shared a stage with Doris at one time or another.

"I couldn't believe my eyes," Phillip says in Marc's documentary *Another Goddamn Benefit*, "when I saw them streaming out of the Victoria Theatre and lined up around the corner." Marc himself recalls it as one of the city's great theater events. The Victoria's 480 seats proved woefully insufficient, and several hundred fans had to be turned away. Doris—stunning, despite the way he felt, in an ankle-length gold wrap and an enormous platinum-blonde flip embellished with a black-and-gold silk rose—went down the line in order to personally thank those who couldn't get in. Later he wrote Jackie (probably Jackie: the letter is unfinished and the salutation simply "Darling"), "I managed to go outside and get their donations anyway and disguised it as a gracious apology." Then he entered the full house to an ovation that couldn't have been more impassioned if Judy Garland had risen from the grave, and took his place of honor in the front row.

The curtain rose dramatically on Miss X, his back to the crowd; he turned, uttered a brief, emotional welcome—"And now, let's bring on the Fishnet Girls!" One by one the full cast peacocked in, done up in elaborate showgirl drag, as Miss X sang "Beautiful Girls," from *Follies*, backed by the small house band. The stage cleared for Pearl. "Thank you for the warm hand on my opening," she deadpanned, then told about winning the Tubes' Talent Hunt with Doris in preface to a song full of meaning for them both: an orgasmic rendition of "Don't Touch Me There," Jane Dornacker's extended double entendre for the Tubes. Underneath the motorcycle jacket she kept tearing open, she was bare on top except for duct tape on her nipples. Miss X, Tippi, and Timmy did three numbers from *Blonde Sin*, and the cast of *Naked Brunch* reenacted the "Queens' Court" episode, with Lulu filling in for Doris. Silvana, as Zizi LaFrance, again performed "I'm Blasé," preceded by the same dumb joke. (Zizi: "I want a slight retard in the last four bars." Tippi: "Hey, I'm not in this number!") Timmy and Ramona Fischer, who'd flown in from Florida for the show, sang the "Love Theme from *Vegas in Space*," and Phillip announced that they'd finally secured the funding to complete the movie, projecting (accurately) a premiere in the summer or fall of 1991. The first act ended with Sandelle and Tippi leading the cast in the jazz dance from *Nightclub of the Living Dead*. Then Anne Block emerged in the same shoulderless polka-dot sheath she had worn at Tommy's benefit to make the same cheerful appeal for funds.

Throughout, there were video clips of Doris—going over the balcony at the Oasis, in *Blonde Sin* and *Vegas in Space* and the Club 181 shows, musing on the afterlife from the makeup table at Chuck Solomon's party. Miss X and Tippi were onstage a great deal of the time, and no one watching Tippi sparkle (I assume speed was involved) would have guessed how ill she was. She had been exhausted during rehearsals, mostly supine when she was offstage. The story given out was that she had a cold, but she was running a high fever, which by then everyone recognized as a symptom of *Pneumocystis carinii* pneumonia, a deadly threat to people with AIDS.

Several cast members had only tenuous connections to Doris's career. He had never performed with the Popstitutes, but as representatives of the new generation of genderfuck drag they provided several minutes of chaos. Debora Iyall, of Romeo Void—rock royalty in '80s San Francisco—sang a torchy number; the band had been on the bill at the 1980 show in which Doris retrieved a tomato from the stage and scrabbled over several rows of seats to grind it into the hair of the young woman who'd thrown it.

And then there was Bambi—Bambi Lake, a trans drag queen (she claimed both tags) with voluptuous breasts and a voice to match, who had performed early on with the Cockettes and the Angels of Light. She was also a hooker who'd been in the slammer more than once and hadn't cultivated a reputation for stability. (A bomb threat she had once been arrested for phoning in had earned her the nickname "Bombi.") Bambi admired the Sluts and had come to some holiday meals on 18th Street, and in the *Still Alive!* benefit she'd sung a glamorous version of an old Cockettes song. Miss X introduced her and did his best to adjust the mike for a singer who stood six-three in heels. Bambi entered, looking beautiful—long blonde hair, purple sequins, dark tinsel boa— and the pianist played the opening bars of "Waltzing Matilda."

The dressing rooms were equipped with speakers, to keep performers waiting to go on abreast of a show's progress. Doris, who was backstage with Connie Champagne preparing for his own big number, groaned, "Oh God, not *that*." He hated "Waltzing Matilda."

Bambi, in fine voice, sang the first words, and then, *whomp*—the mike came loose and dropped to crotch level with an amplified thud. The whole house broke up. It was a classic moment of cold water thrown on a drag queen trying to do something earnest.

She waited impatiently as Miss X ("I didn't do it, I swear!") and a stage tech struggled to tighten the mike. The piano began again. Bambi began again. "Waltzing Matilda" is about a tramp (a swagman) who steals a sheep and leaps into a pond (a billabong) to avoid capture; the story means little to most Americans, but I'm told it speaks powerfully to the antiauthoritarian streak in the early Australian settlers and their descendants. I'm not sure that Bambi's interpretation was appropriate to those feelings—she sang it as Tosca might have sung it—but it was certainly true to the emotions of that evening. She was hypnotic, bringing such astute musicality and such pure anguished force to the old song that at the end the audience rose to vindicate her with the longest ovation of the evening until Doris took the stage.

Before he did, there was a slideshow that Daniel Nicoletta had compiled (as he'd done for Tommy's benefit) in close consultation with Doris, whom he'd been photographing since Doris's days with the Tubes. Funny and touching, it included images by several photographers, including Barry Kay's study of Doris and Jasper, James Moss's picture of Doris surrounded by naked studs, Doris as a naked stud himself (shot for business purposes), wacky stills from shows and cards, and painted self-portraits. The background music ended—"And now, ladies and gentleman, Miss Doris Fish!"—and as the screen rose there was Doris, white-caftaned, golden-gloved, fists on hips. He made modest "sit down" gestures over the shouts and applause, which only the start of the tape quieted down.

Shirley Bassey's "This Is My Life"—like "And I Am Telling You I'm Not Going," the song that sent him over the balcony at the Oasis—verges on hysteria, which makes it a somewhat odd signature number for a performer whose stage persona was controlled and coolly cynical. Or it would have if it weren't utterly prototypical drag queen ground. The moves were the familiar ones, done with élan: the madly wobbling lips, the head bowed in fake humility or quickly tossed, the gloved fingers tracing zigzags in the air. The audience laughed appreciatively at every overdone gesture. And then, when the chorus came—"This is my life . . . / This is me! / This is me!"—and Doris spread his wings into a screen and the slides of his many looks started flashing, near pandemonium. The effect was so powerful and so valedictory that quite a few spectators who had seen the number previously now think they saw it for the first and only time that night. Bassey's overwrought cry "Let me live! Let me live!" was no longer ludicrous. Susan Sontag was probably right when she wrote, "Camp and tragedy are antitheses," but not when she insisted that "there is never, never tragedy" in camp. *This* was tragic—and valiant and moving and stupendous and, as Doris raced upstage and downstage with his arms swept wide for the slides, ridiculous and side-splitting. He even attempted a cartwheel. "That was the absolute crystalline moment," Connie says, "a performer giving it all. Because how many of us truly know what is our last time to be onstage?"

There were some glitches. At first the same images of Doris kept coming up. ("God damn it! Can't you work that fucking slide projector?" Marc screamed at David Weissman.) The cartwheel didn't fully come off—Doris couldn't hoist his legs—but what seemed to be a momentary faltering by the spotlight operator was actually a clever move to conceal the screwup. When it was over, instead of soaking in the applause, Doris waved divaishly and quickly left the stage.

Marc and Silvana emerged in tuxes, Silvana still in makeup and rhinestone earrings. Marc, ever emotional, said, "I just think that it's so incredible that this evening is showing how *alive* we are—and I am so fuckin' proud to be a queen tonight!" They thanked the volunteer crew by name and then, taking turns, read a proclamation from the mayor, Art Agnos, recognizing Doris's "peerless record of theatrical accomplishment," saluting him "for so proudly representing the spirit of our City," and officially naming November 3, 1990, Doris Fish Day in San Francisco. Doris joined them, clad in gold sequins and a lime-green boa, to accept the plaque. (It was the dress Sandelle had sung "Happy Birthday" to Chuck in; Doris bequeathed it to her after the show.) Phillip and Miss X, on behalf of the cast, presented a giant trophy inscribed DORIS FISH, AN INSPIRATION TO MILLIONS. David Lindsey bounded onstage with a check for $2,000 from West Graphics. Ambi Sextrous tore one for $1,000 from his own checkbook. A good Samaritan named Charly Zukow—already on his way to becoming one of the city's leading publicists—had taken it upon himself to contact various airlines; Continental had assented, and he came up to hand over a round-trip ticket to Australia.

The stage emptied, leaving Doris alone to address the crowd. "Well, thank you all a lot. That was quite nice, wasn't it?" he said drily. Laughter. "It's not very often that one, especially one with an ego like mine, gets to indulge it in such a lavish style as this evening," he continued, adding, "I did no work on this show, none whatsoever. You might have noticed." More laughter. "I know when you applaud for those people, you're really applauding for *me*"—he went on making wry jokes, his voice, unlike Marc's, without a hint of tears:

Of course, it is ironic that one has to be almost dying to get such massive attention, but I shouldn't complain, because I've had a pretty good time of it here. I've had some wonderful audiences. I know some of you have been in them. And although I am ailing, that's certainly a fact, I'm not planning to die right away. But after a show like this, I mean, what can I follow it with? I either have to die or leave town. Of course, it would be very embarrassing if I do live through the epidemic. Five years from now we'll pass on the street and you'll say, "I gave that bitch twenty bucks and what did she do? She went to the South Pacific and got a new VCR!" I shouldn't say that before we collect the money, should I? All right, well, I'm not going to thank everybody personally in the cast because that will take too long and I actually don't know a lot of them. I mean, there's hordes of people down here—some of them are all sort of dressed up in glitter and you know they've done a number though I don't remember what it was. Anyway, if I am lucky enough to come back and perform for you again, I know it will be because of your support this evening, and the support of all the wonderful cast and crew, who've given me so much this evening. I know this will, this will last me a long, long time. And I thank you all a lot. And I love you, I really do. Good night.

14

SAINT DORIS

After Doris's death, at the premiere of *Vegas in Space*, Sister Vicious Power Hungry Bitch of the Sisters of Perpetual Indulgence read a proclamation declaring him a saint. Sanctity had always been a part of Doris's comedy, mostly by way of its opposite. "Perhaps I'll become a saint," he'd speculated in his stand-up routine, "and then God will reward me with younger-looking skin!" He and Jackie had been Mary Magdalene and the Virgin at the foot of the cross; with Miss Abood he'd performed *The Martyrdom of Maria Goretti*. When I interviewed Tippi about Doris, practically the first thing out of her mouth was "She's a saint and a goddess!"

Doris wasn't either, but it isn't too much of a stretch to say that as he neared death those around him had an impression of light. As I write

Mildred and Doris, probably 1990. Courtesy of Peggy Darm.

that I can practically hear Jackie groaning and Miss Abood howling, but they weren't there at the end. Gwyn Waters says that each time she locked gazes with Doris across a room it was like suddenly encountering the love of your life: "There was so much love in her eyes, and it was directed toward me. That is the effect Doris had on many, many people."

The benefit took place on November 3, 1990; afterward Doris declined so swiftly that he had to be hospitalized, at Ralph K. Davies Medical Center, close to Maurice's house in the Duboce Triangle. Following his release he returned daily for intravenous pentamidine treatments to control his *Pneumocystis* pneumonia. Gwyn remembers leaving her workplace in Oakland to cross the bridge and pick him up at Maurice's, where he was staying temporarily, and drive him the two blocks uphill and sit with him: "Doris was in so much pain and it was so hard for her to move, but never a complaint—just hope that the *Pneumocystis* would go away." His comment in the *Sentinel* about envying the ones who died quickly had been the mood of a moment. "Boy, she wanted to be here."

But Doris knew it wasn't for long. One evening Robin Clark, the artist who'd shot *Vegas in Space*, went out with the Sluts on the eve of a trip he was planning. When he and Phillip and X were dropping Doris and Tippi at their door, Doris asked him to get out of the car. "And she gave me a hug," Robin recalls. "She said, 'Let's not make a big deal of this.' I knew what she meant."

Once again Doris tried to cut out the painkillers. Bob says, "Doris had a lacerated esophagus and would howl, *howl* in pain. I don't mean just moan, I don't mean just groan, I mean *scream*. Tippi was sleeping with earphones and earplugs and her hands in her ears. But she wouldn't leave Doris."

In Silvana's files I came across a schedule he'd drawn up and distributed: "For at least the next couple of weeks Doris will be staying at Maurice's. If it's your day to check in, please try calling over there. . . . If you want to be included and take a day or two, just let me know." Dozens of similar calendars were floating around the city then. Sometimes it was easier to take care of those you weren't so close to. Bob Burnside, a friend of Janice's, didn't know Doris well, but he lived near his apartment and had a car; he took charge of coordinating rides to the hospital. A care group formed before Doris was discharged.

Happily, Doris wasn't shy about asking for help. Pearl would prepare "very simple things, grains and vegetables, fresh fruits, simple soups—no big meals." Janice thought potatoes and squash would absorb the toxic chemicals from the meds and recalls that a clump of cold butter helped him swallow—"That's the only way she could get food down." Connie remembers making Doris soft scrambled eggs. "And she'd say, 'Oh, darling, you make the most divine scrambled eggs of anyone!' Then I found out she told that to everybody."

Doris kept his sense of humor and a semblance of good cheer, but obviously he was in no condition to clean, and Tippi didn't take up the slack. Janice was furious. "I didn't know Tippi was also sick. Every time I came over she'd say, 'Hi!' and I'd say, 'Drop it'—and she'd hide in her room till I left. I thought, *What a selfish piece of shit, after she's done so much for you.*" Finally she learned from Lulu that Tippi had KS lesions on her feet—she'd told him, "Honey, I got these flea bites on my feet and I'm gonna have them taken off. Bob's gonna take me to the hospital, 'cause I have to go-go dance!"

If illness brought out what was most ethereal in Doris, it made Tippi furl up further. She fastened a semicircular French table to the outside of her bedroom door, with a vase on the tabletop and a rose in the vase, to make it look like part of the wall. Janice described what was behind it in a memoir she wrote about those last days: "Tippi's room turned into a hornets' nest of rumpled fishnets and Day-Glo tights she just couldn't unsnaggle by herself. Her TV had to be on twenty-four hours and she had to have a constant supply of vodka, which she called tweetsy water. She'd nurse her tweetsy water through a pink plastic straw in a large pink plastic tumbler." She did see a lot of Bob (while refusing to leave Doris and move in with him) and remained especially close to Pearl and to Carmela.

And yet to the end she was full of surprises. Their building stood next to a twenty-four-hour Cala Foods, where she would buy her Lucky

Charms and vodka very late, when customers were sparse. Going over one night she heard screams and saw a small elderly Asian woman in the parking lot holding on to the purse a thief was trying to wrest from her. Tippi kicked the mugger in the back of the knees hard enough to throw him off balance, grabbed his intended victim, and ran with her into the supermarket. As she told the security guard what had happened, the beaming woman repeated, "My hero! My hero!"

The cat population was back down to two: Cookie, a small white-and-gray female that Doris claimed, and Varla, who belonged to Tippi—fittingly, since no one else ever caught more than a glimpse of her. She hid behind the bathtub or the water heater. Doris also liked to feed the pack of feral cats next door, and he had "adopted" a rabbit, Dutch, who lived on a farm sanctuary he sent donations to and whose picture he kept on the mantel in his bedroom.

Timmy, who'd been a friend since he provided the music for *Blonde Sin*, and Doris grew closer during this period, partly because Timmy had received his own HIV diagnosis five years earlier, almost as soon as the test became available. Unlike Doris, he had never been secretive about it. "It's different," he says, "when you're talking about it with someone who's in the same position you are." But they weren't in the same position, since Timmy wasn't symptomatic yet. They'd always had a rapport but with a distance. Doris razzed him and introduced him as "one of my drivers." Then one Friday afternoon as Timmy was leaving, Doris told him he wished he could stay. "There was something about it that was unlike her. It wasn't in a pleading way, but it was very sincere." The distance was gone.

Mildred arrived in December and stayed for five weeks. She was mostly a help, but with her continual chatter, she was an irritant, too. Janice's memoir describes the idiosyncrasies of her speech:

> She had one of those light musical voices and always designed her sentence structure to end in a question. This made you feel included immediately, since it required a response. "How are you, darling? It's lovely today, isn't it? Care for some tea? Tea would be nice, wouldn't it? I have

some lovely biscuits, you like biscuits, don't you, darling? Your blouse is a beautiful color, isn't it, Philip? Isn't it, Doris? Doris loves that shade of pink, don't you, Philip, don't you, Doris?

Janice had always assumed that Doris's eloquent elocution was a put-on, so this was a discovery: "She had the same voice!"

Mildred's arrival meant constant excursions—to Fisherman's Wharf to view the sea lions that had taken up residence there, to Golden Gate Park, to Sausalito and Bolinas and so on. She tried to arrange an outing daily, even when a walk down the street had become a challenge for Doris. Occasionally she convinced Tippi to join them. She disapproved of her reclusiveness—"I'd be sick, too, stuck in that room all day, wouldn't you?"

Mildred was fond of Maurice and delighted when his mother drove down to visit for a few days. "We went out to China Town for dinner," Mildred wrote Marianne and Tony, "and browsed round the shops. She had trouble understanding my Australian accent!" They had a pleasant Christmas at Maurice's. Connie remembers Christmas shopping with Doris for figurines of the Virgin Mary: "We went all up and down 24th Street in the Mission getting those. I probably had a whole trunkful. That image of the Madonna—female energy—was very big with Doris."

In fact, there were Virgins all over the apartment. By far his favorite incarnation was the Virgin of Guadalupe, the radiant Madonna said to have appeared before a Mexican Indian in 1531. Doris was living in the Mission, the most Mexican part of the city, and he had a Mexican American boyfriend for whom, as a birthday present, he'd painted the holy image on the back of a jeans jacket. And not as camp, or not entirely: Maurice was a practicing Catholic, with a large image of a thorn-crowned Jesus in his living room that certainly would have pleased Mildred.

After the holidays Doris grew weaker. Cytomegalovirus (CMV), a pathogen deadly to AIDS patients, was spreading from his digestive system to his eyes. "Everything was bad news," Pearl says, speaking of several friends she was helping to care for. "When you would leave the doctor's office it was always very sad, and everybody would cry" because they'd been told "something else awful, like 'You're probably gonna go blind.' It was just a matter of being sweet, not talking about too many things, just massaging or holding somebody."

Janice remembers a horrible day when she and Mildred took Doris to Ralph K. Davies for an MRI; the regular machine was out of service, and to reach its replacement required going outside and up a rickety, precarious ramp. "I turned around and looked at Doris in the wheelchair and thought, *Oh my God, she looks so sick.* She was nervous. She was cold. And she was afraid." Doris asked her to hold his legs as they slid him headfirst into the deafening machine. "And Mildred was talking, talking."

On February 1, Mildred sent Ace a West Graphics Doris card for his approaching sixty-sixth birthday:

> Philip is in hospital. He went in to have a catheter put in his chest. It's only small and doesn't hurt—so he can have more nourishment of various kinds. He went in Monday and has already gained five pounds. He will be in till about next Tuesday or Wednesday so they can assess his needs. He can still eat but the trouble is eating usually gives him pain because of the esophagus. The little tube bypasses the trouble spot. . . .
>
>   The room gets the morning sun and looks over the park and towards the city. I usually have lunch in the cafeteria which is quite cheap. Philip looked well last night. All going well he should make it home [i.e., to Australia] in March.

If Mildred was right, then Doris got out of the hospital on February 5 or 6. On February 7, he met the last person who would assume a major role in his life, as he would in hers. Peggy Darm was a visiting nurse who came to the apartment that Thursday to show Maurice and other members of the care group how to administer total parenteral nutrition (TPN) using what Doris called his "'90s jewelry," the new portal in his chest.

PEGGY WAS BORN IN TURLOCK, CALIFORNIA, IN 1949 AND GREW UP A few minutes south of San Francisco, on the peninsula. By the age of fifteen she was hitching up to the Haight-Ashbury, whose flower-child mysticism provided the foundation for her worldview. Her father, hoping for the best, sent her to a Catholic girls' college in Minnesota. There she met a young man who brought her into the far-left Students for a Democratic Society; she moved to Madison, Wisconsin, then a beehive of radical politics, went to Cuba in 1969 with the first Venceremos Brigade, and returned four months later to organize a women's-liberation collective. Her son, Silas, was born on a commune in Pennsylvania in 1972. Having decided to raise him on her own, she came back to the Bay Area and enrolled in nursing school—"It had been in the back of my mind that I could help people."

She got her degree in 1976 and moved into the city, where she fell in love with the Castro, though she isn't gay herself. "It was like having a fair all the time. The Haight went bad so fast; that never happened on Castro Street. It still hasn't happened." One of her few experiences of drag queens, outside of Halloween, occurred on an evening at the Happy Boy drive-in restaurant at Market and 15th, where she and Silas encountered a man with a glitter-dusted beard wearing a sequined green tulle '50s prom dress. Years later she figured out it was Ambi.

She loved working on the trauma ward and then the neurology ward at San Francisco General Hospital. She wanted, she says, to perform an extraordinary service. She took up Nichiren Buddhism— ardently, as she did everything—and the twice-daily chanting of *nam-myoho-renge-kyo* became a lifelong practice. More degrees followed, and with them more jobs. Late in 1990 she accepted a salary cut in order to take a position with an organization that provided visiting nurses to patients with terminal illnesses. In retrospect, her becoming an AIDS nurse seems inevitable; the work suited the urgency of her need to give. She was strongly drawn to the dying men whose homes she visited. "If they had AIDS, I wanted to love them," she says. And she admits, "I had no boundaries."

That didn't make her unique. As the deaths mounted and the epidemic exploded, the long-accepted rules about boundaries between caregiver and patient were increasingly ignored. Peggy is intense, voluble, and large—when she met Doris she weighed around two hundred pounds. She understood that her patients needed her touch as much as they needed her nursing skills; other people were frightened of physical contact with the infected. "I was so big and buxom," she says, "that I could hold anybody in my arms and make them feel like their mom was holding them. I'd gotten obsessed with the *Pietà*."

Driving through the city on her rounds, she saw the coroner's vans everywhere. That year, 1991, there would be more than fifteen hundred AIDS deaths in San Francisco, more than thirty-seven thousand nationwide. The first invasion of Iraq, Operation Desert Storm, began in mid-January, and she was among the San Franciscans who marched in protest. As the chanting crowd advanced through the streets, she looked at the buildings they were passing and thought, *There's a sick person in every one.*

On February 7 her office sent her to Philip Mills's apartment to explain how to use and sterilize the TPN portal. She was bedazzled by the brightly painted pink-and-blue entryway and even more by all the Virgins; there must have been two hundred. She knew her new patient was Australian, since they had talked briefly on the phone, but that was about it. Maurice and Doris—or, as she always knew him, Philip—immediately struck her as "beautiful, magic people." Their first collective goal was to fatten Philip for the trip to Australia he was bent on making. His initial reaction to the medical equipment was a strangely modest one: "This costs so much!" Peggy, still angry about the war, shot back, "Every one of those missiles costs a million dollars! This is *nothing*."

What she mainly remembers from that first month is "standing at the foot of the bed, while Maurice sat in the chair, giving Philip foot rubs. He really reminded me of a calf—those big eyes. The sun coming in in the afternoon over Twin Peaks, how beautiful it was." One day they were sitting at the kitchen table, which Doris had collaged with photos and cards under plastic, and she looked down and had a moment like Maurice's moment coming up the stairs at Oak Street: "Holy shit—that's you!" Doris began to tell her about his life. "He talked about Australia. He talked about the sun. He talked about Jackie. He and Maurice talked a lot about their drag queen friends." The idea of drag fascinated her because "like LSD—which is something I haven't taken since I was in my twenties—it was another reality. And I don't really like this one so much."

Doris told Peggy about his siblings, about Gina, and, with a good deal of humor, about Mildred and Ace's relationship. He described his life as a prostitute, and of course he talked about the movie, which he still thought he was going to see finished. Every day they grew closer. "I was wide open. Philip was wide open. Many, many people in the city were at that time." One day when Doris was out of the room Maurice told her, "Philip is a control freak. He made that movie, and he insisted on doing every single little bit of it—he built the sets, he did the makeup, he did everything. And now he can't control his own body."

When Peggy first arrived, Mildred was still in town. "I said, 'Mildred, how could you be a Catholic? They're terrible to gay people!' She said, 'Oh, no—that was a big mistake! That's all straightened out now, they don't believe that anymore.'" Peggy's heart went out to her even as Mildred tried her patience. "She went on and on and on and on and on. She was often kind of inappropriate." Mildred told her that in Sydney she was a person of status who got to ride around in limousines, and she was losing all that. "And her heart was breaking."

But Peggy's exposure to Mildred was limited because Doris's friends had made a project of keeping his mother entertained and occupied. Janice was at the apartment one Friday evening in March, shortly before Doris and Mildred's scheduled departure for Sydney. Choosing a restaurant was always a fun ritual, and with dinnertime approaching Mildred urged Doris to phone Maurice. "I just called him, but there's no answer," he told her. Then he added, "He has a new boyfriend."

It was true. Whether Doris felt betrayed I can't say, though I tend to doubt it. Gay mores were different then. Monogamy was the exception.

Romantic commitment meant something different than it did in the straight world, partly because, in gay circles, the intimacy of friendship was so profound. Maybe the arrival of Peggy and the strength of her bond with Doris—with both of them—gave Maurice permission to pull back a little. After all, he had been with Doris for three years of accelerating decline, and Doris was no longer functioning sexually.

But having a second relationship didn't shake his commitment to Doris. "He was a really faithful lover," Janice says. "He didn't desert her. There were times when he just would say, 'I'm not going to be here.'" She sees it as something he had to do in order to stay connected to life. "We weren't trained. We didn't know what we were doing and needed to take our *selves* back occasionally." Janice, too, would sometimes disappear for a few days, using work—she was then the manager of a small catering kitchen—as an excuse until she was ready to return. Doris was always delighted when she did: "I would embrace his outstretched hand in both of mine, kiss it, tell him how much I'd missed him, too, because I had."

"Let's get going then," Mildred said, once it became clear that they were on their own that evening. The three of them set off, walking slowly, arms linked, for the inexpensive Chinese restaurant on Mission Street they had chosen. As they settled at one of the pink Formica tables, the waitress slapped down menus and reeled off the specials.

"I can't hear," Doris whispered.

Janice asked the waitress to speak more slowly. "I can't hear, I can't hear," he repeated, then slipped from his chair and onto the floor, thrashing violently. Janice went with him, guiding his fall and blocking his hands from the portal in his chest, which they were seeking. As the seizure continued, Mildred panicked. *"Is he going to die right here?"* It was the first time Janice had heard her acknowledge the gravity of his condition.

The ambulance was slow to arrive. By the time it did, Doris had come to, but he was still having trouble hearing and now seeing, as well as comprehending. "What happened to me?" he kept asking, over and over.

At the hospital, the doctors ordered another MRI, and he started to cry. "I'm not going into that machine again, I'm not! You don't know what it's like! It's like being in a coffin!" Janice told him, "You don't have to. They'll test you forever. Look at them and don't blink and say no." Which is what he did.

Instead of providing the calming atmosphere you might expect for a patient who had just suffered a grand mal seizure, the staff put him in a room under bright lights. He became even more agitated when he heard one of the doctors say, "Make sure you stay with him because when people have a seizure, they usually have more." After that he was too frightened to shut his eyes. Another doctor arrived with antiseizure medication, which he managed to swallow. Despite the first doctor's warning, there were no more.

Mildred phoned Maurice, and this time he answered. He came immediately. Not only hadn't Mildred eaten; she'd left her blood pressure medication at the apartment, and she was exhausted and unsteady. Maurice drove her home; it's not clear whether Doris went with them or was discharged the following day. He and Mildred departed for Australia shortly afterward.

The night before they left was hard because Doris was afraid he wasn't coming back. Peggy remembers it as "the only time she ever really broke down and showed me a certain part of herself. What she said to me is, 'I haven't done enough. I haven't done enough in this life.'"

He stayed in Australia for a month, mostly utilizing a wheelchair, not only because he was weak but also because something like gangrene (Marianne and Ron both used the word) was ulcerating one foot. He spent time with his mother and his father and traveled down to Wolumla and Merimbula to see his siblings and their families, then returned to Manly Vale. It wasn't all sad. Andrew came up from Merimbula for a few days and wheeled Doris around the Sydney Royal Easter Show, a huge agricultural fair they had always attended as kids. The livestock delighted Doris, and he had a wonderful time, "except," he complained, "for this funny little woman"—Mildred, of course—"who kept standing in front of me all day."

Doris telephoned his old flame Bernard and they had lunch together. Ace and Mildred came along, and Doris spent part of the meal telling them about the ache of losing him. "Oh, bless his heart!" Bernard said affectionately, remembering how wounded Doris sounded that day. Nostalgia hasn't totally softened Bernard, though, because then he added, "He was such an evil bitch! I mean, the last thing she said to me was, 'You broke my heart.' *When she's dying.*" But he said it with a laugh.

Despite being skeletal and barely able to walk, Doris generally kept his spirits up, although he lost his temper with Mildred one morning when she informed him that a priest was on his way over. But he was always happy in the company of his sisters and brothers. They did their best to keep up a semblance of normalcy. "My deepest regret," Liz told me, "was the fear of the disease—holding back when he was quite ill. He was lying on the bed, back in his old bedroom, and I remember later thinking I should've got onto the bed and held him. We were all scared of AIDS then." I know how she felt. Silvana and I put up a friend with AIDS, and I can recall staring uneasily at his toothbrush in our toothbrush glass. I knew very well what the avenues of transmission were, and I was ashamed of my worry. But it was hard not to be unnerved.

Some doctors were less than professional themselves. One orthopedic surgeon at San Francisco General Hospital tried to spread panic among her colleagues about the dangers of operating on HIV-positive patients; they were disgusted, but *60 Minutes* offered her a platform on national TV. (She later became a Holocaust denier.) She might have gotten a sympathetic ear at Manly Hospital, where Doris had to go for his infected foot. Marianne, who'd come up to Sydney for his last weekend at home, accompanied him. "Because Philip had AIDS, they didn't want to treat him. They were *rude*—they were awful." When she put a question to the doctor, he snapped, "I just told you that! What did I say!" She repeated his words verbatim and then let him have it. "I just couldn't believe that a medical person could be so unsympathetic and uncharitable! Philip didn't get upset"—he maintained the same serene calm he'd shown in the hospital after his bashing years earlier.

When he left Sydney it was agreed that he would summon Mildred when the time came, though they probably didn't put it so explicitly.

He and Peggy had been on the phone constantly, ostensibly discussing medical issues. Once he was back, their intimacy deepened. She would drive him around the city or take him to Golden Gate Park—he loved the arboretum, especially the touching-and-smelling garden, and the ducks. Often she dropped by the apartment when she was on her rounds. Doris wasn't her only terminally ill patient; she'd been sitting with one emaciated young man, gently talking him through his last hours, on the day Doris got back. She would perform her morning and evening prayers, after asking permission, in the room of whatever client she was looking after. Sometimes Doris would chant with her early in the morning, before the sun was above the horizon, when the room was just filling with color.

Peggy began stopping by on her way home at the end of the day; then she started sleeping over. The office grew alarmed. Her supervisor reminded her that nurses weren't allowed to have real relationships with their patients, "because we had power and they didn't." Peggy disagreed, vehemently. Self-restraint isn't a part of her personality, and she was falling in love. Not in a sexual sense; she was straight, Doris was gay, and Maurice was the love of his life—none of which held them back when Doris and Peggy decided that it would be a good idea for her to move in. "It's like a love triangle," Doris observed. But then he added, as if to make sure no one misunderstood, "And, you know, I'm not a lesbian."

The office gave Peggy an ultimatum: She could keep spending time with Doris only if she gave up nursing him. Someone else would step in for her. When she told Doris they were no longer going to let her handle his TPN apparatus, he dragged it over to the window and prepared to fling it down to the street. Doris rarely resorted to melodrama, and it worked. "All right," she relented—"fuck them." What she told her bosses she no longer remembers; events may have moved so quickly that she didn't have to tell them anything.

It's worth noting that no one I spoke to expressed qualms about their relationship. Peggy never tried to take anybody's place or to limit anyone's access. "The most huggable, sensible, smart, warm, cool person" is the way Pearl describes her. "You could always find out what was going on from Peggy," Connie says. "She kept everyone in the loop, and she would tell us what was needed. Peggy is gentle; she's not controlling." They were all happy to let her handle the medical care—especially Maurice, who Peggy told me (admiringly) "actually had boundaries."

Among the things she and Doris talked about a lot was his life as a prostitute. He was worried about the clients he'd abandoned, one paraplegic in particular: "Doris told me in this funny, cracky, sad voice, 'Who's doing that now?'" He regarded whoring as service to others, the way Peggy sees nursing: "You hook up your personality to another person. It's not just doing tasks." She says that Doris knew he didn't love the paraplegic—or any of his clients—but he also knew that sex, like LSD, can take you to another world, "and that's what he could do for those people."

Still, if there were no regrets ("She regretted she had to stop!"), there was anguish over the outcome. "People, to die beautifully, have to be brave and look at everything they've done. He said, 'I've slept with a lot of men from the suburbs that were hiding who they were.' They were making their own choices, but all those men had infected their women, and Philip had infected their women. It was really hard for him to look at that part. He said it was a terrible thing to do." Doris, she explains, was "preparing herself morally" for death.

When Peggy talks about Doris, she alternates, like many of his friends, between masculine and feminine pronouns. "I actually never met Doris," she reminded me. "I only knew Philip." She got to know Doris later, through stories and videotapes. "One night, really late at night—he was tired and it was hard—I said, 'Where *is* Doris?' and he said, 'I don't know. I don't know where she is.'"

After Doris's return from Australia, Peggy never again saw him put food in his mouth. All his nutrition came through the TPN line. What was happening was obvious, but he wasn't ready to accept it. His refusal to make out a will was maddening because *Vegas in Space* was on the point of completion and the possibility of profit beckoned. Peggy sees it as more than denial, though denial played a part: "When you're that close to the other world, you care more about wherever it is you're going than you care about what's here."

For a long time he also resisted drawing up a durable power of attorney to grant Maurice the authority to make health-care decisions when Doris became unable to. These legal documents were taking wider hold as the families of some AIDS patients shut out their lovers. Maurice told Peggy it was a kind of magical thinking—"He's afraid he's going to die as soon as he does it." Finally Maurice and Peggy prevailed, and on the day the three of them hammered out the provisions they at last talked frankly about how close Doris was to the end. The document made it clear that he didn't want to be treated "heroically," as Peggy put it, but that he wanted to be kept alive until Mildred could get there. Bob and Tippi acted as witnesses.

They signed it on a Sunday evening, June 9. Monday night Peggy slept over. Doris dreamed of the devil. On Tuesday morning he was so feverish and delusional that it was clear he needed to be hospitalized again. In the entryway to Ralph K. Davies he asked, "Peggy, why did the devil take my glasses and hide them?" Maybe he'd been dreaming about his vision because the CMV had gotten into his eyes. "You know that didn't really happen," Peggy told him, and he came back to himself a little: "Yeah, I do know that." But from that point on he drifted in and out of consciousness. According to Peggy, during his five days in the intensive care unit he "retreated to the place between the worlds where people go when they're dying and they're looking for the way across. I spent a lot of time on the terrace at Ralph K. Davies. Venus and Mars were getting closer and closer together in the western sky. And everybody said when they touched, that's when he'll die."

The narcotics he was given in the ICU may be what clinched the turning inward. Subsequently there were few complaints of pain. After five days they came to the decision to end aggressive treatment: Doris officially became a hospice patient, which meant that treatment of the illness ended and palliative care began. Doris was transferred to a private room in Ralph K. Davies, and Mildred was summoned.

"There was this weird thing." Peggy wasn't sure whether to tell me. "The day that Philip came out of the ICU, it was in the afternoon. The light was darkening. And he started playing with himself. I had never seen anything like this! I was like, 'Oh, you want me to leave?' He didn't talk. He didn't talk for a long time in the end—sometimes, really, a sentence a day—but he could communicate. He didn't want me to go. I sat down there." Even though he was no longer capable of an erection, "he was giving off the most intense sexual vibes and looking in my eyes. 'Are you sure you don't want me to leave?' No." Suddenly, unexpectedly, she felt herself responding. "I just started breathing with him. I'm very attuned to doing that from all my years of Lamaze!" And she came. Maybe, she thinks, she came for both of them. Doris had spent his adult life as a bringer of sexual gifts; it was a calling, which was one reason he went on following it after he knew he should stop. This gift to Peggy was his last.

"That night we spent lying on the bed. I don't know how much Philip actually talked. I would let go and just say how great people were and how great love was, and how everything really was OK and going to be OK." She stayed on a cot in the hospital room with him every night. "One night he couldn't sleep, and we lay on the bed together. We cuddled a lot, and watched for the light to come. I sang. I have a very bad voice, as bad as Doris's. But I still sang to people."

One day she went by the apartment on South Van Ness, and while she was there X showed up. He had biked over to see Tippi; he was still a regular if not a frequent visitor. He and Peggy hadn't met, but they'd each heard a lot about the other. X cried, "*Judy!*" (He was as bad with names as he was with lyrics.) They embraced and they cried. Peggy was distraught: "I made her do the durable power of attorney and I promised her she wouldn't die if she did, and look! Now she's really sick!"

"You get emotional and you get crazy," she told me sheepishly.

X replied drily, "That's right. I'm sure she's lying in the hospital right now and saying to herself, *That bitch made me sign that paper and look where it got me!*"

His sarcasm immediately brought her back to earth. ("I miss A-level gay wit!" she says.) They went to the hospital together. X was subdued, but the visit was free of tension. "Did I do OK?" Doris asked her afterward. "It might have been he asked me with his eyes," Peggy recalls. "I think he asked me in words. That was good. You have to make peace with everybody in this world when you're leaving."

X saw Doris once more. A day or two later he phoned Robin and said, "We *have* to go." Robin tried to squirm out of it, he told me, but X was insistent: "Robin, she loved you." So Robin picked X up and they drove over to the hospital. "We went in, and she was getting a bath," Robin remembers. "She was in horrible shape and couldn't speak. I stood there and didn't know what to do. And X looked at Doris and he said, 'This means you're not gonna make the Gay Day parade, right?' And I started laughing and Doris kind of smiled. That made it easy."

The room was bright, with a large window facing south toward the Castro. They put up pictures and brought in a tape player, and there was a stream of visitors. Timmy, who was one of them, knew seven people at Ralph K. Davies that week. At one point they surrounded the bed and sang songs from *Abbey Road*. One day, Peggy recalls, "Connie and I were playing Joan Baez, 'cause we thought he liked Joan Baez, and he said, 'That's really boring.' That's the only thing he said for that whole day."

Some people couldn't handle the hospital. Tippi was one, of course. Ginger was another: "I couldn't bear to go see her. I had planned to do it a couple of times, and then I just couldn't." Phillip didn't make it, either. But by then his absence was well established. "I felt guilty that I couldn't take Doris to this appointment and that appointment because I was obsessed with trying to finish the film. It took a lot of reconciling within my emotional state, but I convinced myself: *I'm doing what I need to do to serve Doris.* And I let go of my guilt."

Two years earlier, in 1989, he'd lost his job at Monaco Film Labs. He had lost count of how many times he'd been caught in the vault snorting coke, but what finally got him fired was his chronic lateness. Naturally he was upset, because up till then he'd been using the lab's facilities to work on the movie. He found a low-paying position at the Shanti Project, the nonprofit agency that serves people with terminal illnesses, and over several years there he honed administrative skills that are still serving him. "I never went to work high once. As they say in the recovery world, it was manageable then." It must have been a strange job for someone invested in not thinking about what was happening to his closest friends. On his first day, he turned in mild panic to the director of client services: "This guy's calling and says he just got an AIDS diagnosis! What do I tell him?" "Tell him he's gonna die!"

The movie tormented him. "I had done it all on paper. I had a timeline: the lab work, the mixing, the prints." All he lacked was the money. X's credit card debt topped $20,000. "We'd already put eight years into it," X says. "I wasn't gonna let it go. Oh-ho no. All the blood, sweat, and tears and sleepless nights that we've both put into this thing, *and* the fact that now Doris and Tippi are dying—we're not quitting now! Even if we're a joke from one end of this town to the other, we're going through with it!"

The following year they found an investor. But that summer Iraq invaded Kuwait, the stock market tanked, and the funds their angel had planned to make use of evaporated.

And then, in late 1990, a friend told Phillip about a rich young woman who might be interested in bankrolling the final stages. He made it his New Year's resolution to give her a call. "I met her at Julie's Supper Club soon after that. I went down there and had a martini with her on a January night and walked home with a check for twenty thousand dollars in my pocket.

"And it was a race against the clock. Doris was dying. I did one final edit, shot the titles, went to Vegas for the background shots, had all the miniatures cut in, and turned it over to Bob Davis, who had volunteered to do the sound." It had been eight years since they'd filmed the first scene.

MILDRED HAD ARRIVED WHILE DORIS WAS STILL IN THE HOSPITAL. The afternoon she drove in from the airport he was inert, but the minute she came in, he started wailing and shouting, "What's she doing here!" Because he knew.

"You have to be good," Maurice told him sternly. "You asked for this. You have to behave yourself."

Peggy took Mildred to a bench outside the hospital while Maurice calmed Doris down. "One of the things that Mildred did was just talk. We were in front of the ER at Ralph K. Davies, it was dusk, Mars and Venus were out there getting closer and closer, and she just talked and I didn't really listen, to tell you the truth. She wasn't crying."

She was the next day. "I think there was still an IV. She was crying and saying how sad it was that we weren't going try to keep him alive anymore—no more IV food, no more medicine." Maurice reassured her that they were going to keep him comfortable. A priest arrived. "This is not extreme unction!" Mildred insisted. "This is the prayer for the sick. They don't have extreme unction anymore!" Inwardly Peggy was rolling her eyes. *Maybe not in Mildred's Catholic Church*, she thought—*the same church that had changed its mind about gay people and apologized*. Fortunately, Doris was absent that day. "He always looked to everybody's eyes like he was there, but starting in the hospital he didn't produce very much speech anymore. It didn't matter to me, because I was producing so much! 'If this is what you think, blink your eyes!' I had been doing that for quite a while with other people, so it didn't seem strange to me."

Lulu and Janice came for a visit, and they were shocked by what they saw. "One of her eyes was gone completely," Lulu says. "It was *gone*. It was not there." The skin on Doris's face had drawn so close around the bone that he could no longer shut his eyelids all the way. "She looked at us, and she couldn't talk. Her mouth was dry—she was pointing toward her mouth." Janice rubbed ice cubes on his lips.

"She was doing this—reaching," Janice recalls. "The TV was on. There was a picture of Our Lady of Guadalupe on the wall there. I said to myself, *Is he seeing someone? Maybe Our Lady of Guadalupe has manifested for him! Or maybe he's trying to tell us to turn off the TV.*"

Lulu told me, "She pointed to the wall, and she was like—" He made gurgling noises. "'Look, there's Judy Garland! There's Marilyn Monroe!' She was seeing a vision—she was seeing famous dead people! That's all I can imagine."

According to Peggy, reaching isn't uncommon at this stage of dying, though she had never seen it go on for so long. Doris did it for a couple of days. "It's encouraging. You *know* that there's something there that you can't see. It's totally my interpretation that they're reaching for angels, or that they're seeing things that are good."

After four or five days, when there was nothing more the hospital could do for him, they moved him to Maurice's house, since Doris's apartment was three flights up. Mildred continued sleeping over on South Van Ness, with the spectral Tippi. Except for the unending gaze of that suffering Jesus, Peggy says, Maurice had beautiful taste. Doris had painted his foyer red. The front parlor was filled with books and records; a double door led to a second parlor, where they put the hospital bed. Maurice stayed with Doris during the day while Peggy slept in a bed on the back porch, and then she took over at night. Visitors came and went; sometimes Doris was lucid, sometimes not. He was no longer in horrible pain, partly because of the liquid morphine he was being given, and partly because his body was shutting down.

Nighttime was the hardest because he had trouble sleeping. "We snuggled a lot," Peggy says. "Sometimes he did sleep. Obviously I'm remembering the things that were important to me, the restless times, the times when I was necessary. It's like what you do with a baby: His teeth were hurting, and I told him the names of all the people who loved him." One night she was swabbing his mouth and removed a gob of brown exudate, worrying her that the end was going to be ugly and gruesome, as it can be. "But he hadn't eaten for a month." There were no excreta, no odors of digestion. "It was very clean, and he smelled sweet to the very end."

Mildred's noisy displays of emotion tended to upset Doris, but Maurice managed her expertly, often with errands that kept her away. He gave her the laundry to do, which surprised Peggy. "No, that's good," he explained. "She will feel useful. She'll feel like she did something for him." Doris's friends still shepherded Mildred around, and what they saw, and admired, was restraint and gentle humor. She put her real feelings on paper in a meditation:

> *The hand of God rests on me gently*
> *He loves me*
> *It rests also on my family*
> *Philip's life is coming to an end*
> *He will see God soon*
> *The angels will lead him into paradise*
> *The pain he has endured so bravely will be at an end*
> *All his sins will be forgiven*
> *and he will see the face of God and life*
> *We will remember how beautiful he is*

She named his brothers and sisters, including Gina—"the ones he loved so well"—and Maurice, and continued:

> *So it is coming to an end or so it seems*
> *The Halcyon days we had*
> *The sweetness of it all*
> *The love we knew & felt will never end*
> *God's will endures*
> *My prayers are answered*
> *life goes on for them*
> *And Tony too who suffered through it all*
> *We eat the bread and drink the wine*
> *God's will be done*
> > *Mildred*

She wanted to be with him when he died, but she was in the habit of going home to bed early, and when Peggy recognized it was happening it was after ten on a Friday night and Mildred had left. The only other people in the house were Maurice and his boyfriend. "He couldn't sleep, and he had a fever. He wasn't seizing, but he was really restless. I was probably chanting, and crying and singing and just being with him. He could see, and he couldn't talk—he was just *restless*. And hot. I gave him anal Tylenol. We didn't use IV anymore. Finally he passed out and he stopped moving. He was still breathing. People go through a thing where they'll breathe for a while, and stop and start. I told them, 'He might be dying, I'm not really sure.' And then, when I knew it was really close—like probably an hour—I left, and they sat by his bed. Maurice didn't tell me I had to leave. I felt that he had been conscious and in my arms until he was unconscious, and then what happened after that didn't matter. And I was an intruder, in a way. Probably I walked for about forty-five minutes. And he left his body as the sun was coming up." It was Saturday, June 22, 1991, the morning after the summer solstice. "I actually got a chart done, and you can see in the death: there are Mars and Venus touching each other." The sun wasn't yet above the horizon when she came back.

Maurice said, "I feel as if I've been on vacation in a marvelous country and I'll never be able to go back there." They began telephoning, and the house filled up quickly. When Mildred got there, she was quiet, not noisy.

X was the one who answered the phone on 18th Street. "We got the call early in the morning," Phillip remembers. "It was dawn and he came in and he was silhouetted against the window and the dawn, and he said, 'Well, it's time to go, she's gone.' And we went over there. I can't believe I'm crying. And who was there? Connie Champagne and Pearl were there, and Peggy, who I'd never met, though I'd heard about Peggy. And Maurice. Doris was there in the bed. Of course, I moved into action and had to issue press releases. I knew that if you didn't do this, it wouldn't be done."

Timmy stayed next to Doris for several hours. "She was still warm. I was so sad she died. But I was still a little bit fascinated with what that looked like. She very slightly cooled down. Not a lot. It was early morning, and the way the light was coming in on her face was other-worldly—the colors. It was weird to feel a face when it's getting cool. The warmth is not there, and the color changes. It's almost like the skin is translucent. It seemed like the light could go very far into her skin, and you could see through. There's still stuff there, but it's leaving the surface."

After the others left, Maurice and his mother, who had driven down to the city that morning, and Mildred and Peggy went to Mission Dolores to pray. They had lunch at a Chinese restaurant in the Castro, and then they went their separate ways.

MOST OF THE SAN FRANCISCO PAPERS GAVE DORIS THE TREATMENT he would have deemed appropriate. The *Examiner* put its obituary, "Queen of Drag a Quiet Man," on the front page, next to a glamour shot from the year before (blonde, skinny, copious necklaces) and, after the jump, a West Graphics image of Doris as Barbara Bush. It was considerably more respectful than the thirteen-line notice that ran in the *Sydney Morning Herald* under the unadorned heading "Drag Queen Dies of AIDS."

Lulu asked Mildred and Janice to dinner on the evening before Mildred's departure. Janice pleaded illness. "Lulu called me up: 'What the fuck are you doing? *Get over here.* Don't start pulling this shit!' I said, 'I'm afraid, I'm afraid.' He says, 'Yeah, we're all afraid. Get over here, I'm makin' pasta, girl!' So I go over there. 'Hi, Mildred! How are you?' Lulu puts down the bottle. 'Don't dig too deep.'"

Janice laughed. "We couldn't even eat. We just drank. She kept saying, 'This is very nice, oh yes, very nice.' She didn't give us any signs that she wanted to talk about it." It was a beautiful night, and driving her home they made a detour through Golden Gate Park. "We watched her walk up the stairs, alone, into that freaky apartment with crazy Tippi hiding in the room with her tweetsy water."

She got to be a celebrity one more time. In Sydney, Ron and Miss Abood organized *Who Did That Bitch Think She Was?* at Kinselas, on Taylor Square, on what would have been Doris's thirty-ninth birthday. The attractions included Jackie ("direct from Paris for one night only"), Miss Abood, two of the Showbags, the singer Wendy Saddington (who had often shared a bill with Sylvia and the Synthetics), and the opera singer Mary Alterator (an old buddy of Doris's), plus "priceless treasures on loan from the Fish Museum" and a sneak preview of *Vegas in Space*. The $19.95 admission barely covered Jackie's airfare and a twenty-four-page souvenir booklet, with a golden-tinted Doris in a blonde bob on the front and handsomely stubbled and bare-chested on the back. As often happened after these events (Tommy's was followed by sniping about Lulu's new VCR), the organizers of the memorial were later accused of profiting from it.

The 1991 San Francisco Lesbian/Gay Freedom Day Parade took place eight days after Doris's death. His friends put the old six-foot-by-six-foot self-portrait in the back of Timmy's '64 Oldsmobile convertible, and as it inched along—the day was warm and it kept threatening to overheat—with some of them perched on the car and some of them marching alongside, the crowd chanted, "Long live Doris!" They had refreshments on Timmy's patio afterward. Poor Tippi was wilting. "I came in," Timmy says, "and I looked in the mirror, and that's the very first time that I saw that white stuff on my tongue—thrush." His own trials with AIDS were about to begin.

Gwyn spoke for many of Doris's friends when she said, "There were times when I was driving on the freeway and I would have to pull over, because I was overcome. I was heaving. I couldn't believe she was gone."

They buried his ashes in Golden Gate Park, in the arboretum, where he loved to wander. "We found an old Monterey pine," Peggy recalls. "You went along this path, and there was a bench in front of it, and you went behind the bench and between the trees, so it was not really secluded, because no place is really secluded, and we dug a hole with a trowel, a pretty big hole—it went pretty deep—and then buried them. We filled it up and filled it in and covered it over and put a big rock on it.

"I think it was common practice in the city at the time. Probably every tree in Golden Gate Park has someone's ashes. And the city is"—she searched for the right word—"consecrated."

15

BEYOND THE VALLEY OF THE DOLLS

PEGGY MOVED INTO DORIS'S APARTMENT ON JULY 4, 1991. IT had been mostly cleared (some would say ransacked) by friends and acquaintances, but there was still a lot of stuff there. The only empty room was Tippi's—she had finally moved to Bob's—and Silas, Peggy's nineteen-year-old son, slept there with a friend; the colors in the other rooms were too much for them. The visiting-nurses company Peggy had worked for let her go. She spent most of the summer just sleeping and reflecting on what she had been through. One weekend when X was out of town she stayed at his and Phillip's place and watched videotapes of all the shows she'd heard about.

A week or two after they had settled in, she was asleep in the living room—it was late—and Varla started howling. Connie Champagne

Phillip at the Castro Theatre, 1991. Photo by Robin Clark.

had adopted Cookie, Doris's cat, but Tippi hadn't been able to take Varla when she left. Peggy tried to wake herself several times, and finally she sat up, half asleep, "and Philip was in front of me. You could see through him. And I said, 'Oh, my—it's a ghost.' And I put up my hand, and he turned into a swirl of golden sparks and flew into my body and went right here—to my heart."

The next morning, they discovered that Varla had slipped through the back window they always left a little bit open and disappeared. Maybe she joined the feral cats next door. "I told Tippi," Peggy says, "but Tippi was too sick to care anymore." Doris, though, stayed in Peggy's heart. "I used to lie down and I'd say, 'If you want to be here for a little while longer, you can be here with me.'"

In January, Silas moved down to his grandmother's house in Los Gatos, south of San Jose, to help take care of her. Early in February he suffered a stroke, unusual for a person so young. He remained stable enough after he was hospitalized, until, on the third evening, his brain began swelling dangerously; he turned bright red, and saliva bubbled from his mouth. As a team of nurses intervened, Peggy stood in a corner, chanting. She could see his blood pressure plunging and his heart rate accelerating on the monitors, and she knew he was dying. "And Philip flew out of my heart." He hovered before her, she says, composed of Evian water, which he had always loved to drink. "She was putting herself between me and Silas so I didn't have to see." That was her last sight of Doris—"sparkling water in the sky."

Silas didn't die. He recovered slowly, with some motor damage and vision loss. Timmy and X and many other friends came down often to hang out with them. By the end of the decade, Peggy had quit nursing. She and Silas still live together in Northern California.

SINCE TIPPI WAS SECRETIVE AND FRAIL TO BEGIN WITH, FOR A LONG time people didn't know she was sick. That's why Janice was so angry about her indolence around the ailing Doris, though it's hard to imagine Tippi as much of a caregiver even at her healthiest. Still, she was in better shape than Doris was. In February 1991 she felt well enough for Bob to squire her down to the famously kitschy Madonna Inn in San Luis Obispo. "It's so pretty here!" she wrote Doris and Mildred on a postcard. "When they say Pink they don't mess around they mean Pink."

In May, she made a trip to Illinois to see her family. "One of the things she wanted to do before she died," Bob says, "was to forgive everybody." He knew that the monstrous dimensions her parents had swollen to in her imagination had less to do with them than with her own deep unhappiness, and when later they flew out with Tippi's brother for her memorial, everyone found them unassuming and kind.

After Tippi's return, the group was sitting around one day talking about high school proms; Tippi mentioned she had never had one, and they realized that proms were a sore spot for a lot of queer people. They came up with the idea of holding a cross-dressing one at the End Up, a popular bar:

You and your date are invited to
TIPPI'S PROM
in the
VALLEY OF THE DOLLS
a Formal Ball in honor of
the oldest living child star in captivity
"TIPPI" of the fabulous SLUTS A-GO-GO'S!!! . . .
FORMAL DRESS REQUIRED!

They propped her up by the door, where she cordially received the crowd. A stage show featured songs by Miss X and Connie Champagne. The date was Wednesday, June 19, three days before Doris's death.

After which she consented to move to Bob's. Carmela Carlyle would go over every Friday. "I'd drive her to doctor's appointments. I would serve her Ensures in cocktail glasses with umbrellas. We would watch *Cinderella* together."

Bob expected she'd be healthy for a couple of years: "It didn't even last a couple of months." She all but stopped eating, dropping from 120 pounds to 90. "She was this little bitty thing," Pearl remembers. "I used to take her to her doctor's appointments and roll her out in the wheelchair, and she was just a little skeleton."

As death approached, she began to worry she'd be hospitalized and treated as a male patient. So Bob took her down to the Department of Motor Vehicles and she procured a California state ID designating her Tippi E. D. B. Mead, female. No one asked for verification. The *Chronicle* reporter who wrote her obituary must have checked the public records, since the story noted, erroneously, that she'd had a sex-change operation.

She died on August 25, 1991, two months after Doris. Officially the cause was complications from AIDS, but everyone knew the real reason. "When Doris left," Pearl says, "Tippi gave up. That poor little angel was waiting to die, wanting to be with Doris. She didn't care about sex, drugs, music, drag—nothing. She just wanted to go." They scattered her ashes in San Francisco Bay, at the foot of Fort Point, where Kim Novak leaps into the water in *Vertigo*.

VEGAS IN SPACE HAD ITS WORLD PREMIERE AT THE CASTRO THEATRE a few weeks later, on Friday, October 11. It was pretty much the opening of Phillip's dreams—"the klieg lights, the limousines, my name in lights on the marquee over Castro Street, and every drag queen in town dressed to the nines and lined up around the block." The cast emerged from stretch limos, with a bullhorn-wielding Diet Popstitute excitedly announcing each new arrival.

The reviews were affectionate and did their best to be respectful. After that, it was a matter of finding a distributor. Miss X took Doris's place alongside Phillip as the film's spokesperson. The two deaths made peddling it a strange experience. "It was an extra angle," Phillip says, "but not a particularly good angle in terms of selling an outer space comedy drag queen movie." With their filmmaking mentor Bob Hawk's help they got a midnight screening at the annual Sundance Film Festival in January, which was heady and exciting, and, since other film festivals often draw their programming from Sundance, invitations poured in. Suddenly Phillip was traveling—to London, Turin, Vancouver, Frankfurt, and, with Miss X, LA and Santa Barbara; Miss X also attended a transgender film festival in Vienna. "Some of it was fun," Phillip says. "I had no money, and a lot of times they don't pay unless you're a celebrity. So I went into debt."

Eventually they sold the movie to Troma Entertainment, an energetic little company specializing in the distribution of Z-grade films. Troma made one demand: for copyright reasons, the lyrics to the songs in the lounge act sequence had to be overdubbed. ("By the time I get to Venus, she'll be rising . . .") The advance didn't come close to making Phillip and X rich, but it did help them pay off some debts. Troma gave the picture's LA opening a glitzy Hollywood lead-up; Phillip, Miss X, Timmy, Connie, and Arturo all went down to perform at various venues. And then it went nowhere. In October 1993 it showed up on the USA Network's *Up All Night with Rhonda Shear*, which is about as cheesy as TV gets. During one of the pauses in the movie, a very perky Phillip and Miss X emerged from under the covers of a big bed.

And that was about it. Maybe if Doris had been around to promote it, the picture would have done more business; without him, it lost a major portion of its glamour. Or maybe at the height of the AIDS epidemic the prospect of seeing a silly movie starring two dead drag queens just wasn't that enticing. But it probably fizzled for a simpler reason: with its stagy acting, its nudge-nudge dialogue, and its longueurs, a lot of people find it hard to sit through.

IN LATE 1993 PHILLIP DECAMPED, WITH MUCH FANFARE, TO LOS Angeles, where he was going to direct a movie featuring the wealthy young woman who had provided the late funding for *Vegas in Space*. Almost as soon as he got down there, she confronted him about his drug problem and put the project on ice. "I got paid to disappear, basically." He went back to San Francisco embarrassed and angry. "In recovery lingo, up till then it had been manageable. It reaches a point where it becomes unmanageable. And I *will* confess that in late '93 I had transitioned to injecting speed."

He also suspects an element of delayed grief: Following Doris and Tippi's deaths, he'd kept his thoughts tightly focused on his career, with a good deal of help from intoxicants. In early 1995 he was drawn into producing another tribute show, this time for the dying Diet Popstitute. "And it nearly killed me. The benefit was very long, four or five hours. Soon after that I ended up in General Hospital with pneumonia, from shooting drugs and exhaustion.

"I started driving a cab to make money. In April of that year I was evicted. Most of my friends had turned their back on me at that point—they said, 'Don't call me anymore.' I know I scared people, because I was drinking constantly when I wasn't using drugs." He became one of those denizens of cheap Tenderloin hotels, hanging out with hustlers and availing himself of their services. "San Francisco is a very small town. It's like Mayberry—you can't walk down the street without seeing someone you know. I didn't want to see anybody. I was embarrassed. I was embarrassed. People would say, 'Phil! Phil! What are you doing?' 'Nothing.' 'Really?' 'Do you want to hear the details? I shoot speed, suck cock'—I said that to somebody."

In December 1996, at noon on a Monday, he banged his cab into a Rolls-Royce. It wasn't clear who had run the light. "I had a suspended driver's license. I had three moving violations that year and didn't deal with them. If they had tested me, I would have gone off the map. It was the day I should have gone to jail. The police saw that nobody was hurt and shrugged and walked away.

"I went back to the garage and filled out the accident report. This grizzled old manager came out and looked at my form and said, 'Well, looks like it wasn't your fault. Why don't you go home and come back tomorrow?' I thought, *OK, I've had enough. Time is up. I want this to stop now.*"

He wound up in a treatment facility for indigent men run by the City and County of San Francisco, and he hasn't touched drugs or alcohol since.

I'm glad to say he isn't eaten up by regret. "I got to have so many lives. I got to have a show-biz life. I got to have a down-and-out romantic Tenderloin Bukowski-esque existence. And now I get to be a successful corporate middle-aged person." The one constant: "Things will continue to change, and they will change for the better and they will change for the worse. And that's life. Enjoy what there is to enjoy, suffer what there is to suffer." The Buddhist ring to those words is no coincidence: After he got back on his feet, a neighbor introduced him to Nichiren Buddhism, and he's now a practitioner. "Doris was a mentor, artistically and spiritually as well. She planted a lot of seeds."

There was one more show-business venture: *Simply Stunning: The Doris Fish Story*, a one-act monologue Phillip compiled from Doris's quips and writings, with Arturo, a fine mimic, in the role of Doris. It ran in August and September 2002 at Theatre Rhinoceros as part of a larger show, *Let's Talk About Me*, bookended by a first act with Phillip as Liberace (the queeny bejeweled pianist, if you're too young to remember) and a third act with Jennifer Blowdryer as herself. The press was enthusiastic, and Phillip is proud of it—he produced it—but, he says, "it convinced me that this is not a path to happiness."

The one he's chosen instead has led him, unlikely as it may seem, to the financial sector, where he's done well. He has a home and a husband. His sense of humor, his sense of camp, and his pompadour are all intact, although over time the latter has grown increasingly vertical. Twice in recent years he's stayed with Silvana and me in Brooklyn, and each visit has been preceded by a last-minute email making sure that we had a blow-dryer he could use.

MILDRED DID ABOUT AS WELL AS COULD BE EXPECTED AFTER Doris's death, even though she suffered the double blow of losing her closest friend to cancer while she was still in San Francisco. She had her faith and her volunteer work, and she still had four children to love and to pester, and their children, and traveling down to Merimbula and Wolumla whenever she felt like it even if they didn't, as was clearly the case in March 1995. "Everyone said, 'Oh, listen, it's a bad week to come down, we're all really busy,'" Michael told me. "She said, 'I'm coming anyway!'"

Liz, who still lives in Sydney, told her she was too busy to drive her to the station, then had a change of heart. "Isn't it funny—I *knew* that morning I had to take her." Mildred spent a week at Michael and Anne's in Merimbula, then went out to Wolumla for a few days at Marianne and Tony's. The night before her departure she told Tony over a gin and tonic that she was at peace, that she was ready to die and looking forward to being with Jesus. The next morning, as Marianne was showering, Mildred told Tony she had a headache. He gave her something for it and sat with her on the couch. She went quiet. When Marianne came out of the bathroom, her mother could neither see her nor hear her: a sudden, fatal stroke. She was seventy-two.

They buried her next to Gina, for whom they'd never had the heart to erect a headstone, and even though Doris's remains aren't there, they put his name on the one they raised. Andrew sent me a snapshot, and sometimes I pull it out and look at it:

MILDRED JUNE (MILLIE) MILLS

WONDERFUL MOTHER OF 6 & WHO LOVED GOD

1. 6. 1922–4. 4. 1995

GEORGINA CLARGO MILLS

OUR SPECIAL GINA

25. 8. 1959–31 .7. 1973 SUDDEN ILLNESS

PHILIP CLARGO "DORIS" MILLS

11. 8. 1952–22. 6. 1991 SAN FRANCISCO

R.I.P.

Ace had a longer, slower, harder death. He remained in Sydney, watched over by Liz, as he slowly succumbed to dementia, and when the situation became untenable—"It was like looking after a two-year-old that wasn't living with you"—they moved him to a facility in Merimbula, where he continued declining until he died, in October 2010, at eighty-five.

Peter Tully died of complications from AIDS at a hospital in Paris, to which he had been transferred from Jackie and Thierry's home, in August 1992. David McDiarmid died of similar causes in Sydney in May 1995. In 2014 his work was honored with an enormous retrospective at the National Gallery of Victoria in Melbourne.

In May 2021, Miss Abood succumbed after decades of miserable health. He had been living in and around Sydney for years, grouchy as ever and loved by all. He and Jackie remained dear friends, something you would never have guessed from the withering things they said about each other.

Some years ago Jackie and Thierry broke up, explosively. Beyond the emotional toll, which is not the kind of thing Jackie talks about, the dissolution of their business left her strapped. She considered moving back to Sydney, but a visit to her hometown scotched that notion. Slowly she put her business and her life back together. She's in Paris for the long haul, I would say, her wit and her capacity for alcohol undiminished.

Timmy went through several years of declining health, developing *Pneumocystis* and severe KS. He was still hanging in there when the first protease inhibitors appeared, in late 1995. After that, the meds kept getting better. Day by day he was able to watch his lesions fade. In 1997 he went back to school, earning a BS in chemistry from Berkeley. He became a high school teacher of chemistry and then math. I like looking at the comments his students have left on his "Brand New Dance" video on YouTube, such as "AP Calculus will never be the same."

Carmel Strelein's marriage to Robert Sanger went sour and ended in an ugly divorce. Several months later, on March 5, 1997, a man in a blue bandanna and a leather jacket walked into her busy South of Market salon, the Pink Tarantula, pulled out a 9 mm semiautomatic pistol, and shot her in the left eye and the lung. She died within minutes. Four years later Robert Sanger plea-bargained ten to twelve years for arranging her murder as part of an insurance scheme—a dismally clichéd motive for snubbing out a life that was originality incarnate. Her mother, two sisters, and the son she'd put up for adoption in 1978 and never met were present at the sentencing.

Sandelle lives in Hollywood with a husband and a teenage son, teaching middle-school English and dancing flamenco—something I would dearly love to see. As if it needs adding, she's still gorgeous.

As for X: The months after Doris and Tippi's deaths were dark for him. That summer Robin was staying with him and Phillip on 18th Street, melancholy after a breakup he'd just been through. Miss X had a regular singing gig at the End Up. "He'd get home at midnight," Robin remembers, "and make this huge pot of spaghetti, and little, skinny, tall X would eat this huge thing. And we'd talk about everything." One night it was love. "He'd just completely given up on relationships, because why even try? It was pointless and blah blah blah."

X came in the next night at midnight, excited: "You won't believe what happened to me!" He had done his show as usual, "and this woman comes up and kisses me. And I'm in love! I'm in love with this woman!'"

Her name was Alison Farmer. She was a lesbian who moved with a younger clique that idolized the Sluts, and they had met a few weeks earlier when a friend had introduced them at another club. X had been in male drag that evening—"some hideous red-and-white seersucker jacket," Alison recalls, "like a car salesman." Which hardly put her off. X says, "It was just like—*pow!* Talking and talking and smoking and talking and talking and smoking and smoking and talking.'" The kiss was planted a few weeks later.

They married in 1994, and after a stint in Portland, Oregon, they moved to Alison's hometown, Phoenix, where they live in a ranch-style house painted an electric pink that you would swear Tippi had picked out but was in fact the hue that Alison's grandmother had selected for it when it was hers. Their first daughter arrived in 1998, then twin girls in 2000. Lily, the eldest, started to experiment with cross-dressing in high school; now Lily is Lance. All three of the girls had grown up with dinosaurs and train sets as well as dolls and stuffed animals and *RuPaul's Drag Race*: their parents didn't want them to feel confined by gender boundaries.

"You did a good job!" I commented to Alison.

She laughed. "I guess so! I always say I raised such strong feminists that one of them became a man."

AFTERWORD
IN MEMORY OF PHILIP MILLS

MILDRED JUNE (MILLIE) MILLS
WONDERFUL MOTHER OF 6 & WHO LOVED GOD
1. 6. 1922   4. 4. 1995
GEORGINA CLARGO MILLS
OUR SPECIAL GINA
25. 8. 1959   31. 7. 1973   SUDDEN ILLNESS
PHILIP CLARGO "DORIS" MILLS
11. 8. 1952   22. 6. 1991 SAN FRANCISCO
R.   I.   P.

I KEEP RETURNING TO THE EXCHANGE DORIS HAD WITH PEGGY late one night when he was so ill. "Where *is* Doris?" Peggy asked, and Doris, struggling, answered, "I don't know. I don't know where she is."

When Peggy told me that story, I thought it showed how far outside the circle she was. He was Philip to her; the rest of us knew him as Doris. I remember the day Silvana told me that Doris's birth name was Philip Mills. He conveyed it as a piece of good, semiconfidential dish. And there was reason to think this way: We knew quite a few people who'd rechristened themselves once they arrived in San Francisco in order to signify that they had left their old lives behind, and they didn't want to be called by their birth names. Silvana was one of them. But

Courtesy of Andrew Mills.

Doris wasn't, as I came to understand in talking to people who knew him well. He may have wanted to escape Australia for the freedom of San Francisco, but he didn't want to leave his life behind. It was the people he loved most (and his cussies) who had the privilege of calling him Philip.

He didn't live to see HIV go from a death sentence to a chronic but treatable (and now preventable) condition. Or to witness the cultural shift that few of us, amid the turmoil of AIDS and the furies it unleashed, perceived was already underway. Almost overnight, it seemed, homosexuality went from being regarded as disgraceful and revolting to not a big deal. In the early 2000s, Silvana and I would go to parties given by my nephew and his girlfriend (now his wife), who were then in their twenties. We knew they had a lot of gay friends, and so we were a little bemused that we couldn't pick them out. That wouldn't have been the case at our own similarly mixed parties back in the '80s, and not because our gay friends were all queeny. You could just tell. And then, twenty years later, you couldn't, because whatever radioactive signals openly gay people had once sent out they'd stopped emitting. I don't want to exaggerate: Young queers still have it hard, and we'll probably always provide demagogues with an opportunity to foam at the mouth. But for my generation, it feels almost dreamlike to be living in a society not just of equal rights (always revocable) but, far more profoundly, of unblinking, unthinking acceptance—a collective shrug—from the world around us, something that will be a lot harder to roll back than regulations and statutes.

And with this tectonic shift, the drag queen—that creature Esther Newton long ago pegged, correctly, as the open declaration and celebration of homosexuality—turned from feared freak into object of fascination. In 1996, five years after Doris's death, a weekly club named Trannyshack opened in San Francisco. (Now the word *tranny* is itself considered offensive.) It featured drag queens, as well as a whole host of performers from every point on the gender spectrum, playing to mixed audiences bigger than the ones at Club 181. Though San Francisco was ahead of the curve on gay issues, the ascent of drag from entertainment for insiders to popular weekly shows reflected changes that were happening around the Western world. RuPaul zoomed to fame in the '90s, and then in 2009 came *RuPaul's Drag Race*, which turned drag into general entertainment. Parents watched it with their kids. Back in 1987, when Doris strode onto the set of *Pittsburgh 2Day*, after some initial banter the host said, "OK, now let me get heavy for a second now. Seriously. You've just mentioned children. . . . How do kids look at you, and what kind of example are you setting, and do you worry about being an example?" Doris answered smoothly, "Oh yes, certainly. I like to think that I have to set a positive example to let children know if they want to be drag queens it's a perfectly all right thing to be!" The audience laughed. No one, including Doris, imagined the prescience of that reply.

Now the queens on *Drag Race* really are, as Tippi would have called them, profeshkonals. Doris and his generation of drag queens made it possible. They turned drag from "female impersonation" for incredulous crowds into self-affirming shows for a queer audience and then campy satire for a mixed one. From there it kept on flourishing and became entertainment for everybody. The whole phenomenon would tickle Doris—he was always a generous performer—even as he would look on a bit wistfully. For Doris, the notion of stardom had a heavy dollop of fantasy, though he made it work for him: self-delusion was part of his comic persona.

It's tempting to call that persona a fiction, but the truth is, as always, more complicated. "As soon as he got into drag, it was like he was on-stage," his brother Andrew says. "It was a personality change." Yet that doesn't mean the personality wasn't real. Of course in its exaggeration and its drollery, Doris's drag queen incarnation did have a heavy dose of caricature, but more fundamentally it was one aspect of Philip Mills's psyche, always there, if under the surface—a personality freed, not invented. The hunky hooker with the succulent voice was another, and just as real.

It was a common observation that when Doris put on heels and a wig and painted his teeth, he got bigger. "She was so enormous as a

presence," David Weissman commented as we were talking. "I remember seeing Doris for the first time out of drag and being amazed at how
she was really boyish, very guyish. It made it easier to see past the big-
ness in her drag, and to see that she was understated as a performer
as well. Or there was *nuance* in the enormity. I don't remember Doris
ever being a flamboyant performer." (I do—but only when he was lip-
synching, which is to say, playing somebody else. When he was using
his own voice, David was right.) "Her teeth were flamboyant," he continued, "but her movements weren't. Her humor was understated, and
her delivery was dry. She was an understated behemoth."

In other words: artful. But we didn't go to Doris's shows, or we didn't
think we did, because they were art—although they were. Naturally we
recognized that they were smart (they had to be, since the young audience was, too) as well as political, insofar as they incarnated the gay
consciousness that was then suppressed in popular culture. We went
because they were funny and subversive and fabulous, and because they
offered us the rush of sneering at the society that had rejected us, but
most of all we went because they were *ours*. They gave us what theater and cinema have always given their audience: a mirror. Not that
we saw ourselves as drag queens, any more than Depression-era movie
audiences saw themselves as gangsters or millionaires or Rogers and
Astaire. But they reflected our sensibility, our sense of humor—every
generation has its own—and our outrage. They were gay culture.

Gayness defined every aspect of Doris's life. And yet he wasn't
trapped by it, unlike so many queer people who preceded him and not a
few who have followed. He was freed by it. He reveled in it, and it suf-
fused his vision.

While *Vegas in Space* was the most extravagant incarnation of that
vision, the West Graphics cards, taken as a group, were wider-ranging.
To me those cards rival Cindy Sherman's innovations in high-art photography during the same period, although they're not high art and
it would never have occurred to Doris to think of them that way. Yet
they fizz with originality and wit and social commentary. The company was churning them out at a time when massive changes were

taking place both in the gay world and in the attitudes of the world around it. The best art is born from the coupling of a highly particular talent with the spirit of an age. When I look at the cards and, especially, *Vegas in Space* now, that's what I see: a vision both born of the moment and unconfined by it.

I was under the impression that the movie had died a quiet death until Silvana and I attended the twenty-fifth-anniversary screening at the San Francisco International LGBTQ Film Festival in 2016. A troupe of young(ish) drag queens performed beforehand, costumed as the major characters and lip-synching lines of dialogue before going into fantastically choreographed numbers with an energy and command that surpassed anything the Sluts ever did. They were a knockout. They hadn't just studied their RuPaul. It turned out that many of them had seen *Vegas in Space* on late-night TV when they were in early puberty, and it had changed their lives. Peaches Christ, the enterprising drag queen who put the show together, later said that at a time when the only image of gay life the media offered queer kids was AIDS, *Vegas in Space* had been an awakening: "It was fun. It was silly. It was hopeful. It was beautiful. It was glamorous. It had a sense of humor."

A cult picture is one with a devoted following whose small size belies its intensity. Among younger drag queens who care about their history, the movie is a touchstone. In 2019 a queen named Sasha Velour (she took her last name from the characters Sandelle and Tommy played in the movie), who had risen to prominence on *Drag Race*, presented a screening of *Vegas in Space* to a New York audience. She talked about how she had learned about it while watching RuPaul's show, tracked down a DVD, and watched it every day for a month. "And it really formed the backbone of my entire perspective on drag, my sense of the colors and the imagination and the crazy ambitions that can go into a drag project. This movie is truly incredible, even though it is tacky and ridiculous and kind of horrible."

I'd say that about nails it.

Especially "ridiculous." Doris was a superlative clown, and the ridiculousness that was his element went beyond satire into the recognition of a cosmic absurdity. His art was classical drag in the sense that it both mocked and glorified the pop lodestars that we shared—the dramas and the divas of stage and screen and LP—and what it mocked and glorified above all was glamour, that artificial incandescence invented and molded largely by twentieth-century show business, an ideal that those of us formed in the era of second-wave feminism recognized as a construct and, at the same time, craved: we loved it and we hated it and we wanted it.

An artist is someone who makes you see the universe through his eyes, feel it through her skin. Doris's vision both encapsulated and influenced the way we experienced the world ourselves. Unlike the Pop artists, who met the commercialization that's everywhere around us with a blank but fascinated stare, Doris saw beauty in the venality and the crassness of the modern world even as he saw the world for what it was. When he looked at *Valley of the Dolls*, to take the most obvious example, he recognized at once that it was a terrible movie, a commercial product whose reason for being was to make money from a naive audience. But as he said, if you kept looking, you saw more. You saw the glamour of the sets and the costumes, which luxuriated in the high style of the '60s that so beguiled him. The tackiness in that melodrama of crushed dreams is what makes it camp, but dreaming itself isn't tacky, and we all do it. If you kept looking at Doris, you saw more, too: a man who wanted to be the most glamorous of glamorous women, yet who didn't want to be a woman—a man who wanted to break free of the confines of the identity he'd been assigned because it couldn't contain him. You saw his freedom and his confidence and the pleasure he took in being himself.

Doris told Peggy that he hadn't done enough. He thought he hadn't mattered—that, in Keats's despairing phrase, his name was writ in water. It's true that his paintings didn't advance the practice of painting, that he couldn't sing and he couldn't dance, and that his shows were mostly slapped together on the fly and on the cheap. But that wasn't where the essence of his genius lay. Though drag borrows from the other arts (as theater and film and opera do, too), drag is an art in its own right, and in that art Doris was a virtuoso.

Those of us he captivated—those of us drag has captivated—have come to think differently about men and women and the border that doesn't quite separate the two. Now the rest of the world seems to be catching up.

ACKNOWLEDGMENTS

SINCE ACKNOWLEDGMENTS TYPICALLY END WITH RECOGNITION OF the long-suffering spouse, I'll claim my gay man's right of perversity by starting with mine. Silvana Nova (now Silvano to many, but always Silvana to me) shared the stage with Doris, introduced me to him and his circle, and was my partner at every stage of this project. In addition to co-conducting most of the interviews and serving as my in-house photography and graphics adviser and travel agent, he read draft after draft and offered continual suggestions, nearly all of which I received with irritation and then grudgingly accepted because they were right. He knows how much I love him and owe him.

Beyond Silvana, my deepest gratitude goes to the friends, colleagues, and siblings of Doris who sat for long interviews and then answered constant follow-up questions, sometimes for years. Since they're listed at the beginning of the notes, I won't repeat all their names here, but a few people deserve special mention. Phillip R. Ford, who was behind the book from the start, plied me with letters, documents, and, most crucially, tapes of almost all Doris's San Francisco shows. I regret that it took me so long to perceive that the mensch he is bears no relation to the schmuck he played onstage. Bradley Chandler—Miss X—and Ms. Bob Davis also supplied me with original documents and photographs and patiently answered dozens if not hundreds of queries. Ron Smith, a superb artist and a true nut, opened Doris's Australian world to me, providing me with information, documents, introductions, and a thousand delectable phone calls.

In the course of interviewing I learned what excellent taste in friends Doris had. You can't choose your family, though, and Doris was lucky to grow up in one that not only adored him but, in far less enlightened times, got a big kick out of his career as a crazy drag queen. I'm grateful to his four surviving siblings and their spouses for their cooperation, their enthusiasm, and, best of all now, their friendship.

Danny Nicoletta, the distinguished photo-historian of LGBT San Francisco (as his magnum opus is titled), has been a supremely informed guide to the period and an indispensable help on pictures. So has Johnny Allen, the founder of Cabaret Conspiracy and the inheritor of Miss Abood's extensive archives.

I owe thanks to the staffs of several institutions: in the States, the GLBT Historical Society in San Francisco; the Gay and Lesbian Collections of the New York Public Library; the James C. Hormel LGBTQIA Center of the San Francisco Public Library; the National History Archive at the LGBT Community Center in New York; and, in Australia, the State Library of New South Wales, which holds a cache of Danny Abood's papers; Sydney's Pride History Group; and the Australian Queer Archives in Melbourne, where I've benefited from Nick Henderson's encyclopedic knowledge of Australian queer history and his always-cheerful readiness to aid me in my search for information and pictures.

I'm grateful to Susan Choi, Caleb Crain, Ian Frazier, and Brenda Wineapple for their early support of this project; and to Jay Carey, Judith Coburn, Jonathan Griffiths, Ruth Henrich, Kate Sekules, and Judy Steinsapir for the excellent suggestions they offered on the first version of the manuscript. I owe a special debt to Judith Coburn, enemy of the semicolon and PI extraordinaire, who tracked down multiple records I needed and people I wanted to talk to.

I've had the good fortune to work with three extraordinary editors. The legendary Alice Truax, besides fixing bad sentences and spotting lapses of logic, gently pointed out psychological connections that were staring me in the face. Alison Lewis, who is also my agent, had as much as anyone to do with shaping the text, improving it in a bunch of places and making me trim it to a reasonable (I hope) length. And though I might have been alarmed at the youth of PublicAffairs' Anupama Roy-Chaudhury—when I was her age, my main editorial skill was typing—her probing questions forced me to really contemplate the significance of events I had merely recounted. All three of them made the book much, much better.

I'm grateful to Andy Young for fact-checking and to Michelle Welsh-Horst for delicately guiding the manuscript (and me) through the production process. Erin Granville, my challengingly smart copy editor, has a feeling for prose and for logic that made me want to have a conversation about every change she suggested; she rescued me from many errors that would have haunted me to my grave. Jen Burton is the queen (in the classic sense) of indexers. And I lucked out when the terrifically talented Pete Garceau was asked to design this book's cover.

Others, both friends and strangers, who helped in ways large and small include Robin Clark, Michael Cotten, Peggy Darm, Ilene and Joe Denaro, Lisa Duggan, John Epperson, Greg Foss, A. P. Gonzalez, Sally Gray, Lawrence Helman, Ling Hsu, Marc Huestis, Fenton Johnson, Sandelle Kincaid, Joshua Kosman, Danny Mangin, Anna McCarthy, Alex Momin, Denis Norton, Benjamin M. Olin, Una Rey, Steven Saylor, Mandy Smith, Morris Spinetti, Janice Sukaitis, Bill Vourvoulias, Gwyn Waters, John Witte, and Charles Zukow. A kiss or a handshake—you choose—to you all.

Finally, I'm grateful to the John Simon Guggenheim Memorial Foundation for a fellowship that not only provided me with funds to complete this book but also offered a vote of confidence in the project at a time when I needed it.

SOURCES

Most of my information about Doris and his world comes from a series of interviews conducted between 2005 and 2017—usually with Silvana Nova as my co-interviewer and often supplemented by later email exchanges (in a couple of instances, consisting wholly of email)—with the following people: the late Daniel Abood (Miss Abood), Mary Alterator, Kathleen Baca, Brian Barrow, Anne Block and the late Wendy Dallas, Jennifer Blowdryer, Justin Vivian Bond, Kate Bornstein, Bob Burnside, Elizabeth Mills Byrne, Carmela Carlyle, Connie Champagne, Bradley (Miss X) and Alison Chandler, Robin Clark, Moira Batley Coops, Michael Cotten, Peggy Darm, Ms. Bob Davis, Ken Davis, Natasha Dennerstein, John Edwards, Tom Faulkenbery, Ramona Fischer, Bernard Fitzgerald, Phillip R. Ford, Greg Foss (Ginger Quest), the late Arturo Galster, A. P. Gonzalez, Marianne and Tony Haid, Pearl Harbour (Pearl E. Gates), Bob Hawk, Marc Huestis, Marsha Hultberg, Jacqueline Hyde, Johnny Kat, Sandelle Kincaid, Scrumbly Koldewyn, David Lindsey, Lulu, Phil Mangano, Magenta Mason, Theresa McGinley, Dwayne Mead, Andrew Mills, Michael and Anne Mills, Daniel Nicoletta, Denis Norton, Lu Read, Martin Ryter, Aaron Shurin, Ron Smith, Timmy Spence, Morris Spinetti, Janice Sukaitis, Gwyn Waters, and David Weissman.

In 1986, for a profile of Doris in *Image*, the Sunday magazine of the *San Francisco Chronicle and Examiner*, I conducted interviews with Doris, Tippi, Miss X, Sandelle Kincaid, Marc Huestis, and Randy West. I've also drawn extensively from those interviews.

After Doris's death, Peggy Darm taped interviews with Pearl Harbour, Miss X, and Timmy Spence for an uncompleted project about

Doris, and Connie Champagne interviewed Jacqueline Hyde in Paris; I've drawn from those tapes as well.

When quoting from all these interviews, I've taken the liberty of correcting small solecisms, except in a few spots where my reasons for leaving them alone should be apparent. For coherence and flow, I've also edited, shortened, and rearranged sentences, sometimes putting together observations from different parts of an interview. I've regularly deleted "I think," "kind of," and similar conversational space fillers. Very occasionally I've added or taken out a minor word, like *and*. In instances when unrecorded dialogue I wasn't present for appears inside quotation marks, I've reported it as it was reported, sometimes secondhand, to me. I've also (though not consistently) corrected inconsequential grammatical and orthographical errors in letters and in articles from community newspapers.

Morris Spinetti and Denis Norton kindly provided me with their unpublished reminiscences of Sylvia and the Synthetics. Gwyn Waters and Janice Sukaitis furnished unpublished memoirs of their time with Doris.

Almost all Doris's shows from *Blonde Sin* (1980) on were videotaped. Miss X provided me with tapes of *Blonde Sin* and *The Balcony*, and Phillip R. Ford supplied the rest. Many of them, or parts of them, have been posted by Phillip, Marc Huestis, and others on YouTube.

Sources cited include the following books, periodicals, films, videos, and podcasts.

Books, Pamphlets, and Theses

Altman, Dennis. *Homosexual: Oppression and Liberation*. New York: New York University Press, 1993. Originally published in New York by Outerbridge and Dienstfrey, 1971.

Bérubé, Allan. *Coming Out Under Fire: The History of Gay Men and Women in World War Two*. New York: Free Press, 1990.

Bidgood, James, and Bruce Benderson. *James Bidgood*. Köln: Taschen, 1999.

Bornstein, Kate. *Gender Outlaw: On Men, Women, and the Rest of Us*. New York: Vintage, 1995. Originally published in New York by Routledge, 1994.

———. *A Queer and Pleasant Danger: A Memoir*. Boston: Beacon, 2012.

Boyd, Nan Alamilla. *Wide-Open Town: A History of Queer San Francisco to 1965.* Berkeley: University of California Press, 2003.

Carbery, Graham. *A History of the Sydney Gay and Lesbian Mardi Gras.* Parkville, Victoria: Australian Lesbian and Gay Archives, 1995.

Chauncey, George. *Gay New York: Gender, Urban Culture, and the Making of the Gay Male World, 1890–1940.* New York: Basic, 1994.

Cole, Shaun. *"Don We Now Our Gay Apparel": Gay Men's Dress in the Twentieth Century.* Oxford: Berg, 2000.

Crowley, Mart. *The Boys in the Band.* New York: Farrar, Straus and Giroux, 1968.

Everingham, Sam. *Madam Lash.* Sydney: Allen and Unwin, 2010.

Gorman, Michael R. *The Empress Is a Man: Stories from the Life of José Sarria.* New York: Harrington Park Press, 1998.

Gray, Sally. *Friends, Fashion and Fabulousness: The Making of an Australian Style.* Melbourne: Australian Scholarly Publishing, 2017.

Harris, Gavin, and John Witte. *Camp as a Row of Tents: The Life and Times of Sydney's Camp Social Clubs.* Pamphlet. Sydney: Pride History Group, 2007.

———. *Camp Nites: Sydney's Emerging Drag Scene in the '60s.* Pamphlet. Sydney: Pride History Group, 2006.

Harris, Gavin, John Witte, and Ken Davis. *New Day Dawning: The Early Years of Sydney's Gay and Lesbian Mardi Gras.* Sydney: Pride History Group, 2008.

Historical Records of New South Wales. Vol. I, Part 2.—Phillip. 1783–1792. Sydney: Charles Potter, Government Printer, 1982.

History of Sydney drag. [No author, no title.] Ca. 1990s. THE340 [Sydney drag history thesis], Australian Queer Archives, Melbourne.

Huestis, Marc. *Impresario of Castro Street: An Intimate Showbiz Memoir.* San Francisco: Outsider Productions, 2019.

Hughes, Robert. *The Fatal Shore.* London: Collins Harvill, 1987.

Irving, Terry, and Rowan Cahill. *Radical Sydney: Places, Portraits and Unruly Episodes.* Sydney: UNSW Press, 2010.

Kay, Barry. *The Other Women.* London: Mathews Miller Dunbar, 1976. Published in the United States as *As a Woman.* New York: St. Martin's, 1976.

Lake, Bambi, with Alvin Orloff. *The Unsinkable Bambi Lake: A Fairy Tale Containing the Dish on Cockettes, Punks, and Angels.* San Francisco: Manic D, 1996.

Langley, Carol. *Beneath the Sequined Surface: An Insight into Sydney Drag.* Sydney: Currency Press, 2006.

Lindner, Laura R. *Public Access Television: America's Electronic Soapbox.* Westport, Conn.: Praeger, 1999.

Lupton, Deborah. *Moral Threats and Dangerous Desires: AIDS in the News Media.* London: Taylor and Francis, 1994.

McDiarmid, David. *When This You See Remember Me.* Exhibition catalogue. National Gallery of Victoria, Melbourne, 2014.

McPhee, John, with Susan McCormack. "Peter Tully: Urban Tribalwear and Beyond." Exhibition brochure. National Gallery of Australia, Canberra, 1991.

Moore, Nicole. *The Censor's Library: Uncovering the Lost History of Australia's Banned Books.* St. Lucia: University of Queensland Press, 2002.

Morgan, Robin. *Going Too Far: The Personal Chronicle of a Feminist*. New York: Random House, 1977.

Newton, Esther. *Margaret Mead Made Me Gay: Personal Essays, Public Ideas*. Durham, NC: Duke University Press, 2000.

———. *Mother Camp: Female Impersonators in America*. Chicago: University of Chicago Press, 1979. Originally published in New York by Prentice-Hall, 1972.

Power, Jennifer. *Movement, Knowledge, Emotion: Gay Activism and HIV-AIDS in Australia*. Canberra: ANU E Press, 2011.

Shilts, Randy. *And the Band Played On: Politics, People, and the AIDS Epidemic*. New York: St. Martin's, 1987.

———. *The Mayor of Castro Street: The Life and Times of Harvey Milk*. New York: St. Martin's, 1982.

Sontag, Susan. *Against Interpretation and Other Essays*. New York: Farrar, Straus and Giroux, 1966.

Streitmatter, Rodger. *Unspeakable: The Rise of the Lesbian and Gay Press in America*. Boston: Faber and Faber, 1995.

Stryker, Susan, and Jim Van Buskirk. *Gay by the Bay: A History of Queer Culture in the San Francisco Bay Area*. San Francisco: Chronicle Books, 1996.

Swieca, Robert, Glynis Jones, and Judith O'Callaghan. *Absolutely Mardi Gras! Costume and Design of the Sydney Lesbian and Gay Mardi Gras*. Sydney: Powerhouse Publishing and Doubleday, 1997.

Talbot, David. *Season of the Witch: Enchantment, Terror, and Deliverance in the City of Love*. New York: Free Press, 2012.

Templin, Jenny. *Mardi Gras Memories*. Adelaide, Australia: Griffin Press, 1996.

Tent, Pam. *Midnight at the Palace: My Life as a Fabulous Cockette*. Los Angeles: Alyson Books, 2004.

Wherrett, Richard, ed. *Mardi Gras! True Stories*. Ringwood, Victoria: Viking, 1999.

White, Edmund. *Genet: A Biography*. New York: Alfred A. Knopf, 1993.

———. *States of Desire: Travels in Gay America*. New York: E. P. Dutton, 1980.

Witkin, Joel-Peter. *Joel-Peter Witkin*. Pasadena, CA: Twelvetrees, 1985.

Wotherspoon, Garry. *City of the Plain: History of a Gay Sub-Culture*. Sydney: Hale and Iremonger, 1991.

———. *Gay Sydney: A History*. Sydney: NewSouth Publishing, 2016.

Periodicals

The Advocate (Los Angeles)

The Age (Melbourne)

American Gay Life (San Francisco)

Bay Area Reporter (BAR) (San Francisco)

The Bulletin (Sydney)

Cake (Sydney)

Campaign (Sydney)

Christopher Street (New York)

Daily Telegraph (Sydney)

The Digger (Melbourne)

Ego (zine) (San Francisco)

Kalendar (San Francisco)

Nation Review (Melbourne)

New York Times

Oxford Lifestyle Magazine (Sydney)

Phoenix New Times

Release Print (San Francisco)

San Francisco Bay Guardian

San Francisco Chronicle

San Francisco Examiner

San Francisco Gay Life—Where It's At

San Francisco Sentinel

SF Weekly (San Francisco)

Santa Cruz (Calif.) Sentinel

Socialist Review (Oakland, Calif.)

Spurt! Magazine (zine) (Sydney)

The Sun (Sydney)

The Sun-Herald (Sydney)

Sydney Morning Herald

Sydney Star Observer

Village Voice (New York)

William and John (Sydney)

Films, Videos, and Podcasts

Christ, Peaches, and Michael Varrati. *Midnight Mass* (podcast).

Cunningham-Reid, Fiona. *Feed Them to the Cannibals!* 1993. Currently on Vimeo, https://vimeo.com/85880302, 51:23.

Ford, Phillip R. *Vegas in Space.* 1991.

Huestis, Marc. *Another Goddamn Benefit.* 1996.

———. *Chuck Solomon: Coming of Age.* 1987.

Partners in Crime. NBC. Episode 7, "Is She or Isn't He?" Aired November 3, 1984. YouTube, 47:30, posted by Don Jack, https://www.youtube.com/watch?v=xlfq_jz-uqk. Doris's short segment begins at 27:00.

Robson, Marc. *Valley of the Dolls.* 1967.

Weissman, David. *We Were Here.* 2011.

Weissman, David, and Bill Weber. *The Cockettes.* 2002.

NOTES

EXCEPT IN A VERY FEW INSTANCES, THE FOLLOWING NOTES DON'T reference information from interviews. Doing so would have made them unwieldy, and my sources are usually obvious enough in the text.

As of this writing, Doris's letters are not fully archived, but I've provided dates in the expectation that in time they will be. Many of those that I've quoted from are among the Danny Abood papers housed at the State Library of New South Wales in Sydney; others, including letters to Doris, have come to me from friends and family members.

Since a list of books, periodicals, and films and videos cited precedes these notes, in the notes themselves I give only the author and title of a source rather than a full citation. I've included URLs where I think they may be useful and they're not too unwieldy, but given the labile nature of the internet, I'm aware that some may change or become inaccessible over time.

Introduction: Doris and His Times

Doris's "What is the point" is from the *Bay Area Reporter*, March 13, 1986, 8. "What a mess!" is from a letter to Miss Abood, October 14–16, 1977.

Citations from Newton's *Mother Camp*: "mingled shock," 132; every state except Illinois, 84; completed the dissertation in 1968, xv; "open declaration," 64; "drag, like violence," 112–113; "Professional drag queens," 3; "Stigma," 3; "downfall," 126; "degradation," 126; "dishonor," 65; "condemnation combined," 104; "Impersonators do not often," 129–130; glamour drag and comic drag, 41–58. Other information about Newton comes from her *Margaret Mead Made Me Gay*: graduate student, 216; "the object solely," 216; "The insight that gays," 216; denied tenure, 108.

Bornstein's observation "Assuming that gay men and lesbians" is from her *Gender Outlaw*, 134.

The 1968 poll on decriminalizing homosexuality is in Wotherspoon's *Gay Sydney*, 170. The survey mentioned by Altman is in his *Homosexual*, 77.

Information on *The Boys in the Band* comes from "Jim Parsons, Zachary Quinto, Andrew Rannells, and Matt Bomer Lead *The Boys in the Band* on Broadway," *Playbill*, May 10, 2018, https://playbill.com/article/jim-parsons-zachary-quinto-andrew-rannells-and -matt-bomer-lead-the-boys-in-the-band-on-broadway; and "The Boys in the Band," Internet Off-Broadway Database, Lucille Lortel Foundation, 1968, http://www.iobdb.com /Production/3106. The line "You show me a happy homosexual" is in Crowley's published text of the play; it's frequently quoted without the initial "You."

Wikipedia offers full documentation on militant resistance at both Cooper Do-nuts ("Cooper Do-Nuts Riot," Wikipedia, last edited June 2, 2022, https://en.wikipedia.org /wiki/Cooper_Do-nuts_Riot) and Compton's Cafeteria ("Compton's Cafeteria Riot," Wikipedia, last edited May 17, 2022, https://en.wikipedia.org/wiki/Compton%27s _Cafeteria_riot). Victor Silverman and Susan Stryker have made a documentary on the latter, *Screaming Queens: The Riot at Compton's Cafeteria* (2005), on YouTube at https:// www.youtube.com/watch?v=G-WASW9dRBU, 56:11.

1. Manly Vale

For the name "Manly Vale," see Hughes, *The Fatal Shore*, 15; and *Historical Records of New South Wales*, accessible via Google Books.

"I was a perfect Catholic child" and "For my parents" are from Doris Fish, "Catholic Kids," *San Francisco Sentinel*, March 1, 1990, 14.

The "Happy Little Vegemites" commercial is on YouTube.

The Australia Hotel as a cruising spot comes from Wotherspoon, *Gay Sydney*, 41–42, 83, 155–156.

Andrew Mills mentioned the censorship of "White Rabbit," which is in keeping with the Australia of that era, in our interview.

Doris's skating is reported in "Phil Got His Skates On," *Daily Telegraph*, December 2, 1971, 2; and "Bus Strike Roller Man Skating on Thin Ice," *The Sun* (Sydney), December 7, 1971.

2. Sylvia and the Synthetics

Doris called Sydney the drag capital of the world in "Meanwhile, on the Other Side of the Planet," *San Francisco Sentinel*, February 16, 1990, 15. And see, for example, a review of Barry Kay's *The Other Women* in the Sydney gay newspaper *Campaign*, December 1976, 22.

Hughes's "doubly damned" is in his *The Fatal Shore*, 272.

Citations from Wotherspoon's *Gay Sydney*: cruising spots in addition to parks and "beats," 41–46; Cold War–era persecution, 101ff.; shock at the Kinsey Report, 94–97; Colin Delaney, 108 (as well as Wotherspoon's "'This Nest of Perverts': Policing Male Homosexuality in Cold War Australia," Working Paper No. 52, Sir Robert Menzies Centre for Australian Studies, Institute of Commonwealth Studies, University of London, 14); "doctors, criminologists and politicians," 138; tradition of elaborate balls, 63ff.; Stork Club, 159; *camp* as Australian for *gay*, 199–200; opening of a spate of gay clubs, 161–162; Purple Onion, 203; Glitter Strip or Golden Mile, 197; first public meeting of CAMP Inc., 175. The quotation beginning "The very attempts" is in Wotherspoon, *City of the Plain*, an earlier version of *Gay Sydney*, 110.

An excellent academic thesis on the history of Sydney drag in the collection of the Australian Queer Archives in Melbourne—regrettably missing its title page and byline (THE340 [Sydney drag history thesis], c. 1990s)—offers information on the Stork Club, 17, 29; the low pay of drag performers, 26; and the fires in the city's drag clubs, 34.

The definitive study of World War II and homosexuality is Bérubé's *Coming Out Under Fire*.

On Vidal's *The City and the Pillar*, see Moore, *The Censor's Library*, 151.

The "culture of blackmail" quotation is in Harris and Witte, *Camp as a Row of Tents*, 4, which also offers information on the drag balls, 7ff.; Karen Chant's Marie Antoinette, cover photo and caption, 7; and Claudia Wagner, 7, 10. Cecil Beaton is mentioned in their *Camp Nites*, 3.

Citations from Langley's *Beneath the Sequined Surface*: illegality of cross-dressing, 6; the various balls, 6; Karen Chant, 6–7, Les Girls, 11; Purple Onion, 8–9; Jewel Box, 7 (according to the thesis on Sydney's drag history, the wife saw the show in Miami, op. cit., 23); starvation wages, 13; the legally "penumbral zone," 8–9; and the fires at the drag clubs, 11–12. That the fires resulted from nonpayment of protection money is my deduction from several interviews, including those with Jacqueline Hyde and Ken Davis, and also from the thesis on Sydney's drag history in the collection of the Australian Queer Archives, op. cit., 34.

For Finocchio's, see, e.g., "What a Drag: Finocchio's to Close," *San Francisco Chronicle*, November 4, 1999, 1; or "Finocchio's Club," Wikipedia, last edited June 5, 2022, https://en.wikipedia.org/wiki/Finocchio%27s_Club.

On the Whitlam government's support of community projects, see Dr. John Gardiner-Garden, "Arts Policy in Australia: A History of Commonwealth Involvement in the Arts," Parliamentary Research Service Background Paper No. 5, 1994, esp. 9–10, https://www.aph.gov.au/binaries/library/pubs/bp/1994-95/94bp05.pdf. For the mood of optimism it produced, see, e.g., Altman, "Afterword," *Homosexual* (1993 New York edition), 254–255.

Information on Sylvia and the Synthetics is drawn from a number of sources, starting with Barry Prothero, "Putting in the High-Heeled Boot," *The Digger*, January 13–27, 1973: a huge sculptured nose; a trio of gay friends; the Roxy Collective's snakes-and-ladders game; formerly been the Purple Onion (also in Wotherspoon, *Gay Sydney*, 203); the quotation beginning "Even before the main show begins"; "Unfortunately Sylvia won't be performing"; "The noise is tremendous"; "If you get too close to the stage"; they couldn't publicize their shows. Another is Michael Delaney, "Sylvia's Dead," *William and John*, early 1973, 25–27, which mentions Andrew Sharp's participation and "Would you like to stroke it?"

Citations from Doris's own "What Ever Happened to Sylvia and the Synthetics?" in *Campaign*, May 1977, 11–12: as many as twenty; an actor, Andrew Sharp; the debut at the Roxy; "I wore a red suit"; a large one named Rona; Cherry Ripe; "electrifying"; lip-synched, to a set list; "dance to a Stravinsky piano piece"; "Slaughter on Tenth Avenue"; "I'm Gonna Wash That Man Right Outa My Hair"; Snow Whip; the Andrews Sisters' "Hold Tight"; hung drag queens from meat hooks; EMI secured their services (also covered in "What's Going On Out There?," *The Bulletin* [Sydney], June 30, 1973, 44); paper bag, which often got lost or stolen; Del Fricker; Morris left early; traveling porn show (also in Everingham, *Madam Lash*, 88–92); reduced to three.

Morris Spinetti's "it's a wonder" is from his unpublished 2015 memoir, "Sylvia and the Synthetics: My Vague Story as I Remember"; he kindly gave me a copy.

The date of the second show (Saturday, November 11)—the Superman Ball—is on a flyer, in the Danny Abood papers at the State Library of New South Wales.

Newton's taxonomy of misogynistic responses is in *Mother Camp*, 26.

On the Cockettes, see Tent's *Midnight at the Palace*: the first of their legendary midnight shows, 33–35; until October 1972, 226–228; "You could always see which direction," 37; "a surprise to everyone," 48. The John Waters quotations are from the interview with him in Weissman and Weber's documentary *The Cockettes*.

For a fuller (and fascinating) discussion of gay men as "inverts," see Chauncey, *Gay New York*, especially the introduction and chapters 1, 2, and 4.

Doris's "I didn't give anything a second thought" is in Wendell Ricketts, "Portfolio: An Interview with Doris Fish," March 24, 1989, http://ricketts-portfolio.blogspot .com/2010/04/interview-with-doris-fish-24-march-1989 (accessed December 10, 2010, page since removed).

Miss Abood remembered the butcher shop as the group's third show, but none of the sources that describe the November 25 show at the old Onion mention it. The description of that show (the date and name are on a flyer) is drawn from Prothero, "Putting in the High-Heeled Boot"; Delaney, "Sylvia's Dead"; and Fish, "What Ever Happened to Sylvia and the Synthetics?," op. cit.; as well as from interviews. Both Brian Barrow and Miss Abood remembered this performance as having been shut down by the police, but there's no mention in newspaper articles on the show, including Doris's.

The "grotesque denigration" critique is from "Mandies Mincing," *Nation Review*, April 28, 1977, 667.

For the *Australian Women's Weekly* World Discovery Tour, see, e.g., the ads in *The Age*, March 20, 1972, 6, and the Sydney *Sun-Herald*, October 1, 1972, 121.

For Richard Neville's obscenity trial, see Irving and Cahill, *Radical Sydney*, 285–291. The special issue of *POL* was vol. 5, no. 7 (n.d., 1973); see especially the table of contents and 35–38, 47–50. Neville's "theatrical politicians" comment is on p. 35.

3. Working Girl

On Barry Kay: nurturing a new interest in photography, Jill Sykes, "The 'Liberated' Male," *Sydney Morning Herald*, November 25, 1976, 7; opened at the Australian Centre for Photography, *Campaign*, no. 15, December 1976, 22.

Doris's "Sexual liberation was a major issue" is from his "What Ever Happened to Sylvia and the Synthetics?," *Campaign*, May 1977, 11–12, which also refers to his first trip to San Francisco.

Citations from Doris's letters: "$13 a week," to Abood, November 15, 1974; "I believe in succumbing," to Abood, July 15, 1974; "I can't begin to tell you," to Abood, March 6, 1975; stopping first in, to his parents from Vancouver, October 15, 1975; "I'm working as a real life whore," to Mildred et al., November 10, 1981 (reproduced in *Doris Fish: A Celebration of Her Life and Career*, booklet produced for his August 11, 1991, memorial at Kinsela's in Sydney).

Information on Doris's beating comes from interviews with Jacqueline Hyde and with Doris's siblings and from Doris's own (somewhat differing) versions in "What Ever

Happened . . . ?," op. cit., and in answer to a reporter's question in "Cabaret Queen," *Nation Review*, February 1980, 46.

Gucci shoes is from "Husband-Hunting in S.F.," *Campaign*, April 1980, 28. The lovely apartment on Telegraph Hill is in "Doris Fish," *Cake*, July 1979, 12.

Doris spoke of clergymen, lawyers, and judges as clients in his "Gays and Gods," *San Francisco Sentinel*, June 7, 1990, 17; and "Fishy Tidbits," *San Francisco Sentinel*, August 2, 1990, 24.

"The unlovable, the sexually untouchable" is from my interview with Jennifer Blowdryer.

4. The Tubes

"Glamour was in my blood" is from "Doris Fish," *Cake*, July 1979, 12.

Doris's "I broke my first heart" is in "Husband-Hunting in S.F.," *Campaign*, April 1980, 28; so is "'true love' twenty-two times" and the bodybuilding carpenter.

Doris remembered Cheryl as a "gorilla of party animals," as well as his using and selling drugs, in "Castro Memories," *San Francisco Sentinel*, October 11, 1990, 20.

You can occasionally find images of the poster for the Tubes' Talent Hunt on eBay and other internet sites. Descriptions of Doris's audition are from the tape of it that Michael Cotten kindly showed me.

Doris mentions joking about love affairs with the boys in the band in his "What Ever Happened to Sylvia and the Synthetics?," *Campaign*, May 1977, 11–12. Boz Scaggs, Julie Christie, Holly Woodlawn, and Grace Slick are mentioned in "Doris Fish," *Cake*, op. cit., and in "What Ever Happened to Sylvia and the Synthetics?"

Information on Ambi Sextrous is from Jennifer Blowdryer, "Transvestite of the Month," *Ego* (my photocopy is undated), 45; his obituary in the *Bay Area Reporter*, May 21, 1992, 19, http://obit.glbthistory.org/olo/index.jsp; "Robert Lee Graham, 1952–1992," Ancestry.com; and a flyer for the *Halloween Harlots* show in my possession.

The descriptions of Tippi are from interviews with Lulu and Aaron Shurin and from John F. Karr's "Tippi: June 6, 1952–Aug. 25, 1991," *Bay Area Reporter*, August 29, 1991, 23, 26; Karr also mentions Tippi's role as a mouse in *Aesop's Fables*.

Information on James Moss comes mainly from the biography he supplied *Kalendar* (January 7, 1977), from IMBD.com, and from letters and published writings in which Doris mentions the movie.

Citations from Doris's letters: "Last Sunday Ambi Sextrous," to Abood, September 21, 1977; "almost constantly in drag," he and Doris played maids, "in charge of drug distribution," "the Australian Quaalude (Mandrax) Champion," "I'm still recovering," "All goes well except," rugs and carpets, to Abood, January 7, 1977; Jane Dornacker (now going by Leila T. Snake), "Victoriana and butch men," to Jackie, January 15, 1977; "for added 'cinema vérité' impact," he claimed not to have had a Quaalude, "I remember saving," to Abood, January 18, 1977; Melons, to Abood from Fiji, summer 1977; "mattress actress," to Abood, February 12, 1977 (this term for drag prostitutes goes back at least to the early twentieth century; see Boyd, *Wide-Open Town*, 37).

Jasper's "Darling, there's a lot of drugs" is in "Doris Fish," *Cake*, op. cit. Citations from "Night of the Living Dead," *Spurt! Magazine* (a punk zine) 1, no. 8, no pagination or date, though it's page 15 of fifteen pages and internal evidence points to a date of May or early

June 1979 (the article was probably written by Carmel Strelein, who is listed among the contributing writers on the masthead): reported to have crawled into cabs; fourteen, according to one count; he collapsed, dramatically; Ambi Sextrous also competed.

"Jasper was the hostess" and "sitting up in a hozzie bed" are in a letter from Jackie to Doris, September 26, 1977.

The scathing review was Adrian Rawlins, "Synthetics Drag Show Is a Real Drag," *Campaign*, July 1977, 45.

5. Romantic Cruelism

Citations from Boyd, *Wide-Open Town*: San Francisco population figures 2–3; distribution of sexes, 41; 90 percent male, 27 (also in Stryker and Van Buskirk, *Gay by the Bay*, 18); The Dash, 25; easiest city in the country to get a drink in, 44ff.; Finocchio's, 52–56; panicked reactions, 53; two thousand a year, 120 (citing Bérubé, *Coming Out Under Fire*, 262); police raids on bars, 17, 136, 216–218; Black Cat Café addresses, 56; native San Franciscan, 26; cross-dressing from an early age, 210; *Stouman v. Reilly*, 121–122; the police then decided, 137; warned the crowd, 222 (also Shilts, *Mayor of Castro Street*, 52); "United we stand," 59 (according to Shilts, op. cit. 52, the line was "United we stand, divided they catch us one by one"); Dianne Feinstein, 198.

Sodom by the Sea: Stryker and Van Buskirk, *Gay by the Bay*, 18; Shilts, op cit., 48.

From John D'Emilio, "Gay Politics, Gay Community: San Francisco's Experience," *Socialist Review*, January–February 1981: single-person households, 82; fighting back, 94–95; six thousand votes, 88.

Austrian Holocaust survivor: Gary Kamiya, "Portals of the Past: Drag Performer Led Black Cat to Become Gay Bar in 2nd Life," *San Francisco Chronicle*, November 8, 2014, C-2.

From Gorman, *Empress Is a Man*: José Sarria in 1947, 124; Colombian-Nicaraguan descent, 13, 25; "I became the Black Cat," 126; first openly gay American to run, 207.

Citations from Shilts, *Mayor of Castro Street*: warned the crowd, 52; "God Save Us Nelly Queens," 52; "United we stand," 52; some forty local governments, 155 (also in Streitmatter, *Unspeakable*, 211); had voted their own antidiscrimination measure in, 155; "Homosexuals cannot reproduce," 156.

"*We know what's at work*" is in Morgan, "Lesbian and Feminism: Synonyms or Contradictions?," in *Going Too Far*, 180. The essay was originally written for a conference in 1973.

"The scorn directed against drags" is in White, *States of Desire*, 51.

The "flagrant behavior" citation is from Chauncey, *Gay New York*, 103, 105.

Effeminacy had been the mark: Cole, *Don We Now*, 183.

Moss put Tippi in a magazine: *American Gay Life*, no. 12 (n.d., probably 1977), 14.

The Anita Bryant Look-Alike Contest was covered in "Having a Gay Time Looking Like Anita," *San Francisco Examiner*, May 30, 1977, 3, and Kathy MacKay, "Who's Afraid of Anita Bryant?," *Los Angeles Times*, June 2, 1977, H-14.

Estimated parade attendance of 250,000 is cited in "San Francisco Pride," Wikipedia, last edited June 1, 2022, https://en.wikipedia.org/wiki/San_Francisco_Pride, among other sources.

The Miami Gay Support Committee boycott is from a flyer.

That in 1980 Bryant's contract was not renewed is in Laurie Johnston, "Notes on People: Orange Juice Contract Runs Dry for Anita Bryant," *New York Times*, September 2, 1980, B-6.

Tippi even wrote a speech: in Ms. Bob Davis's collection, now part of the Louise Lawrence Transgender Archive in Vallejo, CA.

Citations from Doris's letters: "You'd love her," to Jackie, September 26, 1978; "So glad you're coming," to Abood, October 21, 1977; "We're all anxiously awaiting," to Abood, September 26, 1977; "You've gotta get here!," to Abood, October 14, 1977; "What the fuck are you doing," to Abood, November 12, 1977; "a nice bland publication," to Jackie, November 19, 1977; cover his living expenses, to Abood, November 12, 1977; the launch party, to Abood, October 14–16, 1977, and to Jackie, October 17, 1977; "I'm really missing Bernard," to Abood, October 14, 1977; "were sitting in the lounge," Bernard Fitzgerald announced, and signs, posters, and carpet designs, to Jackie (with Abood), n.d. (spring 1978); "This honeymoon will cost," to Mildred, September 30, 1978; "Good in small doses" and "he sounded well," to Jackie and Carmel (with Abood), October 8, 1978; cross-country road trip, to Mildred, September 30, 1978; by getting back into prostitution and Eddie Troia, to Jackie, November 26, 1978; "An absolute riot," to Abood, January 9, 1979; "is sleeping in parks," The scuttlebutt on Carmel, and "Needless to say," to Abood, December 20, 1978; "We split up last week," to Abood, January 9, 1979; "I was very thin-lipped," to Abood, February 5, 1979; "fuck/suck bar," to Abood, December 20, 1978; "dicks & bums & graffiti," to Abood, February 22, 1979; Doris moved in with him, to Abood, January 9, 1979, and February 5, 1979; ads in the gay papers, to Abood, February 22, 1979; "She seems to be improving," to Abood, February 5, 1979; Linda Ronstadt, Andrew's twenty-first birthday, and they asked Jasper to perform, to Abood, February 20, 1979; "I was so proud of her," to Abood, March 7, 1979.

By mid-decade there were some three hundred: Streitmatter, *Unspeakable*, 185, and Chapter 7, "Defining Gay Male Culture," passim.

Citations from *San Francisco Gay Life—Where It's At*: "Halloween Makeup by Doris Fish," no. 1, 1; appeared in a French maid's outfit, no. 1, 5–6; profiles, no. 3, 18–19, and no. 4, 51; restaurant reviews, no. 3, 17; illustrated ads, no. 2, 19, 24; comic strips, no. 2, 38; cover portrait of Patti LaBelle, no. 4; editorial assistant, no. 4, 1 (masthead); "Photo Creature Feature," no. 4, 57 ("Fifi La Zhoosh").

Pearl peeving Jane is in Julie Green, "Pearl Harbour: She's a Blast," *Patterns and Tones* (blog), May 25, 2013; http://patternsandtones.blogspot.com/2013/05/pearl-harbour -shes-blast.html.

There's a flyer for the Halloween show at Bimbo's.

Jackie's news about Carmel and "We'll be inviting" are from a letter of hers to Doris, August 8 to September 2, 1978.

For Cabaret Conspiracy, see Doris's letter to Abood, February 20, 1979; and John Allen's "A Potted History of the Cabaret," in the photos section of the Cabaret Conspiracy Facebook page, posted August 19, 2012, https://www.facebook.com/Cabaret Conspiracy.

My narrative of the fire, including quoted dialogue (obviously a reconstruction, but from my sources, not invented by me), is taken from the following: Doris to Abood

March 7, 1979; my interviews with Miss Abood and Jackie; and Connie Champagne's interview with Jackie (Paris, n.d.), in my possession.

For Jasper's funeral, see Doris's letter to Abood, March 7, 1979; and "Night of the Living Dead," *Spurt! Magazine* 1, no. 8, 15, May or early June 1979 (more information on this source is in the notes to Chapter 4).

Clayton's death is from Doris's "Wicked, Wicked Friends," *San Francisco Sentinel*, August 30, 1990, 20.

6. Sluts a-Go-Go

Citations from Doris's letters: "I still wake up," "with lovely views," "just too fabulously gorgeous," and ramped up his '60s look, all to Abood, n.d. (almost certainly March 1979); by early April he was turning tricks, "I keep worrying," to Abood, April 5, 1979; He took his final bow, he'd saved up $4,000, to Abood, May 27, 1979; he flew to New York, to Abood, April 10, 1979; "I ended up swinging," to Johnny Allen, August 18, 1979; "She's a clever queen," to Jackie, November 10, 1979; parade in June 1980, to Jackie, July 1980; a nearly nude Adam and Eve (also in Doris's "Gee, Mother, I Love It Here!," *Campaign*, January 1981), to Jackie (with Miss X), July 1980; *Slumber Party* show, earning twenty dollars a night, to "Zelda & the Modern Zonites" (with Miss X), September 1, 1980; "I'm absolutely broke," to (probably) Jackie, n.d. (late 1980); "no good news last month," "I'm working as a prossie again," "Swedish/Norwegian," to Mildred, June 12, 1981; Christmas card to his parents, "nearly Xmas 1981."

Dennis Altman wrote about Cabaret Conspiracy in "Altman," his regular column, *Campaign*, April 1979, 19.

The name Sandra La Moan is on a flyer for a show at Syd's, 256 Crown Street, January 10, 1980.

Information on *As Time Goes By* is from a listing of theater programs posted by the Australian Queer Archives, http://www.alga.org.au/files/theatreprograms.pdf; an online obituary of its director, Ron Owen, http://www.josken.net/sp-obit2.htm#ron; "Doris Fish," *Cake*, July 1979, 12 ("using trick makeup"); and "As Time Goes By: Gay Theatre Stands Centre Stage in Sydney," *Campaign*, June 1979, 34.

Bradley Chandler as a John Waters look-alike is in Dewey Webb, "From Queer to Paternity," *Phoenix New Times*, August 10, 2000; https://www.phoenixnewtimes.com/news/from-queer-to-paternity-6416326.

I have a flyer for the show at the Pride Center on Grove Street.

Doris's being "resplendent in black fishnet stockings" is in Roger Crawford, "Fish Tales," *Campaign*, March 1980, 11.

Citations from Doris's column in *Campaign*: back to San Francisco on March 18, In April he got a call from Martin Ryter, Rehearsals began in early May, a nearly nude Adam and Eve, Michael Cotten invited them, performance at the San Francisco Art Institute, "Gee, Mother, I Love It Here!," January 1981, 32; Mr. Castro pageant, *Can't Stop the Music*, Joan Baez and Lily Tomlin, "Life in a Goldfish Bowl," August 1980, 12; National Reno Gay Rodeo, "Gay in the Saddle," October 1980, 42.

"Brand New Dance": "timmy spence—brand new dance," YouTube video, 3:31, posted by Bill Barton on April 26, 2010, https://www.youtube.com/watch?v=yWPJDQ6ClxM.

Timmy himself later posted the same video as "Timmy Spence Brand New Dance 1981" on May 28, 2020, https://www.youtube.com/watch?v=PX1LrlpNqxU.

There's a video of Doris, Tippi, and Miss X performing "Drag Queen" in 1989: "'Drag Queen' and 'You're the Top' by SLUTS A GO-GO," YouTube video, 5:53, posted by Johnny Kat on June 18, 2010, https://www.youtube.com/watch?v=lyHNm_U-tlU.

"The sin they left out of the Bible" is on a flyer in my possession.

X's 2000 explanation to a reporter is in Webb, "From Queer to Paternity," op. cit.

7. Vegas in Space

The appearance at the On Broadway is mentioned in *Punk Globe* (a San Francisco zine), February 1982.

Citations from Doris's letters: passed out on heroin, to Ace, January 20, 1982; "Hopefully the filming," to Ace, March 1, 1983.

Citations from Jackie's letters to Doris: "charmingly sensitive," February 9, 1982; new French boyfriend, August 24, 1981.

"We don't wish to announce" is in "Out and Out," *Campaign*, August 1981, 19.

Thanksgiving at the "gorgeous house" is in Doris Fish, "Gee, Mother, I Love It Here!," *Campaign*, January 1981, 32.

Doris's excursion to Canal Street and spending a thousand dollars is in Phillip R. Ford, "The Making of *Vegas in Space*," http://vegasinspace.blogspot.com.

Carmel mentions her heroin habit in a letter to Jackie, n.d. (1985).

Mildred's "Well, if that's what outer space is like" is in Kate Bornstein, "The Most Glamorous Opening of the Decade," *Bay Area Reporter*, October 10, 1991, 34.

8. Naked Brunch

"By living together" is in Newton, *Mother Camp*, 13.

Citations from Ms. Bob Davis and Carol Kleinmaier, "Drama Queen: An Interview with Sandelle Kincaid of Sluts a Go-Go," *LadyLike*, no. 47 (2001), 33–34, available online: a room was painted with the eyes; "I had one take"; introducing himself as a student.

For the fifty pairs of eyelashes, etc., see Craig Seligman, "Aggressive Glamour," *Image* magazine, *San Francisco Chronicle and Examiner*, August 17, 1986, 28–31, 38.

Citations from Doris's letters: a weight-lifting routine, to Jackie, April 18, 1982; "Tonight we're trekking" and "lots of enthusiasm," to Jackie, September 22, 1983; rented Project Artaud and "My life may be interesting," to Mildred, March 7, 1983; miniatures . . . created in September, to Mildred, August 3, 1984; "Yes, I'm really 32!" and "I signed hundreds," to Ace, September 10, 1984; 50 percent raise, to Mildred, February 9, 1984; "all expenses paid," to Marianne Haid, June 28, 1984; was going to cost $15,000, to Mildred, September 10, 1984.

"Only years later" is in Huestis, *Impresario of Castro Street*, 56.

The San Francisco International LGBTQ+ Film Festival—it's been known by various names over the years—as the largest festival of its kind is on the "About" page of the website for Frameline, the organization that runs it: https://www.frameline.org/about/frameline.

The soap opera at the Pyramid Club is in "Swinging Sickniks," *Bay Area Reporter*, November 3, 1983, 23.

Club 181's 1954 opening and later history is in Boyd, *Wide-Open Town*, 135.

For Lynne Carter, see Newton, *Mother Camp*, 88–89.

The club's being "so jammed that people actually fainted" is in Michael Snyder, "'Naked Brunch: Episode III'—They Do Soap Opera in the Tenderloin," *Datebook* (the Pink Section), *San Francisco Sunday Examiner and Chronicle*, March 25, 1984, 40.

Citations from Phillip R. Ford, "The Making of *Vegas in Space*," http://vegasinspace .blogspot.com: Phillip says he stayed awake on speed; He let Doris put him in drag; "Get me out of here!"; those five days as pure pleasure; final footage their best work.

Citations from Sontag, *Against Interpretation*: "Camp refuses," 287; "The hallmark of Camp," 283; distinction between "naive" or "pure" camp, 282; "Intending to be campy," 282; "Camp taste is a kind of love," 291; "aristocratic posture," 290–291.

The monograph *James Bidgood* includes the information that he worked as a drag queen (8) and that he shot *Pink Narcisscus* between 1964 and 1970 (40), though other sources, including Bidgood's *New York Times* obituary (February 4, 2022, A-16), give the start date as 1963.

"It took more than one man" is from *Shanghai Express* (1932), and "Gif me that cobra jewel!" is from *Cobra Woman* (1944).

9. Political Theater

Citations from Carbery, *A History of the Sydney Gay and Lesbian Mardi Gras*: "and Lesbian" was added, 107; organized it for late June, 10–11; "Mardi Gras" was used from the outset, 9; Tension arose, 10, 26–29 (also in Harris, Witte, and Davis, *New Day Dawning*, 14 ff.); Outrage broke out, 13; fifty-three . . . arrested, 16; revocation . . . of the Summary Offences Act, 16–17; ballooned to forty thousand by 1984, 242; shift of date . . . to February, 33; grant of $6,000, 47; Eight thousand revelers, 75; thirty-three separate events, 79; one artist among more than fifty, 79.

The thousand-revelers figure is from an interview with Lance Gowland and Barry Power in Templin, *Mardi Gras Memories*, 10.

"Out of the bars and into the streets!" is quoted in David Marr, "A Night Out at the Cross," in Wherrett, *Mardi Gras!*, 12.

The fierceness of the lesbians is mentioned in Gowland and Power, op. cit., 10, and by David McDiarmid in Cunningham-Reed's documentary *Feed Them to the Cannibals!* at 7:48.

Tully's travels to Papua New Guinea and elsewhere are documented in Gray, *Friends, Fashion and Fabulousness*, 33–39 (also in McPhee with McCormack, "Peter Tully," n.p.). Other citations from Gray: they moved to Sydney, 109 ff.; there for the first Mardi Gras, 168; Tully wangled a travel-study grant, 169–170.

There's more on Tully in Sally Gray's essay "When This You See Remember Me: David McDiarmid's Life as Art" in McDiarmid, *When This You See*, including meeting McDiarmid in Melbourne in 1973, 7; moved to Sydney, 7; New York . . . for the annual Gay Pride march, 11.

Tully's "They played the best music" is in Swieca, Jones, and O'Callaghan, *Absolutely Mardi Gras!*, 64; so is the workshop's location on Forbes Street, 82, 88.

"I was looking at urban groups" is quoted in McPhee with McCormack, "Peter Tully," op. cit.

Tully's genius with a glue gun and "very aware, from demo experience" is from Ron Smith's interview (June 19, 2007) with Sydney's Pride History Group, previously posted on the organization's website (https://www.pridehistory.org.au/oral-histories) but unavailable at the time of this writing; so is the workshop as a rat's nest—"literally."

McDiarmid's "marriage of art and politics" is in Cunningham-Reed, *Feed Them to the Cannibals*, op. cit., at 45:15.

Lupton, *Moral Threats and Dangerous Desires*, provides information about the first Australian case of AIDS 44; the three Queensland babies, 45; "GAYS ACCUSED," "'EXTERMINATE GAYS,'" 45.

The Queensland babies are also in Power, *Movement, Knowledge, Emotion*, 41, as is the headline "'DIE, YOU DEVIATE,'" 43.

"If Jesus wept over Jerusalem" is quoted in David Marr, "The Power of One," *Sydney Morning Herald*, January 5, 2008.

That Nile had already called for their cancellation is in Bill Watt, "Gays Risk AIDS at Mardi Gras," *Daily Sun* (Brisbane), February 1, 1985, 18, as is "Bacchanalian orgy."

Opposition to the parade by some members of the organizing committee is mentioned by Bruce Pollack in his interview with Sydney's Pride History Group (December 1, 1995), previously posted on the organization's website (https://www.pridehistory.org.au/oral-histories) but unavailable at the time of this writing; and in Jim Jenkins, "1985," in Wherrett, *Mardi Gras!*, 56.

That Doris got back to San Francisco at the end of February is in Kerry Leves, "The Burden of Glamour," *Oxford Lifestyle Magazine*, January 31, 1985, 23.

The *Vegas in Space* screening notice is in *Release Print*, May 1985, 10.

For the rise of public-access TV, see Lindner, *Public Access Television*, esp. 7.

On Lou Maletta, see "Lou Maletta, Pioneer of Gay-Oriented TV Programming, Dies at 74," *New York Times*, November 9, 2011, A-28.

Mildred's icing-soiled handbag is recounted in Doris's "My Mother, Mildred," *San Francisco Sentinel*, May 10, 1990, 15.

10. Nightclub of the Living Dead

Citations from Doris's letters: announcing his diagnosis, to Ace, April 20, 1989; "You don't have to worry," to Mildred, November 29, 1983; "I'm in no mood," to Mildred, August 12, 1987; "I'm too talented," to Mildred, June 10, 1982; "probably read by about 1 million people!" to Ace, August 18, 1986; "The reaction has been," to Natasha Haid, September 8, 1986.

"Every man was once a woman" is in Kerry Leves, "The Burden of Glamour," *Oxford Lifestyle Magazine*, January 31, 1985, 23.

Figures for AIDS deaths in San Francisco and nationwide were kindly supplied by Ling Hsu, MPH, San Francisco Department of Public Health, citing the department's *HIV Semi-annual Surveillance Report*, June 2017, Table 10, https://www.sfdph.org/dph/files/reports/RptsHIVAIDS/HIVSemiAnnualReportJun2017.pdf, and the Centers for Disease Control and Prevention's *HIV/AIDS Surveillance Report: U.S. HIV and AIDS Cases Reported Through December 2001*, vol. 13, no. 2, Table 21, https://www.cdc.gov/hiv/pdf/statistics_2001_HIV_Surveillance_Report_vol_13_no2.pdf.

On the 1985 and 1986 AIDS budgets, see Hank Plante, "Reagan's Legacy," SF AIDS Foundation, https://www.sfaf.org/collections/status/reagans-legacy/; and Shilts, *And the Band Played On*, 311.

The quotations from Harry Britt and Paul Volberding are in Talbot, *Season of the Witch*, 395–396.

He was dead before the end of the year: December 2, according to a brief obituary in the *Bay Area Reporter*, December 4, 1986, 20.

Letters in the *Bay Area Reporter*: "I was not prepared," March 13, 1986, 8; "Doesn't anybody have any pride," February 20, 1986, 7; "akin to having Aunt Jemima," March 6, 1986, 8; "I am not interested," March 13, 1986, 8.

The Barbie contest is in Mark MacNamara, "Will the Real Barbie Please Stand Up?," *San Francisco Chronicle*, December 1, 1986 (People section), 17.

On the *Times*'s prohibition of *gay*, see David W. Dunlap, "A Liberating Stand," *New York Times*, June 19, 2017, F-2.

My profile of Doris, "Aggressive Glamour," was in *Image* magazine, *San Francisco Chronicle and Examiner*, August 17, 1986, 28–31, 38.

The profile in the *BAR* is Mike Hippler, "Will Success Spoil Doris? She Hopes So," *Bay Area Reporter*, September 18, 1986, 11, 19.

11. Couples

Information on Jane Dornacker's death and memorial is from Michael Norman, "Traffic Copter Crash in Hudson Kills Reporter," *New York Times*, October 23, 1986, B-9; Joel Selvin, "Good-by, Jane, and Amen," *San Francisco Chronicle*, November 24, 1986, 54; David Armstrong, "82 Performers Do Their Best Stuff at Weekend Dornacker Benefit," *San Francisco Examiner*, November 24, 1986, E-1, E-3. Much of the show is at "The Tubes and Friends—Benefit for Jane Dornacker," YouTube video, 49:55, posted by Jeff Dorman on July 10, 2017, https://www.youtube.com/watch?v=FdGtW7jq-_Y; "Señor Jalapeño" is at 36:50.

Citations from Doris's letters: "You may see more," to Ace, August 18, 1986; "terribly sweet and kind," to Mildred, August 12, 1987.

The note from Tippi, kindly supplied by Ms. Bob Davis, is now in the Louise Lawrence Transgender Archive in Vallejo, California.

The *Pittsburgh 2Day* interview, in two parts, is at "DORIS FISH Interviewed on 'Pittsburgh 2 Day' 1986," YouTube videos, both posted by Johnny Kat on July 24, 2010: Part 1, 6:36, https://www.youtube.com/watch?v=coiHZSHCaes; Part 2, 7:43, https://www.youtube.com/watch?v=FxvMtZrAIuk. Video of the *People Are Talking* interview was kindly supplied by Greg Foss (Ginger Quest).

12. Still Alive!

Tommy's naming his benefit is in Edward Guthmann, "Classy Benefit for AIDS Victim," *San Francisco Chronicle*, July 4, 1988, F-2.

Song from an Angel: https://vimeo.com/194060016.

Rodney Price's and Tommy Pace's dates of death are in Steven Winn et al., "AIDS at 25," *San Francisco Chronicle*, June 8, 2006, E-1.

Citations from Doris's letters: working behind the counter, to Ace, October 19, 1988; "It's very hard work" and "Living with Maurice," to Ace, April 20, 1989; "I was taken aback" and "And the rent is only $625!" to Ace, May 9, 1989; south to Santa Cruz, to Andrew and Sally Mills, December 2, 1989.

Nile's trying to have the Sisters arrested is in John Stapleton, "Fred, the Gay Parade Anti-hero," *Sydney Morning Herald*, February 20, 1989, 7. His fuming to the press is in Frank Walker, "It's on Fred's Own Head," *The Sun-Herald*, February 19, 1989, 3.

Background on *The Balcony* is from White, *Genet*, 413, 417–418, 422.

Misha Berson's review, "Queen for a Day," ran in the *San Francisco Bay Guardian*, April 26, 1989, 38.

"I know I'm not a man" is in Bornstein, *Gender Outlaw*, 8. "Doris Fish became my first drag mom" is in her *A Queer and Pleasant Danger*, 197.

For Leland Moss, see "Leland Moss, 41. The Theatre Director of 'The AIDS Show,'" *New York Times*, January 27, 1990, 32.

"I agree with your Director," "cheery letter," and the family's arrival in LA on July 21 are all from a letter from Ace to Doris, May 22, 1989.

The figure of one hundred thousand AIDS cases in the United States is according to "A Timeline of HIV and AIDS," HIV.gov, US Department of Health and Human Services, accessed May 17, 2022, www.hiv.gov/hiv-basics/overview/history /hiv-and-aids-timeline.

13. Who Does That Bitch Think She Is?

On the *BAR* and the *Sentinel* during the AIDS crisis, see Streitmatter, *Unspeakable*, 274.

Citations from Doris's letters: "I've managed to gather," "the most shocking sore throat," "He's an absolutely lovely fellow," and "to double the dose," to Ace, January 29, 1990; "makes me a bit queasy," to Ace, May 9, 1989; "a new Chinese abortion medicine," to Ace, May 9, 1989, and May 16, 1990; "a few bouts of diarrhea" and "It's a very 'gay' process," to Ace, May 16, 1990; flew to Washington, to Mildred, June 5, 1990; "I managed to go outside," to an unidentified recipient, December 26, 1990.

Doris's *San Francisco Sentinel* column ran from October 26, 1989, to October 25, 1990. Citations are as follows: "that other earth-shaking event," "Putting on the Frock," October 26, 1989, 12; "Who is that old, fat cow?" "Not Another Martini, Darling! Eight Is My Limit," December 7, 1989, 17; "talented and volatile" Popstitutes, "Fish and Dips," December 21, 1989, 16; "just awful" and "just about the nicest folks," "Birthday Boy," June 14, 1990, 18; Miss Romé, "She Who Would Be Empress," January 5, 1990, 13; "gay generation gap," "Hideous Old Queen," July 12, 1990, 19; "If they weren't gay," "She Who Would Be Empress," January 5, 1990, 13; Justin Vivian Bond, "Men, Lesbians and Transsexuals," January 11, 1990, 14; "Lypsinka, Lypsinka, Lypsinka!," "Bad Thoughts, Kind Words," August 16, 1990, 19; "Miss X is like an old wine," "Putting on the Frock," October 26, 1989, 12; "I could hear her face cracking," "I'm Serious About My Career," January 19, 1990, 17; "Many readers have expressed," "Wicked, Wicked Friends," August 30, 1990, 20; Gwyn Waters threw one, "Fish and Dips," December 21, 1989, 16; who the worst person had been, "Not Another Martini, Darling! Eight Is My Limit," December

7, 1989, 17; "A Quiet, Dressy Evening," May 31, 1990, 24; Tom Ammiano, "Don't Hate Me Because I'm Beautiful," March 8, 1990, 21; "going topless," "Hi, I'm Back!," April 12, 1990, 18; West Graphics threw itself, "Yet Another Gay Soiree," August 9, 1990, 22; devoted a whole column to plugging, "I'm Serious About My Career," January 19, 1990, 17; about Sylvia and the Synthetics, "Hideous Old Queen," July 12, 1990, 19; about whoring, "Fishy Tidbits," August 2, 1990, 24; about Cheryl, "Castro Memories," October 11, 1990, 20; about Coco Vega, "So Much to Be Thankful For," November 23, 1989, 20; about old shows, "The Doris Decade," December 14, 1989, 17; February column about Mardi Gras, "Meanwhile, on the Other Side of the Planet," February 16, 1990, 15; Mother's Day column, "My Mother, Mildred," May 10, 1990, 15; "Most people who call," "Send in the Lions," December 29, 1989, 13; "No matter how old," "Catholic Kids," March 1, 1990, 14; a letter from Jackie, "A Letter from Paris," July 19, 1990, 18; "Who is that funny old man?," "Miss Sushi Takes a Walk," July 26, 1990, 17; three-week stay in mid-July, "Bad Thoughts, Kind Words," August 16, 1990, 19; "political couch potato," "Chaos at Court," February 9, 1990, 15; "quite correctly think," "So Much to Be Thankful For," November 23, 1989, 20; "If we demand," "Fake Fur Rules, OK?," November 30, 1989, 15; "Fish on a Soapbox," January 26, 1990, 18; "Our Little Brothers and Sisters," June 28, 1990, 15; "The Dead Animal Crowd," September 20, 1990, 21; "Did I Say Something Wrong?," October 4, 1990, 23; "It's dreary to have AIDS," "Oh No, Not Another Gay Day!," June 21, 1990, 35; "Remember when Percodan," "Castro Memories," October 11, 1990, 20; "I was so sick," "In Memory of Doris," September 6, 1990, 16; "Unfortunately, that challenge," "So Long for Now," October 25, 1990, 23.

For Carmel Strelein/Sanger, see Jack Boulware, "Murder at the Pink Tarantula," *SF Weekly*, June 18, 1997, https://www.sfweekly.com/news/murder-at-the-pink-tarantula/. Her late spring or summer 1990 letter to Doris is undated.

The *Voice* story about Miss Abood is Michael Musto, "Dressed to Overkill," *Village Voice*, March 8, 1983, 27.

Citations from Ace's letters to Doris: a three-week stay, July 10, 1990; stretch of physical agony and "Hi, Louis Philippe," October 21, 1990.

The "looksist" accusation is in Jack Davis, "Questions for Doris" in "Letters," *San Francisco Sentinel*, September 27, 1990, 8.

"I couldn't believe my eyes" is in Marc Huestis's documentary *Another Goddamn Benefit* (1997), as is Doris's aversion to "Waltzing Matilda."

Information on Bambi is in Lake with Orloff, *Unsinkable Bambi Lake*, 72, 150.

On "Waltzing Matilda" and the early Australian settlers, my thanks to Jonathan Griffiths for an illuminating discussion.

"Camp and tragedy are antitheses" and "there is never, never tragedy" are in Sontag, *Against Interpretation*, 287.

The mayor's plaque for Doris, with the proclamation, is in the collection of Miss Abood.

14. Saint Doris

Doris says "Perhaps I'll become a saint" in "Doris Fish Standup Comedy," YouTube video, 11:02, posted by phillipford1 on November 21, 2015, https://www.youtube.com/watch?v=exPMsozVUfc, at 7:26.

Gwyn Waters recalls Doris's last days in "Memories of Doris Fish," an unpublished memoir from 2006.

Citations from Janice Sukaitis's unpublished 1994 memoir, "Our Lady of Guadalupe": "Tippi's room," 4 (I've changed her spelling "twitzie" to "tweetsy," which is how she pronounced it when I interviewed her); "She had one of those light," 1; "I'd be sick, too," 5; "I would embrace," 8.

That Mildred arrived in December is in a letter from Doris to an unidentified recipient (probably Jackie), December 26, 1990.

Letters from Mildred: the excursions to Sausalito and Chinatown, to Marianne and Tony Haid, January 1991; "Philip is in hospital," to Ace, February 1, 1991. A copy of her poem was kindly supplied to me by Andrew Mills.

Figures for AIDS deaths in San Francisco and nationwide (as in chapter 10) were kindly supplied by Ling Hsu, MPH, San Francisco Department of Public Health, citing the department's *HIV Semi-annual Surveillance Report*, June 2017, Table 10, https://www.sfdph.org/dph/files/reports/RptsHIVAIDS/HIVSemiAnnualReportJun2017.pdf, and the Centers for Disease Control and Prevention's *HIV/AIDS Surveillance Report: U.S. HIV and AIDS Cases Reported Through December 2001*, vol. 13, no. 2, Table 21, https://www.cdc.gov/hiv/pdf/statistics_2001_HIV_Surveillance_Report_vol_13_no2.pdf.

On the doctors' ordering another MRI: This incident may have occurred shortly before or afterward, but chronological evidence points to that Friday evening.

The doctor who became a Holocaust denier is Lorraine Day; her websites are drday.com and goodnewsaboutgod.com. For her Holocaust denial, see "Antisemitism? Hogwash!," Good News About God, https://www.goodnewsaboutgod.com/studies/dr_day/Antisemitism%20%20Jews%20have%20slaughtered%20100%20million%20Gentiles.pdf. Her *60 Minutes* appearance is at "Steve Kroft's first 60 Minutes piece," YouTube video, 14:04, posted by 60 Minutes on September 8, 2019, https://www.youtube.com/watch?v=0JWZG8n1mFA.

Obituaries: Elizabeth Fernandez, "Queen of Drag a Quiet Man: Doris Fish, aka Philip Mills, Dies of AIDS at Age 38," *San Francisco Examiner*, June 26, 1991, A-1, A-15; "Drag Queen Dies of AIDS," *Sydney Morning Herald*, June 28, 1991, 6.

Afterword: In Memory of Philip Mills

Peaches Christ's comments are in Peaches Christ and Michael Varrati, "Episode 1—*Vegas in Space*," *Midnight Mass* (podcast), July 28, 2021, 53:40.

Sasha Velour's commentary can be seen at https://vimeo.com/316196484, 6:38 ff.

INDEX

Note: *Italic* page numbers indicate photographs. Page numbers followed by the letter n indicate footnotes.

Craig Seligman, pictured here with Silvana Nova on the set of Doris's movie *Vegas in Space*, has written for and edited at a host of magazines, journals, newspapers, and websites. He is the author of *Sontag and Kael: Opposites Attract Me* (2004). He lives in Brooklyn.

PublicAffairs is a publishing house founded in 1997. It is a tribute to the standards, values, and flair of three persons who have served as mentors to countless reporters, writers, editors, and book people of all kinds, including me.

I. F. Stone, proprietor of *I. F. Stone's Weekly*, combined a commitment to the First Amendment with entrepreneurial zeal and reporting skill and became one of the great independent journalists in American history. At the age of eighty, Izzy published *The Trial of Socrates*, which was a national bestseller. He wrote the book after he taught himself ancient Greek.

Benjamin C. Bradlee was for nearly thirty years the charismatic editorial leader of *The Washington Post*. It was Ben who gave the *Post* the range and courage to pursue such historic issues as Watergate. He supported his reporters with a tenacity that made them fearless and it is no accident that so many became authors of influential, best-selling books.

Robert L. Bernstein, the chief executive of Random House for more than a quarter century, guided one of the nation's premier publishing houses. Bob was personally responsible for many books of political dissent and argument that challenged tyranny around the globe. He is also the founder and longtime chair of Human Rights Watch, one of the most respected human rights organizations in the world.

.   .   .

For fifty years, the banner of Public Affairs Press was carried by its owner Morris B. Schnapper, who published Gandhi, Nasser, Toynbee, Truman, and about 1,500 other authors. In 1983, Schnapper was described by *The Washington Post* as "a redoubtable gadfly." His legacy will endure in the books to come.

Peter Osnos, *Founder*